REAL ALE IN BUCKS

The complete guide to the pubs of Buckinghamshire prepared by the local branches of CAMRA (Campaign for Real Ale)

This book is dedicated to the memory of Peter Morris

Editors:	David Roe Nick Holt
Pub Database:	David Roe
Cover Design:	Bob Keegan
County Map:	Peter Morris Nick Holt
Town Maps:	Nick Holt
Photographs:	Tony Gabriel Geoff Gomm John Sadler John Wood
Pub Surveys:	Tony Austin, Richard Bains, Mike Baker, Richard Baxter, John Bazin, Paul Birch, John Callaghan, Eddie Chambers, Gordon Close, John Conen, Brian & Barbara Cordery, Tim Dawe, Elvis Evans, Kevin & Lynn Finnegan, Tony Gabriel, Rhiannan George, John Gordon, Alex Graham, Geoff Griggs, Nick Holt, Michael Horlock, Steve & Dianne Jennings, Bob Keegan, John Lomax, Barry Mayles, Karl Mumford, John Parker, Steve Pearson, Chris Pontin, Ken Price, David Roe, Dave Rumsey, Neil Rutherford, John Sadler, Jim Scott, Chris & Karen Scoggins, Colin Staines, Bryan Spink, Steve Thomas, Ben Walter, Mike Watkins, Mick White, Carol Williams, John Williamson, Dennis Winkworth, John and Tina Wood
Special Thanks:	P.D. Associates, Aylesbury.
Printed by:	Anthem plc, Luton, Bedfordshire

Every effort has been made to ensure the accuracy of the information contained in REAL ALE IN BUCKS, but no responsibility can be accepted for errors and it is inevitable that changes will occur at the pubs during the currency of this guide.

© Copyright CAMRA (Bucks Branches), 1995

Contents

Introduction	4
The Continuing Campaign	5
Local Breweries	10
How to Use this Guide	12
The Pubs	13
Lost Locals	201
Mild	205
Cider	207
CAMRA Information	209
North Bucks Map	212
South Bucks Map	214

Town maps

Amersham	15
Aylesbury	24
Beaconsfield	32
Bourne End	39
Buckingham	43
Chesham	56
High Wycombe	90
Marlow	118
Milton Keynes	126
Newport Pagnell	148
Wooburn	195
Wycombe Marsh	199

Introduction

This is the first extensive guide to the pubs of Buckinghamshire to be published for 11 years. This 1995 edition includes every pub in the county including the few that do not sell real ale. The previous edition, entitled *"Real Beer in Bucks, 3rd Edition"* was published in 1984 and only included the 602 pubs which were selling real ale at that time. This new book contains details of 709 pubs, of which 96.5% sell real ale.

As a CAMRA (Campaign for Real Ale) publication, the main thrust of this book concerns the beer. Each pub lists the real ales which are regularly on sale and very often guest beers will also be available. There is an increasing tendency for brewers to produce seasonal beers (e.g. Fuller's Summer Ale or Mr Harry in winter) – these are not generally listed in the pub entries. Assume that all beers listed will be served through a traditional handpump. Where pubs serve real ale directly from the cask (by gravity) or via an electric pump it will be mentioned in the pub description.

We hope you will find the pub facilities symbols useful. When lunchtime or evening meals are shown we advise that you check the pub description to make sure on which days food is available. This information is likely to change more quickly than others so it is often advisable to telephone the pub to check on meal times.

As regards to facilities for the disabled, most landlords readily affirm that they make disabled customers welcome, but they do not always have the full range of facilities such as ramps and specially adapted toilets. If there is a disabled symbol in this book it should mean that 'proper' facilities are available. The editors would like to receive any comments on this subject (or any others) as it could be useful for updating any future publications.

All surveys for this guide have been done by unpaid

CAMRA volunteers. To maintain impartiality we do not accept any advertising from pubs but advertisements from brewers and others have enabled us to keep down production costs. All profits generated will be passed on to CAMRA Ltd in St. Albans to be used for national campaigning purposes.

The Continuing Campaign...

There are three main things which concern CAMRA at the present time:

- **Quality**
- **Full measure**
- **Choice**

Of paramount importance is **quality.** The reason people prefer real ale to keg beer is quite simply that it tastes so much better. That is why CAMRA started 24 years ago as a protest against fizzy keg beers that lacked any original or distinctive characteristics.

It has been a highly successful campaign and virtually every pub in this county claims to sell real ale. This high degree of conversion to real ale was once considered a fine achievement but the downside is that too many pubs serve real ale of indifferent quality. Why is this? Perhaps the publican doesn't take enough care in looking after his beer – maybe he's not allowing enough time for cellar conditioning before bringing it on stream. Perhaps the beer has deteriorated before he receives it – this is unlikely if it has come directly from a brewery but could arise due to transportation delays or inadequate storage if delivered by a wholesaler. The answer probably lies in better cellarmanship training for publicans.

Another reason for poor quality is slow turnover. Once tapped, real ale is only at its best for a few days and the lower the alcoholic strength the quicker it will deteriorate. To overcome this, some publicans use various methods to extend the 'shelf life' of beers. The best way to reduce the effects of oxidation is to use the smallest cask size that is practicable, but some breweries don't encourage this. CAMRA doesn't approve of using added gas (blanket pressure or cask breathers) as a way of prolonging the period over which a beer can be served. Your beer may still be served via a handpump but you won't be aware of what tricks are going on in the cellar. Although not everyone can detect any difference in flavour, who wants to drink beer that might have been on tap for a week? The flavour will inevitably suffer: it might be just about drinkable but it won't be pleasurable. Some small country pubs plead that they have to use such things as cask breathers because turnover is slow. Often the reason is that they are offering too many cask beers. We would much rather see every pub selling two real ales in excellent condition than six or more of which only a couple are drinkable.

Swan necks with tight sparklers are now being used increasingly. These cause beer to be 'squirted' into the glass producing a large head on the beer. This may be suitable for Northern style beers but does not suit those brewed in Central or Southern England. Some drinkers claim to like a thick creamy head. No doubt this supposed preference has come about as a result of heavy advertising. Real ale doesn't need all this artificial froth. A good real ale has enough natural condition of its own and serving it through a tight sparkler knocks the condition out of the beer so that after the froth has subsided the natural condition will have deteriorated; so will the flavour.

It seems invidious to mention canned beer in a book about real ale but it is scandalous that brewers are allowed to advertise 'draught beer in a can' as if it were the same as the real draught beer in your pub. This is impossible; the production process is different (canned beer is filtered and pasteurised). Why won't Trading Standards Officers act to stop this disgraceful deception?

Turning to **quantity**, why can't we expect to get a full pint? The Government allows pubs to fob us off with a pint consisting of only 95% of liquid. We are not saying that all pubs adopt this principle – some give fair value. But those that only give 95% or less are cheating the customer of about 8 pence on a pint costing £1.60. If you are given short measure, ask politely for a top-up. CAMRA believes that the only way drinkers can get full measure will be by the general adoption of oversize glasses. This would allow full measure, and head as well.

You may wonder, after this catalogue of problems with quality etc, where you can get a decent pint. In plenty of your local pubs, of course! But to find the very best you should buy the *Good Beer Guide*, published annually in October. This lists about 10% of the country's pubs which have been selected by CAMRA branches all over the country and also has an extensive breweries section where you can find descriptions of the beers and their alcoholic strengths. We have not included a beers listing in this book for reasons of space. The 1984 version of this guide only featured 83 real ales but now we have an enormous choice. For example, the Blackwood Arms (see page 113) sells over 900 different real ales in a year. If you need to know the strengths of the beers you will be drinking, the information is often on the pumpclip (in very small print) or you could refer to the *Good Beer Guide*.

Another way to experiment with today's huge array of real ales is to attend CAMRA beer festivals. The only regular beer festivals in Buckinghamshire are held at Milton Keynes in May and December. In neighbouring counties there are festivals in April (Luton, Beds), July (Woodcote, Oxon), September (Long Hanborough, Oxon), and October (Reading, Berks). The best festival of all is the Great British Beer Festival held at London's Olympia for five days at the beginning of August every year.

So how has the **choice** of beers in Buckinghamshire's pubs changed? We certainly have a much wider choice of beers locally than ten years ago but pub landlords don't necessarily have the *freedom* of choice that the Government intended in its 1992 Beer Orders.

The ownership of hundreds of pubs has changed in that time. Of the major brewers, perhaps Courage has undergone the most changes. Several of their pubs were sold to Morland; the bulk came under the control of Grand Metropolitan's Inntrepreneur Estates although Courage continue to supply the beer. Courage Breweries have just been taken over by Scottish and Newcastle with few objections being raised by the Office of Fair Trading. This will probably not have much impact on the supply of beer in this county but on a national scale CAMRA deplores the prospect of more brewery closures and opposes this takeover. The newly merged company will become Britain's largest brewing group. Bass, up until now the largest, will not take kindly to being pushed into second place and will probably want to take over some regional breweries (with probable closure implications) to retain their market share.

Allied Domecq, owners of Carlsberg-Tetley, once held a stranglehold on Mid and North Bucks with their Benskins and ABC pubs. This monopoly is now much reduced – they have sold pubs to both Fullers and Greene

King which has much improved the choice for drinkers in a very positive way. Others have been sold or leased to Sycamore Taverns and Pubmaster, but both these retailing groups have tie agreements that a proportion of their beers have to come from Allied.

Whitbread's local tied estate has not changed so much as other major breweries. The beer is different – the Wethered Brewery at Marlow closed in 1988 and any so called Wethered beers are now brewed in various locations. Nearly all their pubs now sell Boddingtons and Flowers Original and occasionally more interesting brews from their Castle Eden Brewery in Cleveland.

On the face of it there are now far more beers to choose from, but there are still very few genuine free houses and it is very difficult for the new micro brewers to find enough outlets for their beers.

We hope this book will encourage you to support your local, and discover the rich variety of pubs throughout Buckinghamshire.

NH, July 1995

LOCAL BREWERIES

Buckinghamshire has had a chequered time as far as its breweries are concerned. ABC ceased brewing in the thirties but its presence was still felt until the brewery and warehousing was demolished earlier this year; all ABC beers are produced in Burton. Both Carrs and Phillips came and went during the 1980's and finally Wethered Brewery in Marlow closed in 1988.

This left Chiltern brewery as the sole brewery in the county. However, things have drastically improved with the emergence of three new breweries: Old Luxters, Rebellion and Vale. All these breweries are detailed below.

Chiltern Brewery, Aylesbury

Chiltern Ale (OG 1038, ABV 3.7%)
Beechwood (OG 1043, ABV 4.3%)
Three Hundreds Old Ale (OG 1050, ABV 4.9%)

Set up in 1980 on a small farm, Chiltern specialises in an unusual range of beer related products such as beer mustards, Old Ale chutneys, cheeses and malt marmalade which are sold at the brewery shop (open 9-5 Mon-Sat).
The beer itself is regularly supplied to up to 20 free trade outlets (no tied houses). There is a museum and brewery tours are at noon Saturday, or by arrangement. Bodgers Barley Wine (OG 1080, ABV 8%) is available as a bottle conditioned beer.

Old Luxters Farm Brewery, Hambledon

Barn Ale (OG1042, ABV 4.5%)

Set up in May 1990 in a 17th-century barn by David Ealand, owner of Chiltern Valley Wines. Apart from the brewery and vineyard, the site houses a fine art gallery and a cellar shop. Tutored tastings with expert speakers are also a feature.
The brewery supplies 12 local free trade outlets and pubs further afield via wholesalers. Brewey shop open daily 9-6 and tours available by arrangement. Barn Ale is available in a bottle conditioned version (OG 1052, ABV 5.4%)

Rebellion Beer Company, Marlow

IPA (OG 1037, ABV 3.9%)
Mutiny (OG 1046, ABV 4.5%)

The Rebellion Beer Company was established in early 1993 by two old school friends from Marlow. The new brewery heralded the revival of Marlow's illustrious brewing tradition in the wake of the shameful closure of the old Wethered's brewery in 1988.

The past two years have seen a steady growth in sales and there is now a strong loyal following in the area for the two beers currently brewed by the Rebellion Beer Company.

They plan a major expansion of the brewery in 1995 and the brewing capacity will be increased from 30 brls/wk to around 200 brls/wk with the installation of a 40 brl brewhouse. The beer range will also be developed to include a light golden wheat beer '24 Carat' and a stout or old ale. Seasonal and speciality beers will also be brewed regularly and a bottled beer, possibly conditioned in bottle, is due to be launched towards the end of this year.

Vale Brewery, Haddenham

Wychert Bitter (OG 1040, ABV 3.9%)
Grumpling Old (OG 1046, ABV 4.6%)

After many years working for larger regional breweries and allied industries, brothers Mark and Phil Stevens combined their experience and opened a small purpose built brewery in Haddenham. This revived brewing in the village after the last brewery closed at the end of World War Two.

The inaugural brew, Wychert Ale, is made only from premium malted barley and whole hops and this forms the ethos of the brothers commitment to produce the finest traditional ales possible. It is supplied to approximately fifty freehouses in the locality.

Wychert Ale went on sale in March 1995 and a second brew, Grumpling Old Ale followed in June.

Although not in Bucks, we must mention the
Tring Brewery.
Opened in 1992, they produce three beers: **Ridgeway Bitter (4% ABV)**, **Old Icknield Ale (5% ABV)** and the winter ale **Death or Glory (7.2% ABV)**.

How to understand the layout of the pubs in this guide

SWAN SONG

Map Reference: C4

Made up town name just for the purpose of illustrating the way all towns and pubs work in the guide. These descriptions have been written by various people and we are grateful for all their valiant efforts.

ANATIDAE ARMS
Webbed Feet Road
☎ (01234) 567890
11am-3pm; 6pm-11pm (Opens 11am-11pm Friday and Saturday)

Mute Best Mild; White Feathers Bitter; Wobbly Beak Old Ale

🏠 ❀ ⛌ ✕ ✕ ⬜ ♨ ⛺ ♣ 🚗 🏨

Named after the family name for swans (a swan in chains is the symbol for Buckinghamshire), this pub lies between the largely commuter belt of the southern part of the county to the contrasting northern part of the county which is dominated by Milton Keynes.

Name of Locality

Map Reference (see map at end of guide)

Locality Description

Pub Name
Address
Telephone Number
Opening Times (variations noted in brackets)

Beers available - handpumps are assumed and any variations will be noted in the description.

Pub Facilities - see full listing on following page.

Pub Description

List of Facility Codes

- **Keg pub** : When surveyed, this pub served no real ale and is included in the guide for completeness only.

- **Real fire** : A fire fuelled by coal, logs or smokeless fuel - not one of those useless flame effect things!

- **Quiet pub** : At least one area of the pub is devoid of electronic music, juke boxes etc. but with no guarantee of silence!

- **Family room** : A separate room where children are welcome (legally) without a bar and not just a corridor or use of the restaurant.

- Garden or outdoor drinking area.

- **Accomodation** : Rooms to let - no assessment of quality or price is made.

- Lunchtime meals available (not just snacks).

- Full evening meals available - booking may be required, so a telephone call might be a good idea.

- Separate restaurant area

- Snacks available - no need to have a full meal.

- **Public Bar** : Pub has a distinctly separate public bar, but no price difference is likely in Bucks!

- **Wheelchair access** : Ramps allowing easy access and (in most cases) accessible toilets.

- **Camping** : Facilities in pub grounds or within one mile.

- **British Rail** : Pub is within half a mile of a BR or Underground station.

- **Pub Games** : Pub offers at least two games like darts, dominoes and cards.

- **Bar Billiards** : Superb game but getting rare - why?

- **Pool** : At least one pool table taking up a large part of the bar and forcing drinkers to beware pool cues!

- **Real Cider** : Draught cider - not keg cider - available. Hopefully not one of the fake handpumps that are becoming more common.

- Car Park

- **No Smoking** : At least one bar has been set aside for people who wish to avoid dying from passive smoking!

- **Meeting Room** : Separate room available for use/hire.

- **Regular live music** : further details on frequency and type will be given in the description.

ADSTOCK

Map Reference: C4
Just off the A413 about 3 miles NW of Winslow close to the River Great Ouse. A few timbered and thatched houses and now many more modern properties. St Cecilia's church is worth a visit for the reputedly 800 years old doorway.

FOLLY
Buckingham Road
☎ (01296) 712671
11am-3pm; 6pm-11pm
Hook Norton Best Bitter; ABC Best Bitter; Tetley Bitter

Traditional busy roadside public house providing good home cooked food and is listed in the good food guide, is R.A.C recommended and English Tourist Board approved.

OLD THATCHED INN
Main Street
☎ (01296) 712584
Noon-2.30pm; 6pm-11pm
Hook Norton Best Bitter; Morrells Bitter; Ruddles Best Bitter, County; Webster's Yorkshire Bitter

16th century listed thatched inn at the centre of the village. The inn has been tastefully renovated and extended and still includes many original features such as the flagstone flooring. The vintage car club meets here on the third Thursday evening of every month.

AKELEY

Map Reference: C3
A pretty but rapidly expanding village situated 3 miles N of Buckingham on the A413.

BULL & BUTCHER
The Square (O.S. Ref. 709377)
☎ (01280) 860257
Noon-3.30pm; 6pm-11pm
Marston's Pedigree; Morland Original Bitter, Old Speckled Hen; Regular Guest Beer

Dating from the 17th century this pub is a mixture of ancient and modern. A wealth of exposed beams and stones at one end of the comfortable bar and a more modern wooden rafter and plaster finish to the other. No food on Sundays at all and no food on Monday evening. A shove Ha'penny board is available. Car parking is very limited. Camping at Scotts Farm, Maids Moreton.

AMERSHAM

Map Reference: F8
The old town with its broad street retains many fine period buildings including the old Market Hall, spared demolition despite pressure of ever increasing road

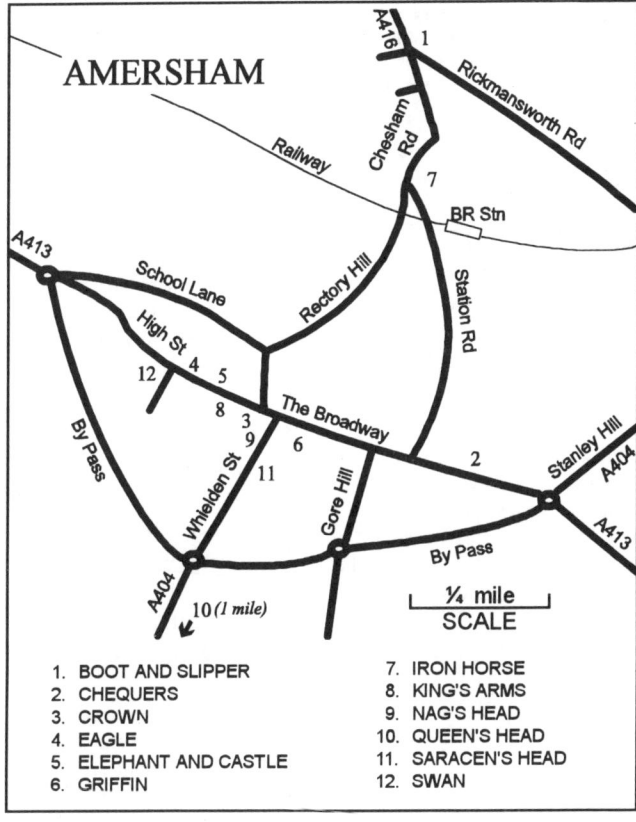

1. BOOT AND SLIPPER
2. CHEQUERS
3. CROWN
4. EAGLE
5. ELEPHANT AND CASTLE
6. GRIFFIN
7. IRON HORSE
8. KING'S ARMS
9. NAG'S HEAD
10. QUEEN'S HEAD
11. SARACEN'S HEAD
12. SWAN

traffic. Now it is hopefully saved as a new by-pass has been constructed. Amersham on the Hill is in complete contrast however - 'Metroland'.

BOOT AND SLIPPER

2 Rickmansworth Road
☎ (01494) 727082
11am-11pm
Courage Best Bitter, Directors; John Smith's Bitter; Theakston's Best Bitter

Large traditional locals pub, dating back to 1611, with one large bar and a small quiet snug. Recent refurbishment has given it a more traditional look.
Discos/live music every Sunday.
No evening meals on Sunday.

CHEQUERS

51, London Road East
☎ (01494) 727866
11am-3pm; 5.30pm-11pm
(Closes 2.30pm-5pm Saturday afternoon)
Ind Coope Burton Ale; Marston's Pedigree; Tetley Bitter; Wadworth 6X

Comfortable one-bar pub, on the outskirts of the old town, with cobbled verandah. Previously a bakehouse and a prison, the building is over 500 years old, was mentioned by Cromwell's brother in his diaries, and is reputed to be haunted. Quiz night on Tuesdays.

CROWN
16 High Street
☎ (01494) 721541
11am-2.30pm; 6pm-11pm
Draught Bass; Courage Directors

Comfortable and thoroughly civilised Forte Heritage hotel, opposite Market Hall. Large restaurant which specialises in English cuisine. The cockatoo, now stuffed, saved the hotel in the thirties by warning the owner of a fire. The interior was featured in the film 'Four Weddings and a Funeral'.

EAGLE
145 High Street
☎ (01494) 725262
11am-3pm; 6pm-11pm
Fuller's London Pride; Greene King IPA; Tetley Bitter

Traditional, comfy and friendly old-town pub with narrow frontage, it is often dominated by diners at lunchtimes. A footbridge over the River Misbourne at the rear allows access to meadows and cricket and football pitches. Evening meals available on Saturdays.

ELEPHANT AND CASTLE
97 High Street
☎ (01494) 726410
11am-3pm; 5.30pm-11pm
Boddingtons Bitter; Brakspear Bitter; Marston's Pedigree; Wadworth 6X; Flowers Original; Occasional Guest Beers

Smart pub with a reputation for good food. Re-landscaped garden and new conservatory garden. No food Sunday evening.

GRIFFIN
12 Broadway
☎ (01494) 725175
11am-3pm; 6pm-11pm
(Open all day Sunday for diners)
Theakston's Best Bitter; Regular Guest Beer

Comfortable and spacious old inn with a cosy snug bar and a large lounge bar-cum-dining area with a small window which reveals the original wattle and daub walls. Oliver Cromwell is reputed to have dined here. Fun quiz Thursday evening. Theakston's 'Particular Pint' award winners.

IRON HORSE
Station Road
☎ (01494) 433831
11am-11pm
Draught Bass; Charrington IPA

Previously called the 'Station Hotel', it is now known locally as 'The Iron Lung'. Basic public bar and comfortable lounge with Sky TV and video juke box. Regular discos.

King's Arms, Amersham   *GG, 1993*

KING'S ARMS
30 High Street
☎ (01494) 726333
11am-11pm
Greene King IPA; Benskins Best Bitter; Tetley Bitter; Regular Guest Beers

Magnificent 15th century coaching inn, the many rooms are authentically decorated and furnished. Award-winning restaurant specialising in international cuisine. The exterior featured in the film 'Four Weddings and a Funeral'. The guest beers are served by gravity.

NAGS HEAD
3 Whielden Street
☎ (01494) 725430
11am-11pm
Boddingtons Bitter; Brakspear Bitter; Marston's Pedigree; Castle Eden Ale

Popular locals pub, part of which used to be an old jail house, dating back to the early 19th century. Caters for all ages and has regular live entertainment.

QUEENS HEAD
Whielden Gate (O.S. Ref. 941957)
(Just off A404 1½ miles outside Amersham)
☎ (01494) 725240
11am-2.30pm; 5.30pm-11pm
(Opens 11am-3pm; 6pm-11pm Saturday)
Adnams Bitter; Rebellion Mutiny; Regular Guest Beer

Friendly local on site of 'Red Lyon' dating back over 300 years. Large garden with small animals, two horses (carriage rides available) and 'Monty', the door-opening dalmation! Excellent family room where smoking is not permitted. Occasional folk evenings. No food Sunday evening and only pizza available on Monday evening.

SARACEN'S HEAD
Whielden Street
☎ (01494) 721958
11am-3pm; 6pm-11pm
Draught Bass; Morland Original Bitter, Old Masters, Old Speckled Hen

🐾 ❀ ⋈ 🗡✕ 🔲 ♨ 🏠

Traditional family inn, which is reputably haunted, with function suite at back. Home-made food available all sessions except Sunday evenings with giant Yorkshire puddings a speciality. Has a very successful quiz league team.

SWAN
122 High Street
☎ (01494) 727079
11am-11pm
(Opens all day Sunday for diners)
Boddingtons Bitter; Flowers Original

❀ 🗡✕ 🔲 ♨ 🚗

Beefeater restaurant and pub.

ASHENDON

Map Reference: C6
Waddesdon 3 miles NW

GATEHANGERS
Lower End (O.S. Ref. 704143)
(Down lane by church)
☎ (01296) 651296
Noon-2.30pm; 7pm-11pm
Adnams Bitter; Hall & Woodhouse Badger Best; Wadworth IPA, 6X; Regular Guest Beer

🐾 ❀ 🗡✕ ♨ ♣ ✓ 🚗

Formerly the 'Red Lion', this 400 year old building was used by magistrates as a courtroom before becoming a pub. On hilltop overlooking the northern Vale of Aylesbury. Imaginative food served seven days a week.

ASHERIDGE

Map Reference: E7
Mainly modern village on the chiltern ridge, 2 miles NW of Chesham.

BLUE BALL
(O.S. Ref. 937046)
☎ (01494) 758263
Noon-2.30pm; 5.30pm-11pm
(Opens Noon-11pm Friday & Saturday)
Courage Best Bitter; Regular Guest Beers

🐾 ❀ 🗡✕ ♨ ♿ ♣ ✓ 🚗 ♪

Isolated pub with one comfortable bar containing a large open fireplace. Large garden. Three guest beers usually available. No meals Sunday evening.

ASHLEY GREEN

Map Reference: F7
On the A416, 2 miles south of Berkhamsted.

GOLDEN EAGLE
☎ (01442) 863549

11am-3pm; 5.30pm-11pm
(Opens Noon-4pm; 7pm-11pm
Saturday)
Adnams Bitter; Draught Bass; Shipstones Bitter; Greenalls Cask Bitter, Thomas Greenall's Bitter; Wadworth 6X

❀ ✕ ✕ ♣ 🚗

Traditional village pub dating from 17th century. The Eagle has its own football team and classic car clubs.

ASKETT

Map Reference: D7
Tiny village just off the edge of the Chilterns. A mixture of cottages surround the Three Crowns pub, which is one of the best looking buildings.

BLACK HORSE

Aylesbury Road
☎ (01844) 345296
11am-3pm; 5.30pm-11pm
Fuller's Chiswick Bitter, London Pride, ESB

🍺 ❀ ✕ ✕ ▢ ♟ ♿ 🚗

1930's roadside pub with one long bar and restaurant area.

THREE CROWNS

(150 yards from A4030)
☎ (01844) 343041
Noon-2.30pm; 5.30pm-11pm
Hancock's HB, Worthington Best Bitter; Flowers Original

🍴 🍺 ❀ ✕ ✕ ♣ 🚗

Village pub with two simple bars.

Superior food freshly cooked to order featuring specialist dishes. No food Mondays, other times subject to availability.

ASTON ABBOTTS

Map Reference: D5
An attractive village which surveys the surrounding Vale from a small hill; there is a good view of 'Fred's Folly' in Aylesbury! Some timbered and thatched cottages remain. The village gets half its name from the Abbot of St. Albans, who had a house there.

BULL AND BUTCHER

85 The Green
☎ (01296) 681520
Noon-2.30pm; 5.30pm-11pm
(Closes 3pm and reopens 6.30pm Saturdays)
Courage Best Bitter; John Smith's Bitter; Regular Guest Beers

🍴 ❀ 🛏 ✕ ✕ ♟ ♣ ⑧ 🚗 👪 ♪

A free house, enlarged during summer of 1994. Front bar mainly for food and new extended bar for regular live music, games or special functions.

ROYAL OAK

Wingrave Road
☎ (01296) 681262
Noon-3pm; 6pm-11pm
ABC Best Bitter; Marston's

Pedigree; Flowers Original

16th century half-thatched inn. Very attractive beamed interior and fine display of brassware. Secure garden with play equipment for children. No meals Sunday evening.

ASTON CLINTON

Map Reference: E6
On the northern slope of the Chilterns, the village was once a centre for straw preparation and has strong associations with the de Rothschilds. Sports car trials on nearby Aston Hill originated a famous motoring marque.

BULLS HEAD
52 Aylesbury Road
☎ (01296) 630385
11am-3pm; 6pm-11pm
(Opens 11am-11pm Friday & Saturday)
Adnams Bitter; Tetley Bitter

1930's style roadhouse now in need of exterior renovation. Plain, but clean, interior with two bars and separate eating area. Surrounding gardens sold by brewery for housing development.

CROWS NEST
Tring Hill (O.S. Ref. 904113)
☎ (01442) 824819
11am-11pm
Boddingtons Bitter; Morland Old Speckled Hen; Flowers Original

Extremely popular Beefeater Steakhouse clone in standard interior style. Separate bar area (bar meals available) and restaurant (open all day at weekends - booking advisable). Adjoining accomodation in Travel Lodge and large garden/childrens area giving extensive views over the vale.

OAK
119 Green End Street
☎ (01296) 630466
11am-3pm; 6pm-11pm
(Opens 6.30pm Saturday)
Fuller's Chiswick Bitter, London Pride, ESB

Following sensitive restoration in 1993, this pub retains many appealing features such as wooden floors and settles, low beams and a no-smoking area in the rear bar. Converted from electric dispense to blanket pressure in March 1995.

PARTRIDGE ARMS
50 Green End Street
☎ (01296) 630572
11am-3pm; 5.30pm-11pm
Draught Bass; ABC Best Bitter; Marston's Pedigree

An unaltered house-like frontage hide two small cosy bars with open fires. Separate room with full size snooker table available for private hire. No food on Sunday.

Rothschild Arms, Aston Clinton *JW, 1993*

RISING SUN
132 London Road
☎ (01296) 630399
11am-11pm
Draught Bass; Courage Best Bitter, Directors
🏠 ❀ ✕ ✕ 🅾 🍴 🚗

Lively and cheerful main road pub, near Green Park education centre. "Conservatory" restaurant and beer garden at rear. No meals Sunday evening.

ROTHSCHILD ARMS
82 Weston Road (O.S. Ref. 872171)
☎ (01296) 630320
Noon-2.30pm; 5pm-11pm
(Opens 11.30am-11pm Friday & Saturday)
Worthington Best Bitter; M&B Highgate Mild; Flowers Original
🏠 ❀ 🛏 ✕ ✕ 🍴 ♿ ♣ ⑧ 🚗 🅿 ♪

Expect a high level of banter from the landlord in this friendly one-bar mid terrace local on road to Weston Turville. Food only until 8.30pm (8pm on Saturday) and none on Sundays. Barbecues in summer. Live music once a month.

ASTWOOD

Map Reference: F2
On the A422, just 7 miles NE of Milton Keynes. It is the most easterly village in North Bucks.

OLD SWAN
8 Main Road (O.S. Ref. 953474)
☎ (01234) 391351
11.30am-3pm; 6pm-11pm
Courage Bitter Ale, Directors; Ruddles County
🏠 ❀ ✕ ✕ 🅾 🍴 ♣ 🚗 ♪

Extended 17th century roadside inn with a mix of red tiles and thatch roof. Much of the original interior still on display despite some alterations. Open all day during summer. Enthusiastic manageress working hard to build up a good customer base. Occasional live music mid week and beer festivals periodically (see local press for details). Part of the Old English Pub Chain, a small three pub affair owned by some old English gents whose love of pubs has driven them to this!

AYLESBURY

Map Reference: D6
Mention Aylesbury to a stranger and he will probably say "Oh, where the ducks come from...". Admittedly duckbreeding was an important part of the local economy in the 18th and 19th centuries, but nowadays the most likely place you will see a handsome white Aylesbury duck is depicted on the plaques outside some A.B.C. pubs.

For centuries the town's prosperity was based on its agriculture and markets. There are still open-air markets on three days a week, but the cattle market closed in the 1980's and the area is now used as a car park. Until the 1970's, printing and engineering companies were the main employers but now local government, light industry and corporate offices provide most of the employment.

Aylesbury has been the county town since 1725 when it took over from Buckingham. The eleven storey tower block above County Hall dominates the Aylesbury skyline and can be seen from miles around the Vale. This was completed in 1966 following the destruction of many Georgian buildings and the creation of Friars Square shopping area. The brutalist 60's architecture soon went out of fashion and Friars Square was rebuilt 20 years later as a covered shopping mall. The quaint character of old Aylesbury, however, has not been totally destroyed. Looking down the market Square, the Clock Tower, the Old County Hall (now the Crown Court), the Town Hall Arches and the Bell Hotel present a pleasant panorama. The square contains statues of John Hampden, Disraeli and Lord Chesham. At the northern end, the King's Head, a remarkable 15th century inn, is largely obscured by shops which should never have been allowed to be rebuilt so close. The most unspoilt part of the town comprises Church Street (with Georgian town houses, earlier almshouses and the County Museum), St. Mary's Square and surrounding lanes such as Parson's Fee. The fine facade of the late lamented Derby Arms can be seen beside the Parish Church.

Ten years ago only 60% of Aylesbury's pubs sold Real Ale - now 95% of them claim to do so.

ARISTOCRAT

1 Wendover Road
☎ (01296) 415366
11am-3pm; 4.45pm-11pm
(11.30am-11pm Friday,
11am-11pm Saturday)

Fuller's Summer Ale, IPA, Chiswick Bitter, London Pride, Mr Harry, ESB

A warm welcome awaits everyone at this popular Fuller's pub on the outskirts of Aylesbury. It has retained a good atmosphere and its facination for young and old alike with a mixture of regular quizzes, pub games, discos, karaoke and live music. Attractive garden area with hanging baskets. Good value, home cooked food daily including vegetarian dishes.

BELL HOTEL
Market Square
☎ (01296) 89835
10.30am-11pm
Boddingtons Bitter; Courage Directors; John Smith's Bitter; Marston's Pedigree; Flowers Original

Busy hotel, part of the Inn Leisure Group, refurbished in the early 90's with low beams and county artifacts. Two bars, also plenty of accomodation and catering facilities. À La Carte meals every session except Sunday evening and tea, coffee and sandwiches 10am - 5pm.

BRICKLAYERS ARMS
Walton Terrace
☎ (01296) 82930
11am-3pm; 5.30pm-11pm
(Open all day Saturday)
Fuller's London Pride; Hook Norton Best Bitter; Marston's Pedigree; Morland Original Bitter, Old Speckled Hen; Tetley Bitter;

Bricklayers Arms   NH, 1995

Wadworth 6X

Cosy and friendly 17th century family pub. Provides many pub games focusing on a very strong darts following. Extensive bar menu and a sandwich bar with an extensive selection with food also available in the recently opened restaurant. Free house since 1990 when it was acquired from ABC.

BRITANNIA
9 Buckingham Road
☎ (01296) 436713
11am-11pm
Tetley Bitter

Fairly basic town pub opposite former Royal Bucks Hospital. Large games room, also used for discos.

BROAD LEYS
8 Wendover Road
☎ (01296) 23727
11am-11pm
Tetley Bitter

Originally dates back to the 17th Century but occasionally known as the 'New Inn' by some locals. Large family pub with garden including children's bar, tree house and swings. Regular discos.

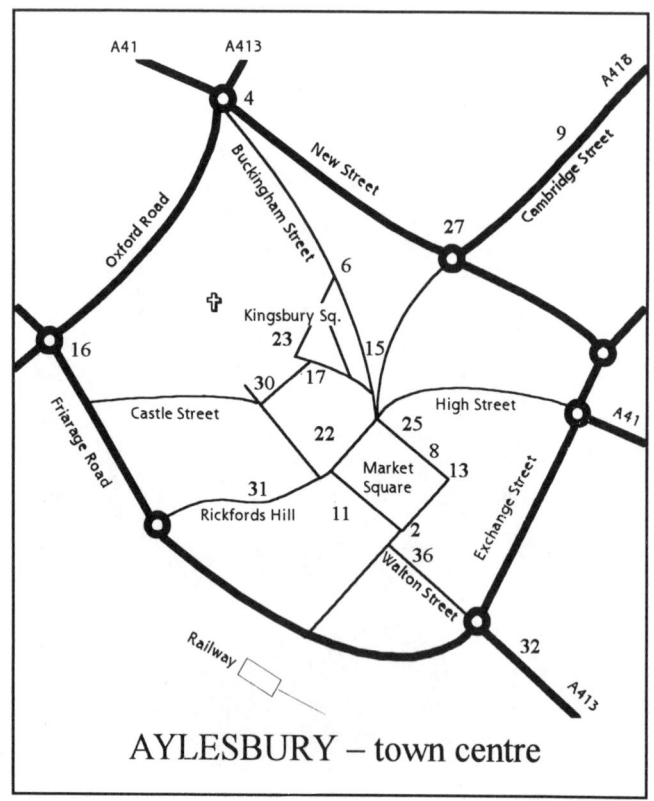

AYLESBURY – town centre

AYLESBURY – outskirts

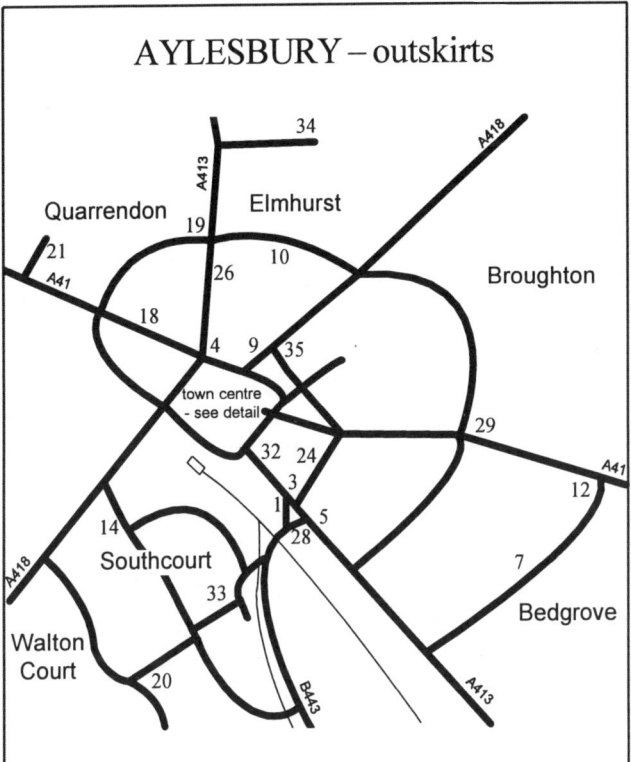

AYLESBURY – key to both maps

1. ARISTOCRAT
2. BELL HOTEL
3. BRICKLAYERS ARMS
4. BRITANNIA
5. BROAD LEYS
6. BUCKINGHAM ARMS
7. BUCKINGHAMSHIRE YEOMAN
8. BUTLER'S
9. COUNTY ARMS
10. DAIRY MAID
11. DARK LANTERN
12. DUCK
13. GRAPES
14. GREYHOUND
15. HARROW AND BARLEYCORN
16. HEN AND CHICKENS
17. HOBGOBLIN
18. HOP POLE
19. HORSE AND JOCKEY
20. HUNTSMAN
21. JOHN KENNEDY
22. KING'S HEAD HOTEL
23. LOBSTER POT
24. MILLWRIGHTS
25. MUSWELL'S
26. NEW ZEALAND
27. ODDFELLOW'S ARMS
28. OLD PLOUGH AND HARROW
29. PLOUGH
30. QUEEN'S HEAD
31. SARACEN'S HEAD
32. SHIP
33. STEEPLECHASE
34. WATERMEAD INN
35. WEAVERS
36. WHITE SWAN

BUCKINGHAM ARMS
Buckingham Street
☎ (01296) 399037
11am-11pm

Two-bar town centre pub. Prints of old Aylesbury decorate the walls. Used to have a wide range of real ales on offer but is now keg only. Discos every other Friday. Live bands.

BUCKINGHAMSHIRE YEOMAN
Cambourne Avenue, Bedgrove
☎ (01296) 86615
11am-11pm
ABC Best Bitter; Tetley Bitter

Theme pub based round family bar with food, ball pond, videos etc, and outdoor play area. Kiddies parties catered for.

BUTLERS
Market Square
☎ (01296) 82382
11am-11pm
(Opens 9am-11pm Saturday)
Draught Bass; Tetley Bitter

Formerly The Green Man and Saints wine bar, the pub overlooks the Market Square and has an attractive first floor balustrade. A narrow main bar plus two upstairs rooms (games and small restaurant). Discos on Friday and Sunday. Evening meals for group functions only.

COUNTY ARMS
124 Cambridge Street
☎ (01296) 23552
11am-3pm; 5pm-11pm
(Opens 11am-11pm Friday & Saturday)
Tetley Bitter; Regular Guest Beer

A pub which is one of Aylesbury's few remaining 'boozers'. A traditional 1890's pub with cellar cooled by stream.

DAIRY MAID
Elmhurst Road
☎ (01296) 81397
Noon-11pm
Morrells Dark, Bitter, Graduate

1960's estate pub with large saloon bar situated on ring road connecting Buckingham and Leighton Buzzard roads. Much improved since a major refurbishment in early 1995.

DARK LANTERN
1 Silver Street
☎ (01296) 82409
11am-11pm
Tetley Bitter

Historic pub with Civil War connections but a chequered (sometimes notorious) history over the last 25 years. Has undergone many brewery inspired interior design themes, the latest of which is 'Mr. Q's'.

DUCK
Queens Mead, Bedgrove
☎ (01296) 24878
Noon-11pm
Tetley Bitter

Large modern estate pub at end of Bedgrove with comfortable raised drinking area separated from pool and darts playing areas.

FORTE POST HOUSE
Aston Clinton Road
☎ (01296) 393388
11am-11pm

Expensive hotel with a first class range of facilities on eastern outskirts of town.

GRAPES
36 Market Square
☎ (01296) 83735
11am-11pm

Courage Best Bitter, Directors; Vale Wychert; Regular Guest Beer

Narrow bar (formerly the Six Grapes and Pettits Wine Bar) adjacent to Civic Centre. Wooden floorboards and Victorian decor provide a pleasant atmosphere. The upstairs restaurant only takes group bookings for evening meals. Regular live music.

GREYHOUND
Churchill Avenue, Southcourt
☎ (01296) 24826
11am-3pm; 6pm-11pm
(Opens 11am-11pm Saturday)

Tetley Bitter

Estate pub in the Southcourt area. Discos on Fridays, Saturdays and Sundays. Karaoke on Wednesdays. Conservatory at the rear opening into large garden.

HARROW AND BARLEYCORN
4 Cambridge Street
☎ (01296) 81313
11am-11pm

Tetley Bitter

Three split-level bars in imaginative conversion of the two previous pubs. Reputed to be haunted! Regular discos on Thursday, Friday and Saturday.

HEN AND CHICKENS
Oxford Road
☎ (01296) 82193
11am-11pm

Courage Directors; John Smith's Bitter

60's pub by busy roundabout. Huge games area in rear bar - four pool tables, video games, satellite TV etc. Near Aylesbury college and popular with students.

HOBGOBLIN
Kingsbury Square
☎ (01296) 41500
11am-3pm; 5pm-11pm
(Opens 11am-11pm Saturday)

Wychwood Shires Bitter, Dr Thirsty's Draught, Dogs Bollocks; Regular Guest Beers

Previously Mangrove Jacks and before that the Red Lion, it was taken over by Wychwood in 1994. Merlins Nightclub (currently keg) stays open till 1.30am on Wednesday and 2am Friday & Saturday but you have to pay to get in. Not open on Sunday and no food Friday and Saturday evenings.

HOP POLE
83 Bicester Road
☎ (01296) 82129
10am-11pm
Draught Bass; Tetley Bitter; Regular Guest Beer

A multi roomed pub which is Aylesbury's main Blues and Rock venue with live sessions Fridays.

HORSE AND JOCKEY
Buckingham Road
☎ (01296) 23803
11am-2.30pm; 5.30pm-11pm
(Closes 2.30pm Sunday lunchtime)
Ind Coope Burton Ale; Tetley Bitter; Regular Guest Beer

A 'Big Steak' pub situated on the outer ring road at the A413 junction and handy for Aylesbury United football ground. A pleasant, comfortably furnished bar with a 24 room hotel attached.

HUNTSMAN
Hannon Road, Walton Court
☎ (01296) 29588
Noon-11pm
John Smith's Bitter; Theakston's Best Bitter; Webster's Yorkshire Bitter

Two bar modern estate pub hidden in the Walton Court shopping precinct. Originally to be the 'Princess Diana' but prevented for legal reasons.

JOHN KENNEDY
Meadowcroft
☎ (01296) 26541
11am-11pm
Tetley Bitter

Large pub on the Meadowcroft estate. Refurbished in early 1995 on 'Mr. Q's' theme.

KING'S HEAD HOTEL
Market Square
☎ (01296) 415158

Aylesbury's one truly historic inn. Closed in 1993 but is now undergoing a major restoration under the supervision of its owners, the National Trust. The date of re-opening is unknown but building work is expected to finish during 1995.

LOBSTER POT
32 Kingsbury Square
☎ (01296) 23849
11am-11pm
Draught Bass

A 16th century pub, popular with the young, the name of which derived from Cromwellian soldiers headgear. Adjacent to Pebble Lane which contains the old town water pump and leads to St. Mary's Square. Happy hour 5pm-7pm. Discos Friday and Saturday nights.

MILLWRIGHTS
83 Walton Road
☎ (01296) 23405
11am-11pm

Games and music oriented pub. Sold by Ind Coope to Greene King late summer 1995, so details of beers etc. unknown at time of going to press.

MUSWELL'S CAFE BAR
Hale Leys Shopping Centre
☎ (01296) 87590
11am-11pm
(Closed on Sundays)

Previously the Bull and Crown. Built on the site of the old Bull Hotel. Recently redecorated with an American theme. Chess is played here and the pub is available for party hire. DJs every Thursday.

NEW ZEALAND
175 Buckingham Road
☎ (01296) 432219
Noon-11pm
Charles Wells Eagle, Bombardier, Fargo

Bright, open plan bar with framed prints on "New Zealand" theme. Games oriented pub.

ODDFELLOWS ARMS
64 Cambridge Street
☎ (01296) 24160
Run down pub beside new inner ring road. Closed since March 1993.

OLD PLOUGH AND HARROW
22 Stoke Road
☎ (01296) 23306
11am-11pm
Courage Best Bitter, Directors; Ruddles County; Regular Guest Beers

Popular and comfortable pub on busy gyratory road system. Strong local trade with thriving darts, crib, quiz and football teams.

PLOUGH
Tring Road
☎ (01296) 86941
11am-11pm
Boddingtons Bitter; Flowers Original; Regular Guest Beer

Beefeater Inn on main road. Thriving locals drinking area, decorated with prints of old Aylesbury and general Beefeater bric-a-brac. Baby changing facilities available.

QUEEN'S HEAD
1 Temple Square
☎ (01296) 415484
11am-3pm; 5.30pm-11pm
Tetley Bitter; Greenalls Cask Bitter; Wadworth 6X; Regular Guest Beer

Village type pub (c.17th century) in the old part of Aylesbury. Two bars and a small dining area with an interesting collection of water jugs hanging from the beams in the back bar. Always a friendly welcome!

SARACENS HEAD
5 Rickfords Hill
☎ (01296) 21528
11am-3pm; 6pm-11pm
(Opens 11am-11pm Friday & Saturday)
Boddingtons Bitter; Charles Wells Eagle, Bombardier; Regular Guest Beer

Friendly pub near the older part

central Aylesbury. A long one-bar pub with a snug type bar at one end. Discos Wednesday and occasional cabaret. No lunches Sunday.

SHIP
59 Walton Street
☎ (01296) 21888
11am-2.30pm; 5pm-11pm
(Opens till 3pm on Friday)
Greene King Abbot; Tetley Bitter; Wadworth 6X

Cosmopolitan, warm and friendly town pub situated by canal basin at end of Aylesbury arm of the Grand Union Canal; opposite controversial 'blue leanie' office block. Discos Thurdays and occasional bands.

STEEPLECHASE
Taylor Road, Southcourt
☎ (01296) 23030
11am-3pm; 6.30pm-11pm
(Opens 11am-11pm Friday & Saturday)
Draught Bass

Local community pub in the Southcourt estate. Weekend barbecues in the summer. Entertainment on Fridays and Saturdays (bands, entertainers, disco, karaoke).

WATERMEAD INN
Watermead, off Buckingham Road
☎ (01296) 433123
Noon-11pm
Courage Directors; Theakston's Best Bitter, Old Peculier; Webster's Yorkshire Bitter

Built about five years ago at the centre of Aylesbury's new 'waterside village', overlooking the lake. A Chef & Brewer carvery restaurant and bar, rather ostentatiously decorated.

WEAVERS
1 Park Street
☎ (01296) 82210
11am-3pm; 5.30pm-11pm
(Opens 11am-11pm on Saturday)
Tetley Bitter

Queens Head, Aylesbury   *GG, 1994*

Split level drinking areas with walls dripping with old prints, jars, bottles, books and even a mountain bike. Regular discos and very popular with young drinkers. No food evenings or weekends.

WHITE SWAN

3 Walton Street
☎ (01296) 23933
11am-11pm
(Opens 10.30am Saturdays)
Tetley Bitter

17th century pub situated opposite the Public Library. A tasteful renovation with wood panelling has drawn the once separate Stable Bar into main pub area but this is now used as a pool hall. No food Sundays.

BALLINGER COMMON

Map Reference: E7
Quiet and unexceptional Chiltern hamlet, 3 miles west of Chesham.

PHEASANT INN

(O.S. Ref. 912032)
☎ (01494) 837236
Noon-3pm; 6.30pm-11pm
(Closed Sunday evening)
Greene King Abbot; Wadworth 6X; Beer with House Name

Primarily an eating house, this fine old pub is often completely full of diners. It is very tastefully furnished and has what must be some of the cleanest loos around!!

BEACHAMPTON

Map Reference: C3
Hamlet hugging a rivulet supplying the Great Ouse only 2 miles W of Stony Stratford

BELL

☎ (01908) 563861
11am-2.30pm; 5.30pm-11pm
(Opens Noon-3pm; 7pm-11pm on Saturday)
Courage Directors; Greene King IPA; Marston's Pedigree; Morland Old Speckled Hen; Wadworth 6X

Large friendly traditional old village pub with a mixed clientele. Good food, families welcomed. Loud live music on Sunday evenings. Closed on Monday lunchtimes.

BEACONSFIELD

Map Reference: F9
Another Chilterns town of two parts, and notably chiefly for its magnificent wide main street and Georgian houses bestride the A40; politician Edmund Burke lived here, also poets Edmund Waller and G.K Chesterton, whose 'Father Brown' stories were written in Grove Road.

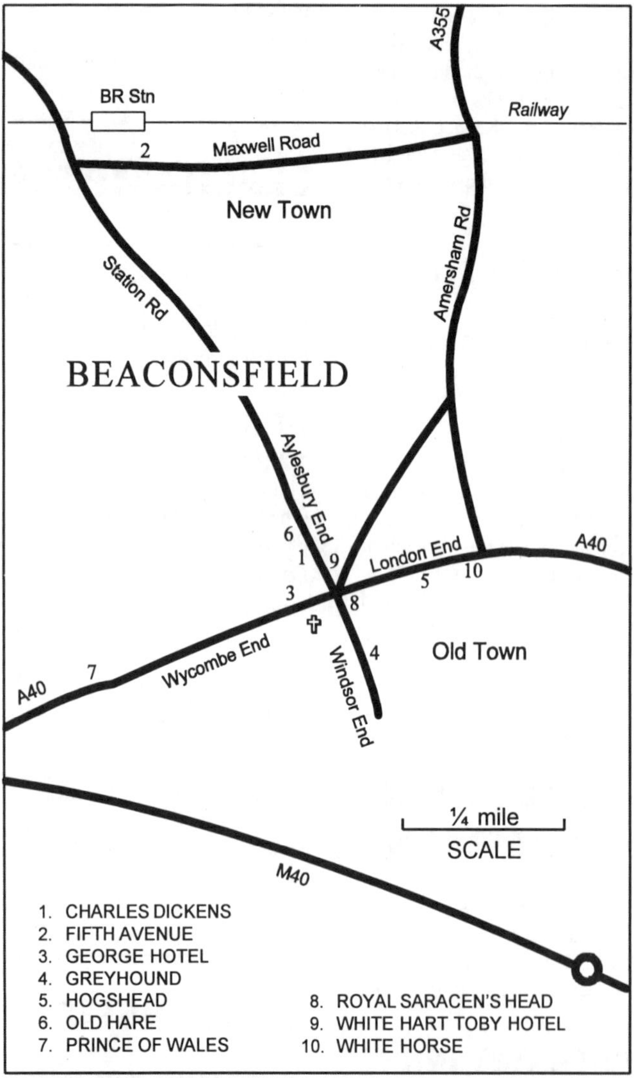

CHARLES DICKENS

35 Aylesbury End
☏ (01494) 674451
Noon-2.30pm; 5.30pm-11pm
*Boddingtons Bitter;
Marston's Pedigree; Flowers
IPA, Original*

Formerly called 'The Star', this pub now has a display of framed pictures of the time of Charles Dickens. No Sunday evening meals.

FIFTH AVENUE

Maxwell Road, New Town
☏ (01494) 672014
11am-3pm; 5.30pm-11pm
*Adnams Bitter; Boddingtons
Bitter; Flowers IPA*

American theme in pub and restaurant. Called the Beech Tree until the mid 1980's. Regular discos.

GEORGE HOTEL
73 Wycombe End
☎ (01494) 673086
Noon-3pm; 6.30pm-11pm
(Closed Mondays)
Greene King IPA, Abbot

Hotel with restaurant specialising in fish dishes. Restaurant area part of the bar. Hunting scenes along one wall. Sunday hours are noon - 6pm.

GREYHOUND
33 Windsor End
☎ (01494) 673823
11am-3pm; 5.30pm-11pm
Courage Best Bitter; Fuller's London Pride; Wadworth 6X; Regular Guest Beers

Small, charming, unspoilt pub with cosy snug bar. Home cooked food can be eaten in bar or restaurant area. Function room upstairs.

HOGSHEAD
London End
☎ (01494) 673800
11am-11pm
Boddingtons Bitter; Brakspear Bitter; Fuller's London Pride; Marston's Pedigree; Morland Old Speckled Hen; Wadworth 6X; Castle Eden Ale; Flowers Original

Renovated pub, previously the Swan, with character and many artifacts. Only one bar, but with different areas within. Juke box and Sky TV difficult to ignore. Landlord in Guild of Master Cellarmen. Live music once a week.

OLD HARE
41 Aylesbury End
☎ (01494) 673380
11am-11pm
Benskins Best Bitter, Ind Coope Burton Ale; Marston's Pedigree; Tetley Bitter; Regular Guest Beer

Cosy pub with low beams, stained glass windows, tempting meals and friendly bar staff. Striking exterior in old town. Appears in CAMRA Good Food Pub Guide.

PRINCE OF WALES
15 Oxford Road
☎ (01494) 674128
11am-3pm; 5.30pm-11pm
(Opens 7pm on Saturday evening)
Wadworth 6X; Flowers IPA

Cosy one-bar pub on edge of old town. Free house with changing range of beers. Favoured by competitors in the annual stretcher race. Beware low beams when negotiating the step! Lunches weekdays only.

ROYAL SARACENS HEAD
London End
☎ (01494) 674119
11am-11pm

Boddingtons Bitter; Flowers Original
✕✕ 🍴

Busy Beefeater at centre of old town. Beers on offer may vary.

WHITE HART TOBY HOTEL
Aylesbury End
☎ (01494) 671211
11am-11pm
Draught Bass
🅡 ⛨ ✕✕ ◻ 🍴 🚗

A Toby restaurant with artifacts dotted around the drinking area which tell the history of old Beaconsfield.

WHITE HORSE
London End
☎ (01494) 673946
11am-11pm
Courage Best Bitter
❀ ✕✕ 🚗 ♪

End of town pub with wine bar attracting all ages. Live music on Thursday, Friday and Saturday evenings. No meals at weekends.

Food orientated country pub with plans to extend in early 1995. No food Sunday evening.

BENNETT END

*Map Reference: C8
Stokenchurch 2 miles W*

THREE HORSESHOES
Horseshoe Road (O.S. Ref. 783973)
☎ (01494) 483273
Noon-2.30pm; 7pm-11pm
(Closed Mondays, except Bank Holidays)
Brakspear Bitter; Flowers Original; Regular Guest Beers
🅡 🍺 ❀ ⛨ ✕✕ ◻ 🍴 ♣ 🚗 ♪

18th century unspoilt inn tucked away in an attractive Chiltern valley. No meals Sunday evenings.

BELLINGDON

*Map Reference: F7
Chesham 3 miles SE*

BULL
(O.S. Ref. 938057)
☎ (01494) 758163
Noon-3pm; 6pm-11pm
Greene King IPA; Marston's Pedigree
🅡 ❀ ✕✕ 🚗

BIERTON

*Map Reference: D6
Linear village 2 miles north east of Aylesbury on the Leighton Buzzard road.*

BELL
191 Aylesbury Road
☎ (01296) 436055
11am-3pm; 6pm-11pm
(Opens all day on Saturday)
Fuller's Chiswick Bitter,

Three Horseshoes, Bennett End   *AG, 1991*

London Pride, ESB

A small two-bar pub within easy access of Aylesbury. It has a thriving food trade at reasonable prices. All food is home prepared, nothing defrosted. Seasonal beers.

BOB'S BARN

Golf Centre, Hulcott Lane
☎ (01296) 399988
11am-11pm
Bateman XB; Fuller's London Pride

Originally a traditional threshing barn converted in 1991 into the club house for a golf course and driving range. The bar is open to the public - you don't need to be a golfer to get a drink! Straightforward, reasonably priced food available from 9am to 9.30pm.

RED LION

68 Aylesbury Road
☎ (01296) 394857
11am-3pm; 6pm-11pm
Draught Bass; Ansells Mild, ABC Best Bitter; Regular Guest Beer

17th century timber framed building opposite church with two low ceilinged bars. Old fashioned public bar with tiled floor. Varied and reasonably priced menu (no meals Sunday or Monday evenings).

BISHOPSTONE

Map Reference: D6
Aylesbury 2 miles North

HARROW

27 Main Street
☎ (01296) 748652
11.30am-2.30pm; 6pm-11pm

(Open until 3pm Saturday, closed Mondays)
Draught Bass; Worthington Best Bitter

🏠 ❀ ✕ ✕ 🎲 ♿ 🚗

Long one-bar pub in linear village. Interesting pub fare with home cooking a speciality. No food Sunday evening and the pub is closed on Mondays. Very accessible for disabled customers.

BLEDLOW

Map Reference: C7
A charming village on a northern slope of the Chilterns, it has a huge turf-cut cross for a landmark. The fine Norman church is full of surprises, including a colossal 600-year old St.Christopher.

LIONS OF BLEDLOW
Church End
☎ (01844) 343345
11am-3pm; 6pm-11pm
Courage Best Bitter; John Smith's Bitter; Ruddles County; Wadworth 6X; Regular Guest Beer

🏠 🍺 👪 ❀ ✕ ✕ 📷 🎲 🚗

Rambling 16th century pub in picturesque setting. Very popular but has ample parking. No food Sunday evening.

BLEDLOW RIDGE

Map Reference: D8
Once a much busier community, little now remains of the one-time post mill or the brickworks, but there are some fine views over a dramatic landscape.

BOOT
Chinnor Road (O.S. Ref. 794982)
☎ (01494) 481659
11am-2.30pm; 5.30pm-11pm
Morland Independent IPA, Original Bitter, Old Masters

🍺 ❀ ✕ ✕ 🎲 ♣ 🚗

Busy, modernised village pub with plush lounge. Popular, with many pub games.

BOLTER END

Map Reference: D9
Just south of the M40, but not accessible to it. Marlow 5 miles SE.

PEACOCK
(O.S. Ref. 797923)
☎ (01494) 881417
11.45am-2.30pm; 6pm-11pm
ABC Best Bitter; Marston's Pedigree; Tetley Bitter; Regular Guest Beer

🏠 🍺 ❀ ✕ ✕ ♣ 🚗

Original building dates back to 1620 and located on corner just west of Lane End. Large room with several distinct areas and emphasis on freshly prepared, home cooked bar meals (no food Sunday evening).

BOOKER

Map Reference: D9
On the western edge of High Wycombe with an Aerodrome and a pleasant common.

LIVE AND LET LIVE
Limmer Lane, Booker Common (O.S. Ref. 835917)
☎ (01494) 520105
11am-3pm; 5.30pm-11pm
Brakspear Bitter; Wadworth 6X

Main problem is to locate it. Down unlit bridle path off side road off minor road between Wycombe & Lane End. Kept going by knowledgeable locals and visitors with detailed maps. Meals can be booked (no meals on Sundays).

SQUIRREL
Squirrel Lane (O.S. Ref. 838919)
☎ (01494) 525517
Noon-3pm; 5.30pm-11pm
Morland Original Bitter

Hard to find pub on outskirts of High Wycombe. Cosy small rooms and attractive, immaculately maintained, stepped garden. Rough track opposite end of garden is driveable and leads to Booker Common. No food at weekends.

TURNPIKE
New Road
☎ (01494) 529419
11.30am-11pm
Draught Bass; Boddingtons Bitter; Webster's Green Label

Large main road pub. Night club atmosphere with American jazz-age decor in main bar. Due to be re-furbished to old world style soon. No meals on Sundays.

BOTLEY

Map Reference: F7
Chesham 2 miles W

FIVE BELLS
Tylers Hill Road (O.S. Ref. 980018)
☎ (01494) 775042
11am-3pm; 6pm-11pm
Draught Bass; Fuller's London Pride; Wadworth 6X; Regular Guest Beers

No food Monday evening and Sunday.

HEN AND CHICKENS
Botley Road (O.S. Ref. 978022)
☎ (01494) 783303
11am-2.30pm; 6pm-11pm
(Closes 3pm Saturday lunchtime)
Draught Bass; Greene King IPA; Tetley Bitter; Flowers Original

Small friendly local. No food Sundays.

BOURNE END

Map Reference: E9
Marlow 3 miles West.
Thames-side bungalow village popular with the boating fraternity - the riverside is its best feature.

BLACK LION
Marlow Road, Well End
☎ (01628) 520421
11am-3pm; 5.30pm-11pm
Draught Bass; Boddingtons Bitter; Brakspear Bitter; Wadworth 6X

Smart roadside pub with mixed clientele. Live music on Sundays.

BOUNTY
Riverside, Cockmarsh
☎ (01628) 520056
Noon-11pm
(Summer only - see description)
Morland Old Speckled Hen; Rebellion IPA, Mutiny; Beer Range Varies

Riverside pub on towpath on Berkshire bank of the Thames - no vehicular access. Pedestrian access via nearby footbridge bolted on to side of railway bridge or by boat from marina - customers may use 240ft of free riverside boat moorings. Open all day during June, July & August and then depending on the weather from Easter to June and to the end of October. Only opens Sunday lunchtime during winter.

FIREFLY
Station Road
☎ (01628) 521197
11am-2.30pm; 5.30pm-11pm
Ind Coope Burton Ale; Regular Guest Beer

Friendly locals pub with games room. Next to station. Nautical flavour. Petanque pistes in garden. Snacks available only lunchtime.

GARIBALDI
Hedsor Road
☎ (01628) 522092
11.30am-2.30pm; 6pm-11pm
Marston's Pedigree; Rebellion Mutiny; Wethered Bitter, Flowers Original

Range of good value pizzas, tasty and home made. Exceptionally cheerful and friendly bar staff. Attractive floral display at front. Pizzas available till 9pm.

HEART IN HAND
Cores End Road
☎ (01628) 523887
Noon-2.30pm; 6pm-11pm
Boddingtons Bitter; Greene King Abbot; Wethered Bitter, Bentley's Yorkshire Bitter

Recently refurbished pub with large restaurant.

MASON'S
Hedsor Road
☎ (01628) 523903
11am-11pm
Fuller's London Pride; Morland Old Speckled Hen; Regular Guest Beers

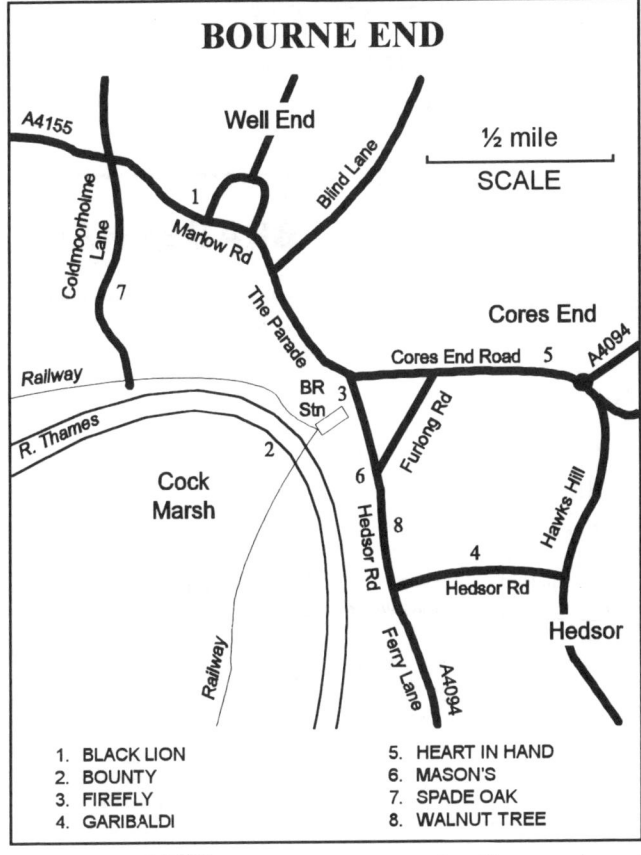

BOURNE END

1. BLACK LION
2. BOUNTY
3. FIREFLY
4. GARIBALDI
5. HEART IN HAND
6. MASON'S
7. SPADE OAK
8. WALNUT TREE

Busy "wine bar" with games room. Popular with young people. Previously known as the Red Lion. Regular live music.

SPADE OAK
Coldmoorholme Lane (O.S. Ref. 884877)
☎ (01628) 520090
11am-11pm
Boddingtons Bitter; Brakspear Bitter; Wadworth 6X; Flowers Original

Full restaurant menu with specials and vegetarian. Sign on main road indicates route down lane. 50 yards from Thames.

WALNUT TREE
Hedsor Road
☎ (01628) 520797
Noon-3pm; 5pm-11pm
Morland Original Bitter, Old Masters, Old Speckled Hen; Regular Guest Beer

Smart low-profile comfortable one-room local pub near centre of Bourne End. Formerly bakery and home brew pub on this site. Large patio garden and forty seater restaurant. Regular live music.

BOVINGDON GREEN

Map Reference: D9
1 mile NW of Marlow.

ROYAL OAK
Frieth Road/Chalkpit Lane (O.S. Ref. 835870)
☏ (01628) 483875
11am-3pm; 5.30pm-11pm
Brakspear Bitter; Wadworth 6X; Wethered Bitter

Extensive menu with very generous portions, all home cooked (no meals on Mondays or Sunday evenings). Floodlit petanque (boules) in large garden. Folk or blues live music in the bar on Friday or Saturday evenings.

BOW BRICKHILL

Map Reference: E3
Attractive village at the foot of Brickhill Woods, close to Woburn Golf & Country Club.

WHEATSHEAF
21 Station Road
☏ (01908) 370947
11am-2.30pm; 5.30pm-11pm
(Opens 11am-11pm Saturdays)
Charles Wells Eagle, Bombardier

A very well kept pub with a quiet lounge and games in the public bar

BRADENHAM

Map Reference: D8
A delightful village, the boyhood home of Benjamin Disraeli, was acquired by the National Trust in 1956. The beechwoods above it are a splendid sight, not only in spring and autumn, but also after a snowfall.

RED LION
☏ (01494) 562212
11am-2.30pm; 6pm-11pm
Adnams Bitter; Brakspear Bitter

Part of National Trust village. Records of building go back to 17th Century; said to be Elizabethan. Internally restored in 1993 to 1900 vintage. No evening meals on Sunday or Monday.

BRILL

Map Reference: B6
In a superb hilltop position, and more small town than large village. It is historically linked with the hunting kings of England and the hillside so pock-marked from clay diggings, is crowned by a fine 17th century post mill.

PHEASANT

39 Windmill Street
☎ (01844) 237104
11am-3pm; 6pm-11pm
Tetley Bitter; Wadworth 6X
🍺 ❀ ✕ ✗ 🔲 ♿ ⚠

17th century free house (purchased from Halls in 1991) situated beside the famous windmill. Fine views across the common of at least five counties. Superbly restored open hearth fire.

RED LION

27 Church Street
☎ (01844) 238339
11.30am-3.30pm; 6pm-11pm
Greene King IPA, Rayments Special, Abbot
🍺 ❀ ✕ ✗ 🔲 ♿ ⚠ ♣ 🏠

A roomy and interesting village inn, dating back to 1540, which is steeped in local history. The original brickwork in the barn (now a function room used as a restaurant at weekends) is some of the oldest in Brill and the bricks were locally made. A large collection of key fobs adorns the ceiling behind the bars. Aunt Sally played in summer. No food Tuesday evening.

SUN INN

2 High Street
☎ (01844) 238208
11am-11pm
Boddingtons Bitter; John Smith's Bitter; Regular Guest Beer
🍺 ❀ 🛏 ✕ ✗ 🔲 ♿ ⚠ ⑧ 🚗 🏠

Small country hotel (free house) with a restaurant and two contrasting bars - a smart tasteful 'snug' and a 'village' bar with pool table etc. Parts of the building date from the 14th century and it was once used as a courthouse. No food Sunday evening.

BROUGHTON

Map Reference: D6
Aylesbury 2 miles West

PRINCE OF WALES

Broughton Crossing (O.S. Ref. 840147)
☎ (01296) 85228
Noon-3pm; 5.30pm-11pm
(Opens 11am-11pm on Saturday)
Draught Bass; Greene King IPA; ABC Best Bitter; Marston's Pedigree; Tetley Bitter
🍺 🏠 ❀ ✕ ✗ 🔲 ♿ 🚗 🏠
♪

Early Victorian pub at what was once a railway level crossing. About ¼ mile from the Grand Union Canal. Cellar bar now known as 'JB's American Rib Shack' and serves grills from Wednesday to Sunday.

BRYANTS BOTTOM

Map Reference: E8
Hamlet in a valley 4 miles SE of Princes Risborough.

GATE
(O.S. Ref. 856996)
☎ (01494) 488632
11am-11pm
Draught Bass; Greene King Abbot; Wadworth 6X

Traditional, friendly village pub with separate lounge bar, public bar and restaurant. There are also three real fires. Food is served in the bars as well as the restaurant.

BUCKINGHAM

Map Reference: B3
Nestling in a loop of the River Great Ouse, Buckingham is no longer the county town of Buckinghamshire. It is neither served by the canal nor served by any trains. What it does have is a market on Tuesdays and regular fairs on bank holidays that block the streets. Thankfully, it has a bypass. The grounds of nearby Stowe School are run by the National Trust and are open to the public.

BARREL
17 West Street
☎ (01280) 817630
Noon-3pm; 6pm-11pm
(Opens Noon-11pm Fridays & Saturdays)
Worthington Best Bitter; Tetley Walker Bitter

L shaped corner pub on the A422 main road out of town, a clone of pubs in Deanshanger and Aylesbury.

BRITANNIA
Gawcott Road
☎ (01280) 812580
11.30am-11pm
ABC Best Bitter; Webster's Yorkshire Bitter

Dating from the mid 1800's this pub is accessed from the street by means of a steep staircase. There is a single L shaped split level bar. Situated very close to the long defunct London & North Western line Bletchley to Banbury spur.

GRAND JUNCTION
13 High Street
☎ (01280) 813260
11am-3pm; 5pm-11pm
(Opens 11am-11pm Tuesday, Friday & Saturday)
ABC Best Bitter; Tetley Bitter

Town centre pub someway short of its former glories.

KINGS HEAD
7 Market Hill
☎ (01280) 815380
11am-11pm
Wadworth 6X; Webster's Green Label, Yorkshire Bitter

This pub's sights are not set too high.

MITRE
Mitre Street
☎ (01280) 813080
Noon-2.30pm; 7pm-11pm
Tetley Bitter; Flowers IPA

BUCKINGHAM

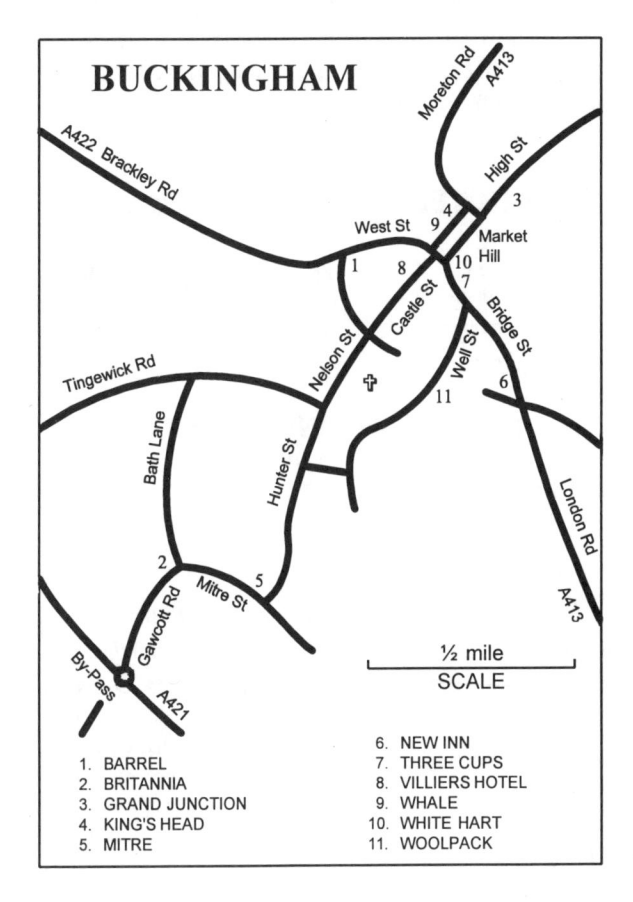

1. BARREL
2. BRITANNIA
3. GRAND JUNCTION
4. KING'S HEAD
5. MITRE
6. NEW INN
7. THREE CUPS
8. VILLIERS HOTEL
9. WHALE
10. WHITE HART
11. WOOLPACK

Situated near the railway viaduct but with little to reward you for finding it, this strange building, dating from the mid 1700's has an arch and a window seemingly from a church. If the London & North Western railway re-opens then this pub will be nearest to the station.

NEW INN
18 Bridge Street
☎ (01280) 815713
10am-11pm
Greene King IPA, Abbot, Winter Ale

Regular entry in the Good Beer Guide. Beers always in good form. Evening meals by arrangement and Sri Lankan cuisine a speciality, advisable to book in advance.

THREE CUPS
24 Bridge Street
☎ (01280) 813348
10am-11pm
*Hook Norton Best Bitter;
John Smith's Bitter;
Webster's Yorkshire Bitter*

Friendly but basic pub on main road. Two Grand Met beers and a guest. Parking in the hotel to the rear but a charge may be incurred. Occasional Irish folk bands to liven things up.

VILLIERS HOTEL
3 Castle Street
☎ (01280) 822444
Noon-2.30pm; 5.30pm-11pm
Boddingtons Bitter; Hook Norton Best Bitter; Wadworth 6X

Dating from the early 1700's, the former Swan & Castle and now Villiers Hotel is not to be confused with the Swan upon the Hoop which predated it by some 200 years. Refurbished and renamed about 5 years ago the small bar down the mews is dominated by an open fire and is ideal for toasting crumpets.
A good but common range of ales at high prices.

WHALE
14 Market Hill
☎ (01280) 815537
10am-11pm
Fuller's Chiswick Bitter, London Pride, ESB; Regular Guest Beers

Typical town centre pub, warm and friendly with a well decorated split level bar. Traditional and not so traditional pub games, pitch and toss, Jenga, Captains Mistress etc. Food noon to 2.30 Monday to Sunday and 6.00 till 9.00 Monday to Friday

WHITE HART
Market Square
☎ (01280) 815151
11am-3pm; 5pm-11pm
(Opens 11am-11pm on Saturdays)
Courage Directors; John Smith's Bitter; Ruddles County

Normal Harvester with large food oriented bar and restaurant. Uninspired range of beers.

WOOLPACK
57 Well Street
☎ (01280) 813286
11am-2.30pm; 5.30pm-11pm
(Opens 11am-11pm on Saturdays)
Cains Bitter; Jennings Bitter; Ruddles Best Bitter; Webster's Yorkshire Bitter

Lively back street basic pub with usual Grand Met beer and two guest ales. Loadsacups for darts and pool. Occasional live bands.

BUCKLAND

Map Reference: E6
Just north of Aston Clinton, half mile off A41.

ROTHSCHILD ARMS
Buckland Road
(On B489)
☎ (01296) 630205
Not to be confused with the pub of same name in Aston Clinton. Currently boarded up with sign saying 'Under Offer' - future uncertain.

BUFFLERS HOLT

Map Reference: B3
A name only. On the A422 and not quite two miles out of Buckingham.

ROBIN HOOD
☎ (01280) 813387
11am-2.30pm; 5.30pm-11pm
(Closes 3pm Saturday afternoons)
Boddingtons Bitter; Wadworth 6X; Charles Wells Eagle; Regular Guest Beer

Ancient drovers inn with one bar serving two small rooms, one almost entirely given over to dining, a picture gallery and a display of memorabilia.
A scorching hot fire to thaw you out on cold winter evenings. Three letting rooms if the attraction proves too much.

BURNHAM

Map Reference: E10
Slough 3m SE.
The old village is surrounded by the characterless environs of Slough, but some original buildings survive in the High Street including an interesting church. In Burnham Park the timber-framed County Library is one of the more worthy efforts of erstwhile County Architect, Fred Pooley.

CRISPIN
1 Britwell Road
☎ (01628) 602827
11am-11pm
(Closes 3pm - 5.30pm Monday & Tuesday)
Draught Bass; Charrington IPA

L-shaped pub with low ceiling. More refined saloon bar to the left with boisterous locals bar at front. General atmosphere is intimate.

GARIBALDI
11-13 High Street
☎ (01628) 602911
Noon-3pm; 5pm-11pm
Courage Best Bitter; John Smith's Bitter; Wadworth 6X; Regular Guest Beer

Originally cottages, this 500 year old pub has original beams and a Victorian style fireplace. Bars and restaurant give a cosy, intimate atmosphere. No evening meals on Sunday.

GEORGE
20 High Street
☎ (01628) 605047
11am-11pm
Courage Best Bitter, Directors; Ruddles Best Bitter

Old coaching inn with archway courtyard and stables, open plan bar with bare boards. Directors tap protrudes from mirror and locals call it 'Alice through the looking glass'. No food Sunday.

OLD FIVE BELLS
14 Church Street
☎ (01628) 604276
11am-11pm
Boddingtons Bitter; Brakspear Bitter; Flowers IPA; Regular Guest Beer

Modern single bar opposite church with mainly young clientele. Large comfy children's room looks out on to garden which has two petanque pitches and a small but well equipped play area. No Sunday lunches or evening meals at the weekend. Live music every month either on Thursday or Sunday.

RED LION
101 High Street
☎ (01628) 605939
11am-11pm
Tetley Bitter; Regular Guest Beer

Large, single bar pub on High Street. Separate raised area with pool table. Mixed clientele, popular with young people at weekends. Main bar decor is Mid-Atlantic style. Separate dining area which serves breakfast from 9.30am.

SWAN
34 High Street
☎ (01628) 661690
11am-3pm; 5.30pm-11pm
Courage Best Bitter; Regular Guest Beer

The original coaching inn, now long gone, straddled the present site with the building to the north part of the old Swan Hotel. Long single bar is split into two by dividing wall and fireplace frequented by all types. No food Sunday.

BURNHAM BEECHES

Map Reference: F10
About 300 acres of woodland are open to the public. To wander through these beautiful and astonishing beechwoods is an experience not to be missed; some of the knarled specimens are thought to be almost 1000 years old.

CROWN
Crown Lane, East Burnham
☎ (01753) 644125
11am-11pm
Courage Best Bitter, Directors; Regular Guest Beers

Originally mentioned in Domesday book, the present building is 500 years old. Has patioed frontage where you can sit under the second oldest wysteria in the country (confirmed by Kew Gardens). One bar with two distinct drinking areas. Dark wood and floorboards give pub a feeling of age.

GRENVILLE LODGE
Hawthorne Lane
☎ (01753) 643227
11am-11pm
Hogs Back Traditional

English Ale

Single bar pub with 'Henry's Nightclub' attached. Open plan bar looks out on to large garden. Outer wall of original buildings now forms an arched corridor which helps break up the bar area. Modern beams give pub a traditional feel.

STAG

Hawthorne Lane
☎ (01753) 642226
11am-3pm; 5.30pm-11pm
(Opens 11am-11pm on Saturday)
Boddingtons Bitter;
Brakspear Bitter; Wadworth
6X; Regular Guest Beers

Large, single bar pub with two raised drinking areas, armchair seating, bare wooden floor and stripped pine giving a country feel. The conservatory to the rear doubles as a dining room and family area. Very popular with the young, especially on music nights.

BURROUGHS GROVE

Map Reference: D9
Between Wycombe and Marlow, one and a half miles south of M40 Junction 4, towards Marlow Bottom.

THREE HORSESHOES
(O.S. Ref. 876890)
☎ (01628) 483109
11am-12pm
(Supper licence)
Boddingtons Bitter;
Brakspear Bitter; Flowers
Original

A whitewashed inn on old main road to Marlow. Has a large room with sections and a spacious conservatory restaurant. Wayside Inn concept: no-smoking areas; no loud music, open all day Sunday for food etc. Occasional Dixieland Jazz nights.

BUTLERS CROSS

Map Reference: D7
Wendover 2 miles East.

RUSSELL ARMS
(O.S. Ref. 842071)
☎ (01296) 622618
11am-3pm; 6pm-11pm
ABC Best Bitter; Marston's
Pedigree

Two-bar pub at the foot of Coombe Hill. Formerly owned by Aylesbury Brewery Co. it was taken over by the Pubmaster chain in 1993. Large secluded garden with childrens play area. Somewhat under utilised as restaurant is rarely used. No food Monday evening.

Squirrel, Booker   *AG, 1994*

CADMORE END

Map Reference: D9
The village is on the B482, its centre lying to the south of the main road. The church offers one of the warmest welcomes to participants in the annual sponsored walk and bicycle ride in aid of historic churches.

BLUE FLAG
(O.S. Ref. 777931)
☎ (01494) 881183
11am-2.30pm; 5.30pm-11pm
Fuller's London Pride; Morland Original Bitter; Old Luxter's Barn Ale; Wadworth 6X; Occasional Guest Beers

Impeccable service and a warm pub. Strong emphasis on food including fish specialities. High quality hotel accomodation.

OLD SHIP
(O.S. Ref. 788925)
☎ (01494) 883496
11am-3.30pm; 6pm-11pm
Brakspear Bitter, Special, Old

Tiny, totally unspoilt, traditional country pub. All beer carried up from cellar. One of the classic Hambleden Valley pubs on road between Stokenchurch and Lane End. Limited parking nearby. No food Sunday lunchtime.

CADSDEN

Map Reference: D7
On the Ridgeway long distance path. Princes Risborough 2 miles SW. Nearest BR station is Monks Risborough.

PLOUGH

Cadsden Road
☎ (01844) 343302
Noon-2.30pm; 5.30pm-11pm
(Closes 3pm-6pm Saturday afternoon)

Greene King IPA, Abbot; Hook Norton Best Bitter, Old Hooky; Regular Guest Beers

In a secluded setting suurrounded by beech woods, this pub, built in 1830, has the Ridgeway long distance path passing the front door. Popular lunchtime and weekend stop for ramblers and cyclists. Recent change of owner and management.

CALVERTON

Map Reference: D3
A pretty village, satellite to Stony Stratford, but if the present building rate continues, not for much longer.

SHOULDER OF MUTTON

Lower Weald
☎ (01908) 562183
11am-2.30pm; 5.30pm-11pm
(Opens 11.45am-2.30pm; 6pm-11pm Saturday)

Courage Directors; John Smith's Bitter; Ruddles Best Bitter, County; Wadworth 6X

This large single roomed friendly pub dating in parts back almost three hundred years caters to a good mixed age group. It has plenty of seating. Bar meals on all days though the main menu is not available on Sunday evenings. The pub has a strong quiz team. Separate accommodation is available. In addition to the wide range of regular ales there is usually a guest.

CASTLETHORPE

Map Reference: D2
Small attractive village in the Carrington estate about 3 miles N of Wolverton. It has a noted Norman church. Served at one time by a surprisingly large railway station but less surprisingly no longer operational.

CARRINGTON ARMS

1 South Street
☎ (01908) 510257
Noon-2.30pm; 6pm-11pm
(Opens 7pm Saturday evenings)

Greene King IPA; John Smith's Bitter; Wadworth 6X

Lively village pub with an imposing frontage. Rare outlet for Northants skittles. No food available. A real fire in the lounge bar and games, juke box and other entertainment in the public bar. Folk music on first Sunday every month.

CHACKMORE

Map Reference: B3
Remote village about 1 mile NW of Buckingham and very near Stowe School, former seat of the Dukes of Buckingham.

QUEEN'S HEAD
Main Street (O.S. Ref. 686358)
☎ (01280) 813004
Noon-2.30pm; 6.30pm-11pm
Draught Bass; Worthington Best Bitter; Charrington IPA

Welcoming and well run village pub, if a little remote. Can get very crowded. For the historians amongst us the queen's head in question was that of Queen Anne.

CHALFONT ST GILES

Map Reference: F9
An overgrown village in the Misbourne Valley. Milton came here to escape the Plague; the ploy obviously worked, as he succeeded in completing 'Paradise Lost' and beginning 'Paradise Regained'. His cottage has been kept as a museum.

CROWN
High Street
☎ (01494) 872110
11am-3.30pm; 5.30pm-11pm
Benskins Best Bitter; Marston's Pedigree; Flowers Original

Quiet and totally traditional, one-bar, street-corner local with its own off license attached. No food Sunday lunchtimes.

FEATHERS
High Street
☎ (01494) 874039
11am-3pm; 5.30pm-11pm
(Opens 11am-11pm Friday & Saturday)
Boddingtons Bitter; Brakspear Bitter; Fuller's London Pride

Pub situated in centre of village, popular and pleasant atmosphere.

FOX AND HOUNDS
Silver Hill (O.S. Ref. 987936)
☎ (01494) 872151
11am-3pm; 5.30pm-11pm
Benskins Best Bitter; Marston's Pedigree; Occasional Guest Beers

Quiet, two-bar pub, off the beaten track. No lunches Sunday or Monday.

IVY HOUSE
London Road
☎ (01494) 872184
11.30am-3.30pm; 6.30pm-11pm
Boddingtons Bitter; John Smith's Bitter; Ushers Founders Ale; Regular Guest Beer

Country pub/restaurant very much geared towards food. Comfortable and civilized with a French theme. No evening meals on Sunday.

MERLIN'S CAVE
Village Green
☎ (01494) 875101
11am-2.30pm; 5.30pm-11pm
ABC Best Bitter, Ind Coope Burton Ale; Tetley Bitter; Regular Guest Beer

Popular and comfortable, two bar pub which appeals to a wide ranging clientele. Pool table in rear bar and jazz every Sunday lunchtime in the attached barn.

MILTON'S HEAD
20 Dean Way
☎ (01494) 875856
11am-11pm
Morland Original Bitter

Down to earth local with one bar offering regular discos or karaoke on Friday nights.

PHEASANT INN
London Road
☎ (01494) 872113
11am-3pm; 5.30pm-11pm
ABC Best Bitter, Benskins Best Bitter, Ind Coope Burton Ale; Tetley Bitter

Friendly 16th century village inn near Milton's cottage. Children's play area in garden.

WHITE HART
Three Households
☎ (01494) 872441
11am-2.30pm; 6pm-11pm
Morland Original Bitter, Old Speckled Hen; Theakston's XB; Regular Guest Beer

Much improved in recent years, this pub has much to recommend it. It offers two smart and clean bars, a friendly welcome and appeals to a mixed clientele.

CHALFONT ST PETER

Map Reference: F9
By-passed village which has suffered much from modern development but fortunately retains some charm. The dreaded Judge Jeffreys once lived here. The Chalfont centre for epilepsy was founded here in 1895.

GEORGE
137 High Street
☎ (01753) 886637
11am-11pm
Courage Best Bitter; Ruddles County

An ancient inn which is now very much a noisy, young persons pub.

GREYHOUND
High Street
☎ (01753) 883404
11am-11pm
Courage Best Bitter, Directors; John Smith's Bitter; Marston's Pedigree; Ruddles County; Wadworth 6X

14th century residential inn which once doubled as a courthouse. Judge Jeffries, the hanging judge, held court here and it is reputed that the last man to be sentenced to death for sheep stealing was hanged from a tree next to the inn. No food on Sunday evening. The beers are all kept under blanket pressure.

JOLLY FARMER
Gold Hill West
☎ (01753) 882464
11.30am-3pm; 5.30pm-11pm
(Opens 11.30am-11pm on Saturday)
Taylor Walker Best Bitter; Tetley Bitter; Regular Guest Beer

Large two-bar, 'Big Steak' pub facing Gold Hill Common. The public bar is lively with locals playing pool and darts and has a juke box. The comfortable and friendly lounge bar is now less food orientated than previously. A no smoking area is planned.

POACHERS
High Street
☎ (01753) 882454
11.30am-11pm
(Opens Noon-11pm on Saturday)
Tetley Bitter; Beer with House Name

Long narrow one-bar pub with two pool tables. Very much a centre of life for the young. Poachers Bitter is a low priced house beer.

WAGGON AND HORSES
Copthall Lane
☎ (01753) 888755
11am-11pm
Courage Best Bitter; Fuller's London Pride

Small one-bar locals pub with a warm welcome.

WHITE HART
High Street
☎ (01753) 887725
11am-11pm
(Opens 11.30am-11pm on Saturday)
Benskins Best Bitter, Ind Coope Burton Ale; Marston's Pedigree; Tetley Bitter; Regular Guest Beer

Fine 16th century coaching inn with many low beams and an unusual fireplace. The ghost of a former landlord, Fiddler Ross, is reputed to play his violin in the dead of night. An excellent selection of board games is available. No food Sunday.

CHARTRIDGE

Map Reference: E7
Chesham 2 miles SE

BELL
☎ (01494) 782878
11am-2.30pm; 6pm-11pm
(Closes 3pm Saturday lunchtime)
Greene King IPA; Benskins

Best Bitter, Ind Coope Burton Ale; Marston's Pedigree

Genuine village pub with a welcome for all. The pub dates back to the 16th century and the games/family room was formerly the stables.

CHEARSLEY

*Map Reference: C6
Aylesbury 7 miles NE.
Pretty village close to the Thame, with a 13th century church. The nearby Notley Abbey was founded in 1162 by the first Earl of Buckingham.*

BELL

Church Lane
(Near A418)
☎ (01844) 208263
Noon-2pm; 6pm-11pm
(Opens 12am-4pm; 6pm-11pm on Saturday)
Fuller's Chiswick Bitter, London Pride

An attractive thatched one-bar local, overlooking the village green. Open hearth fire. Annual pumpkin competition in the autumn.

CHEDDINGTON

*Map Reference: E6
Straggling village once linked with the fortunes of nearby Mentmore Estate. Attained brief notoriety as the scene of the Great Train Robbery in 1963.*

OLD SWAN

58 High Street
☎ (01296) 668226
11am-2.30pm; 6pm-11pm
(Opens 11am-11pm Friday & Saturday)
ABC Best Bitter; Tring Ridgeway Bitter; Wadworth 6X; Regular Guest Beer

450 year old rural pub with attached restaurant attracting a mixed clientele. The pub has regular theme nights and a golf society. A gated childrens area is provided in the garden.

ROSEBERY ARMS

Station Road
☎ (01296) 668222
11.30am-2.30pm; 5.30pm-11pm
Brakspear Special; Charles Wells Eagle, Bombardier; Regular Guest Beer

Fine old ex-hotel, now a free house, offering good value food and drink near the scene of the Great Train Robbery. The bar has recently changed sides! No food Sunday evening.

BEER IS BEST

THE TRING BREWERY
Brewers of finest traditional Ales
Come along and pick up your own beer
if you wish

*We accommodate customers' requirements for
fine
locally brewed real ales from quantities
suitable for hotels and drinking establishments
to
private functions and parties
or by individual collection
from the Brewery.*

**81-82 Akeman St Tring
Tel 01442 890721**

21/00000/638

THREE HORSESHOES
13 Mentmore Road
☎ (01296) 668367
Noon-2.30pm; 6pm-11pm
(Closes 2.30pm Sunday lunchtime)

Greene King IPA; Benskins Best Bitter; Flowers Original

Quiet, traditional local with two bars and a 'jug & bottle' serving hatch.

CHENIES

Map Reference: G8
A most most attractive model village with fine Tudor manor house. The church contains monuments of the Russell family, the Dukes of Bedford.

BEDFORD ARMS HOTEL
☎ (01923) 283301
11am-3.30pm; 5.30pm-11pm

Theakston's Best Bitter; Younger's IPA; Occasional Guest Beers

Upmarket Mount Charlotte-Thistle hotel with two comfortable bars (one primarily for cocktails). Bar food is available every session.

RED LION
(O.S. Ref. 022980)
☎ (01923) 282722
11am-2.30pm; 5.30pm-11pm

Adnams Bitter; Benskins Best Bitter; Wadworth 6X; Occasional Guest Beers

Friendly, busy village pub, now a free house, which attracts drinkers and diners from near and far. The pub is notable for its complete lack of electronic machines and has an amazing 'snug', to the rear of the dining room.

CHESHAM

Map Reference: F8
Recent years have seen High Street pedestrianised and a clock tower erected in Market Square, the original Town Hall clock proudly in place once again. The town, formerly industrial, known to many as 'Sleepy Hollow' and for its beer, boots, brushes and Baptists. The last brewery of three in the town sadly closed in the late fifties, but a new public house now occupies the old General Post Office in the town centre.

BLACK CAT
Lycrome Road, Lye Green
(1½ miles NE of town)
☎ (01494) 783850
11am-11pm

Greene King IPA; Marston's Pedigree

Country pub where a good selection of pub games are played. The pub attracts a selection of locals and passing trade. No food Sunday evening.

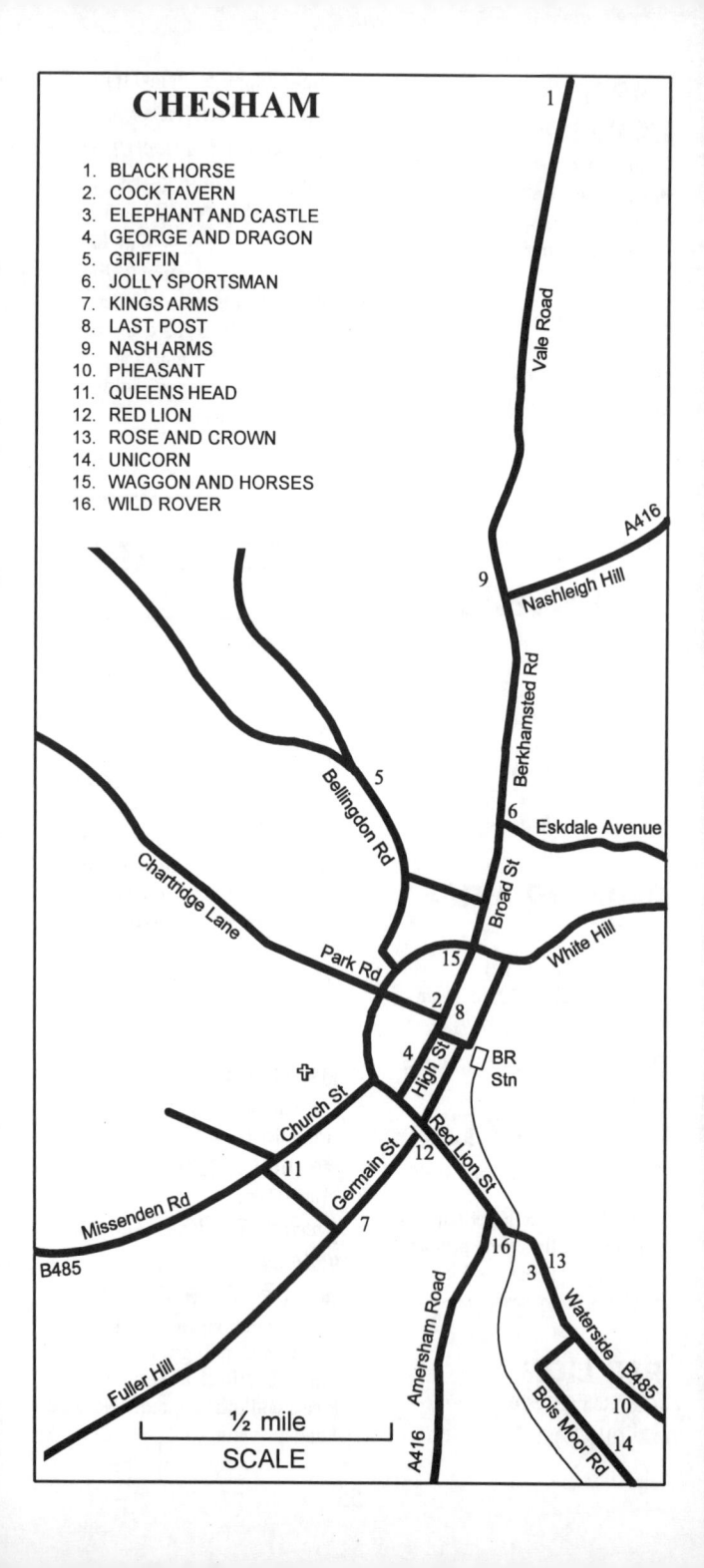

CHESHAM

1. BLACK HORSE
2. COCK TAVERN
3. ELEPHANT AND CASTLE
4. GEORGE AND DRAGON
5. GRIFFIN
6. JOLLY SPORTSMAN
7. KINGS ARMS
8. LAST POST
9. NASH ARMS
10. PHEASANT
11. QUEENS HEAD
12. RED LION
13. ROSE AND CROWN
14. UNICORN
15. WAGGON AND HORSES
16. WILD ROVER

½ mile
SCALE

BLACK HORSE
Chesham Vale (O.S. Ref. 964046)
(Two miles North of Chesham on Cholesbury Road)
☎ (01494) 784656
11am-2.30pm; 6pm-11pm
Adnams Bitter; Benskins Best Bitter, Ind Coope Burton Ale; Tring Ridgeway Bitter; Regular Guest Beer

Comfortable old inn with an enormous garden. Inside the accent is on food, but drinkers are also very welcome. Watch out for the low beam.

COCK
96 Broadway
☎ (01494) 782792
11am-11pm
Shipstones Bitter; Wadworth 6X; Regular Guest Beers

One-bar town centre pub catering mainly for local trade.

ELEPHANT AND CASTLE
Waterside
☎ (01494) 783834
11am-11pm
Courage Best Bitter; Morland Old Speckled Hen; Wadworth 6X; Webster's Yorkshire Bitter

Basic back street local. Note that all beers are served through swan-neck pumps. No food at weekends.

GEORGE AND DRAGON
High Street
☎ (01494) 782402
11am-11pm
Greene King IPA; Tetley Bitter; Wadworth 6X; Regular Guest Beer

Old, town centre coaching inn, dating back to the 16th century.

GRIFFIN
Bellingdon Road
☎ (01494) 783064
11am-11pm
Benskins Best Bitter; Tetley Bitter; Regular Guest Beer

Very much a locals pub with two bars, just out of the centre of town. Recently refurbished, the Sedgwick's sign refers to a former Watford brewer.

JOLLY SPORTSMAN
2 Eskdale Avenue
☎ (01494) 784628
11am-11pm
Ind Coope Burton Ale

Traditional, street corner, locals pub which welcomes families. No food available on Sunday.

KINGS ARMS
King Street
☎ (01494) 783626
11.30am-2.30pm; 6pm-11pm
Greene King IPA; John Smith's Bitter; Webster's

Yorkshire Bitter

Street corner local with a mixed clientele, it is Chesham's oldest town pub, circa 1731. Frequent discos and sing-songs.

LAST POST
77 The Broadway
☎ (01494) 785622
11am-10pm
(Closes 10pm every night including Sunday)
Theakston's Best Bitter, XB; Younger's Scotch; Regular Guest Beers

Typical J.D. Wetherspoon conversion of what used to be the old town post office (hence the name) which opened in 1994.

NASH ARMS
1 Vale Road
☎ (01494) 782440
11am-3pm; 5pm-11pm
(Opens 11am-11pm Friday & Saturday)
Ind Coope Burton Ale; Tetley Bitter

Traditional, solid town local with two bars and the accent on games. Beer is conditioned using cask breathers.

PHEASANT
Waterside
☎ (01494) 783387
11am-3pm; 5.30pm-11pm
(Opens 11am-11pm Saturday)
Adnams Bitter; Ind Coope Burton Ale; Marston's Pedigree; Occasional Guest Beers

Solid, back street, local with bouncy castle in the garden. No food Sunday.

QUEENS HEAD
Church Street
☎ (01494) 783773
11am-2.30pm; 5pm-11pm
(Opens 6pm Saturday evening)
Brakspear Bitter, Special, Old; Fuller's London Pride; Regular Guest Beer

Traditional public bar and comfortable and airy lounge, make this an excellent old-town local. Very much a centre of local life. Brakspear's 'Old' is an occasional winter visitor. No food on Sunday.

RED LION
Red Lion Street
☎ (01494) 784565
11am-3pm; 5.30pm-11pm
(Opens 11am-11pm Friday & Saturday)
Draught Bass; Hancock's HB, Worthington Best Bitter; Charrington IPA

Young people's venue in town centre with the emphasis on games and music.

ROSE AND CROWN
Waterside
☎ (01494) 786564
Noon-11pm
Boddingtons Bitter; Fuller's London Pride; Greene King IPA, Abbot; Morland Old Speckled Hen; Regular Guest Beers

Busy out-of-town local with wide cross-section of drinking clientele.

UNICORN
107 Bois Moor Road
☎ (01494) 783220
11am-3pm; 5pm-11pm
(Opens 11am-11pm Saturday)
Draught Bass; Tetley Bitter

Out of town pub near Chesham Bois. Occasional live music. No food on Sunday.

WAGGON AND HORSES
High Street
☎ (01494) 783111
11am-11pm
Butcombe Bitter; Benskins Best Bitter, Ind Coope Burton Ale

One-bar pub, with garden, in town centre.

WILD ROVER
2 Amersham Road
☎ (01494) 771991
11am-3pm; 5pm-11pm
Ansells Bitter; Tetley Bitter

Recently refurbished one-bar pub, with a distinctly Irish flavour. Formerly 'The White Horse'.

CHESHAM BOIS

Map Reference: F8
Just north of Amersham on the A416.

RED LION
Chestnut Lane (O.S. Ref. 969990)
☎ (01494) 724944
11am-11pm
Greene King IPA; Tetley Bitter; Wadworth 6X

Busy and popular locals pub.

CHICHELEY

Map Reference: E2
2 Miles NE of Newport Pagnell on the A422 Bedford road this very small village was probably inhabited by the staff of Sir John Chester, owner and part architect of Chicheley Hall. Thought to be one of the best surviving examples from the English Baroque period. The hall is now occupied by descendants of the Beatty family.

CHESTER ARMS
☎ (01234) 391214
11am-2.30pm; 6pm-11pm
Greene King IPA, Abbot

Whitewashed roadside pub with red roof tiles. Pleasant interior with some tongue and groove wood panelling. Divided drinking areas and split level restaurant. Horse brasses, plates and notably teapots decorating the walls and shelves.

CLIFTON REYNES

Map Reference: E1
An almost hidden village close to Olney but on the opposite bank of the Ouse.

ROBIN HOOD
(O.S. Ref. 902512)
☎ (01234) 711574
Noon-2.30pm; 6.30pm-11pm
Greene King IPA, Abbot

16th century pub with two bars and a conservatory. A spacious garden where on summer Sundays barbecues can be enjoyed. Caters for local clientele due to its remoteness. Popular with walkers though the landlord doesn't welcome their muddy boots. No food Monday evenings.

COLESHILL

Map Reference: F8
A large hilltop village with some impressive Georgian and Victorian houses. Parish was part of Hertfordshire for centuries.

MAGPIES
Amersham Road
☎ (01494) 726754
11am-11pm
Boddingtons Bitter; Marston's Pedigree; Flowers Original

Isolated pub on Amersham - Beaconsfield road. Recently extended into a 'Brewers Fayre', the Magpies caters for families and offers food all day.

RED LION
Village Road
☎ (01494) 727020
11.30am-3.30pm; 5.30pm-11pm
(Opens 11.30am-11pm on Saturday)
Morrells Bitter; Tetley Bitter; Wadworth 6X; Flowers IPA

Smart village pub with an equal welcome for drinkers and diners. High quality food is served in the one comfortable bar. This pub probably has the smallest gents' loo in the area!

COLNBROOK

Map Reference: G11
Astride the old Bath Road, and formerly an important staging-post, it is famed for its inns and houses of all ages. Royalty has spent nights here down the centuries - the young Elizabeth I, Henry VIII, and Charles I during the Civil War. At the time this guide was prepared Colnbrook was at Buckinghamshire's southernmost tip and we have included all its pubs, despite the fact that the Punch Bowl and the Star & Garter were just over the county boundary in Surrey. All this has now changed, since from 1st April 1995 Colnbrook has become part of Berkshire!

CROWN

Old Bath Road
☎ (01753) 682026
Noon-11pm
(Close 4pm - 7pm on Saturday)
Tetley Bitter; Regular Guest Beers

Large single bar smartly furnished with integral velour buttoned bench seating around the walls, finished in dark wood to match the beams on the high ceiling. The conservatory (suitable for families) has the same styling.

GEORGE

146 High Street
☎ (01753) 682010
11am-3pm; 5pm-11pm
Courage Best Bitter; Marston's Pedigree; Morland Old Speckled Hen

The original pub may date from 1106, there being little proof whether it is older than the Ostrich. In 1558 the inn received Princess Elizabeth as prisoner to Queen Mary on their way from Woodstock to Hampton Court. Now a large single bar with the original beams and old wood panelling. Views of the village of times gone by start at the right hand side of the bar. The staircase to the Georgian restaurant is Edwardian.

GREYHOUND

Colnbrook By-pass
☎ (01753) 684920
(Varied opening with late extensions)
Regular Guest Beer

Originally a 1930's roadside inn, now run as a gay nightclub.

OSTRICH INN

High Street
☎ (01753) 682682
11am-3pm; 6pm-11pm
John Smith's Bitter; Ruddles Best Bitter; Tetley Bitter; Regular Guest Beers

The present building dates from about 1500, but there are records of an inn dating back to 1106 and thus the pub claims to be the third oldest in the land. The building is of timber and plaster with a projected upper storey with gables at either end. The bar is accessed via a door under an archway which leads to a yard which is now the car park. The interior panelling is 17th century as is the staircase which leads up to the function room/restaurant. In the bar is a scale model of a 'Sweeney Todd' type bed, from which a previous owner in the 14th century would hurl guests to their deaths in the cellar, and then dispose of the bodies, pocketing their riches.

PUNCH BOWL

Old Bath Road
☎ (01753) 682683
Noon-3pm; 5pm-11pm
(Opens Noon-11pm Friday, all day Saturday)
Draught Bass; Regular Guest Beer

Possibly the original building is Georgian, but has had many alterations over the years. The narrow L-shaped bar has been modernised with new beams and leaded glass above the bar giving the interior a country style.

RED LION
High Street
☎ (01753) 682685
Noon-3pm; 7pm-11pm
Ushers Founders Ale;
Seasonal Beers

580 year old building with small single bar split into three areas reflecting the original layout. Fitted with wood panelling and original bench seating in bay window. Popular with locals - one of the cheapest pubs in the area. Fish & chip van on forecourt on Wednesdays. Live music on alternate Sundays.

STAR & GARTER
Park Street
☎ (01753) 682157
Noon-11pm
Courage Best Bitter; Morland Old Masters; Regular Guest Beer

500 year old listed building below road level has been a pub for 300 years. Small cosy bar with original oak beams. Interesting display of plates on frieze shelf; note Toby jugs and bottles. Bistro/restaurant in cellar, intimately seating 16, corridor area from which is no smoking area. Garden which overlooks River Coln has swings and wood animals for the kids.

CRYERS HILL

Map Reference: E8
Prestwood 2½ miles North.

WHITE LION
(O.S. Ref. 875969)
☎ (01494) 712303
11am-3pm; 5.30pm-11pm
(11am-11pm Fridays)
Courage Best Bitter;
Wadworth 6X; Regular Guest Beer

17th century pub with extensions. Located at top of Cryers Hill on A4128.

CUBLINGTON

Map Reference: D5
Quiet village in rolling vale countryside, 5 miles north of Aylesbury. One of the sites chosen for the third London airport in the 1970's but, happily reprieved.

UNICORN
High Street
☎ (01296) 681261
Noon-3pm; 5.30pm-11pm
Beer Range Varies

Excellent low-beamed village local with open fires at each end of a long bar. Separate dining room (no meals Sunday evening). Five real ales served from a changing range. Happy hour 5.30pm - 7pm.

62

CUDDINGTON

Map Reference: C6
Aylesbury 5 miles NE. A quiet village with many original buildings, an interesting church, and some fine examples of the traditional 'wichert' walls crested with tile and thatch.

ANNIE BAILEY'S
Upper Church Street
☎ (01844) 291215
Noon-3pm; 6.30pm-11pm
(Closed Sunday night and all day Monday)
Brakspear Bitter; Marston's Pedigree

Formerly the Red Lion, renamed when purchased from ABC, and called after a landlady in the 1840's whose history can be read in the bar. Emphasis on food but drinkers welcome. Don't miss the marinated olives. The Burrow Hill cider is popular.

CROWN
Aylesbury End
☎ (01844) 292222
Noon-2.30pm; 6pm-11pm
Fuller's Chiswick Bitter, London Pride, ESB

Very attractive 13th century thatched building. Extensive interior alteration has kept the character and improved the appearance. Two superb 'corbaling' (inglenook) fireplaces provide winter warmth.

DAGNALL

Map Reference: F6
Wayside village between Whipsnade Zoo and Ivinghoe Beacon. A brewery flourished here until around the turn of the century.

GOLDEN RULE
Main Road South
☎ (01442) 843227
Noon-2.30pm; 6pm-11pm
(Opens 12.30pm Saturday lunchtime)
Boddingtons Bitter; Fuller's London Pride, ESB; Greene King IPA; Wadworth 6X; Regular Guest Beer

Busy free house with one u-shaped bar serving a sixth beer at weekends. An additional car park is available opposite the pub. There is no food available on Sunday.

RED LION
Main Road North
☎ (01442) 843272
11am-3pm; 5.30pm-11pm
(Opens 11am-11pm Saturday)
Greene King IPA, Abbot; Regular Guest Beer

Village pub with bar and separate dining room attracting locals and passers by. No evening meals on Monday.

DENHAM

Map Reference: G9
Near the junction of the M25 and M40. A delightful old-world village cheek by jowl with modern development.

FALCON
Village Road
☎ (01895) 832125
11am-3pm; 5.30pm-11pm
Brakspear Bitter; Marston's Pedigree; Morland Old Speckled Hen; Flowers IPA, Wethered Winter Royal

Excellent, quiet village local with one bar and upstairs toilets. No children under 14. No lunches on Sunday. Fish and chip suppers available on Friday evening between 6.30 and 9pm.

GREEN MAN
Village Road
☎ (01895) 832760
11am-3pm; 5.30pm-11pm
(Opens 5pm Friday evening)
Courage Best Bitter; Fuller's London Pride; Morland Old Speckled Hen; Webster's Yorkshire Bitter

Tastefully furnished one-bar village local with flagstone floor and pale wood panelling on the walls. Large garden with facilities for children at rear. Evening meals Friday to Monday from 7pm - 9pm including à la carte.

NIGHTINGALE
North Orbital Road
☎ (01895) 833848
11am-11pm
Tetley Bitter

25 year old pub, previously called 'The Denham Express', catering for youngsters and locals. One large bar with pool room upstairs complete with video screens.

PLOUGH
Cheapside Lane
☎ (01895) 834098
11am-3pm; 5.30pm-11pm
(Opens 7pm Saturday evening)
Morland Old Speckled Hen; Ruddles Best Bitter, County; Webster's Yorkshire Bitter

One-bar pub with a large restaurant to the rear.

SWAN
Village Road
☎ (01895) 832085
11am-11pm
(Closes 3pm-6pm Saturday afternoon)
Boddingtons Bitter; Courage Best Bitter; Gales HSB; Wadworth 6X; Regular Guest Beer

Large, comfortably furnished, one-bar village pub with large garden to the rear. No evening meals on Sunday. Theme nights on Monday.

DINTON

Map Reference: C6
Aylesbury 4 miles NE.

SEVEN STARS
Stars Lane
☎ (01296) 748241
Noon-2.30pm; 6pm-11pm
(Closed Tuesday evening)
ABC Best Bitter; Tetley Bitter; Wadworth 6X

Lovely 17th century inn with two bars and an à la carte restaurant (booking advisable). Part of the original 'wichert' wall is preserved under a glass panel in the public bar. Large attractive garden, with Aunt Sally and barbecues in summer. No evening meals Sunday or Tuesday.

DORNEY

Map Reference: E10
Between the River Thames and the M4, 3 miles west of Slough.

PALMER ARMS
Village Road
☎ (01628) 666612
11am-3pm; 6pm-11pm
Brakspear Bitter; Regular Guest Beers

Two bar areas and restaurant to the rear, modernised in a country style. Extensive menu with a good selection of vegetarian dishes. Until recently the pub belonged to the Palmer family of Dorney Court where in the past estate workers would get two pints of ale as part of their wages.

PINEAPPLE
Lake End Road
☎ (01628) 662353
11am-2.30pm; 5pm-11pm
Friary Meux Best Bitter, Ind Coope Burton Ale; Tetley Bitter

Originally two cottages dating from 1743. Fronted by a picturesque porch with its own post box. The saloon bar is the original pub and the public is the second cottage. There is a small third room behind the Victorian fireplace in the public.

DOWNLEY

Map Reference: D8
Uphill from Wycombe which is 2 miles to the south.

BRICKLAYERS ARMS
High Street
☎ (01494) 520597
11am-11pm
Courage Best Bitter; Wadworth 6X

Comfortable pub in village High Street providing extensive seating with archway between bars. Fresh fish van sells in car park from 2-3.40pm Wednesdays.

Fox, Dunsmore *NH, 1994*

DOWNLEY DONKEY
Plomer Green Lane
☎ (01494) 448235
11am-11pm
Wethered Bitter
❀ ✕ ❽ 🚗 ♪
Modern estate pub with occasional live music. No food Sunday lunchtime.

LE DE SPENCER ARMS
(O.S. Ref. 849959)
☎ (01494) 535317
11am-2.30pm; 5.30pm-11pm
(Opens 11am-11pm Saturdays)
Fuller's London Pride, Mr Harry, ESB
🏠 ❀ ✕ ✗ ♣ 🚗 ♪
Brick and flint pub remotely situated on a track leading off Downley Common. Purchased by Fullers in the early nineties, it has been renovated and an extension added. Opens at 9am for coffee. No food Sunday evenings. Folk music once a month.

MASTERS
Brindley Avenue
☎ (01494) 524032
11am-11pm
Boddingtons Bitter; Greene King Abbot; Wethered Bitter
❀ 🎱 ❽ 🚗 ♪
Modern one-bar estate pub with games area. Devil amongst the tailors available. Live music Sunday and alternate Saturday evenings. Weekly raffle on Sunday evenings up to £1000.

DRAYTON PARSLOW

Map Reference: D4
Attractive but remote village about 3 miles SW of Bletchley. In the church there is a brass plate that tells the sad tale of 14 orphans. At one time this village

had a bell foundry in the area behind the pub now being used to park caravans.

THREE HORSESHOES
10 Main Road
☎ (01296) 720298
10am-11pm
Fuller's Chiswick Bitter, London Pride, ESB
🍺 ❀ ⛳ 🍴 ✗ 🎲 🅰 ♣ 🚗
Recently reopened and pending a major refurbishment in 1995. Popular village pub with a great deal going for it. Plans for extensions, and improvements are currently in the pipeline.

MOLE & CHICKEN
Easington Terrace (O.S. Ref. 687102)
☎ (01844) 208387
11am-3pm; 6pm-11pm
Courage Best Bitter, Directors; John Smith's Bitter
🍺 ❀ 🍴 ✗ 🎲 ♿ ☺ 🚗
This stone built, one-bar building (c.1839), formerly known as the Rising Sun, stands high above Long Crendon with commanding views to the west. A friendly atmosphere, enhanced by two real fires. Strong emphasis on food. Large collection of Malt Whiskies. Beer selection varies.

DUNSMORE

Map Reference: D7
Wendover 2 miles North. Isolated village buried in the Chiltern beeches high above Wendover; good walking country.

FOX
☎ (01296) 623186
Secluded traditional country pub on the Ridgeway walk. Closed since spring 1995, future uncertain.

EASINGTON

Map Reference: B6

EDLESBOROUGH

Map Reference: F5
Leighton Buzzard 5 miles NW Effectively joined to Eton Bray, across the Beds border, and based on a medieval settlement. High on a bare slope of the Chilterns the church stands like a lighthouse and is arguably the most handsome in the county.

BELL
Leighton Road, Church End
☎ (01525) 220314
11am-3pm; 5pm-11pm
Draught Bass; Greene King IPA
🍺 ❀ 🍴 ✗ 🎲 ♣ ⑧ 🚗
Attractive village local opposite the large church. An inglenook fireplace separates the two bars. Interesting display cases on the walls. No evening meals Monday.

RULE AND SQUARE
1 Brownlow Avenue
☎ (01525) 220999
11am-2.30pm; 6pm-11pm
(Opens 11am-11pm Saturday)
*Theakston's Best Bitter, XB;
Webster's Yorkshire Bitter;
Regular Guest Beer*
🍴 🏠 ❀ ✕ ✕ ♣ 🎱 🚗
Friendly locals pub with a large garden. Spot the old Watney Combe & Reid sign on the way in to the car park! Swan neck pumps abound! No meals Sunday evening.

TRAVELLERS REST
Tring Road
☎ (01525) 220750
11.30am-11pm
Tetley Bitter; Regular Guest Beers
🍴 🍺 ❀ ✕ ✕ 🚗
Old coaching inn dating back to 1770. Pleasant views from garden. Two guest beers always available.

EMBERTON

*Map Reference: E1
1 mile S of Olney and dominated by a fine 14th century church with Emberton Country Park within half a mile, providing fishing, boating and camping facilities.*

BELL & BEAR
12 High Street (O.S. Ref. 886495)
☎ (01234) 711565
9am-1.30pm
*John Smith's Bitter;
Webster's Yorkshire Bitter;
Charles Wells Eagle,
Bombardier*
🍴 ❀ ✕ ✕
The landlord declined to provide comprehensive information.

FARNHAM COMMON

*Map Reference: F10
A northern dormitory extension of Farnham Royal.*

FORESTERS
The Broadway
☎ (01753) 643340
11am-3pm; 5pm-11pm
(Opens 11am - 11pm on Saturday)
Draught Bass; M & B Brew XI; Fuller's London Pride
🍴 🍺 ❀ ✕ ✕ 🅿 ♿
Transformed into a 'Bar Restaurant' in 1991 but retains a good drinking ambience. An enterprising food menu (including vegetarian options) attracts a loyal local following to the restaurant area, part of which is for non-smokers.

ROYAL OAK
Beaconsfield Road
☎ (01752) 642032
11am-11pm
Courage Best Bitter; Ruddles County; Occasional Guest Beers
❀ ✕ ✕ 🅿 ♿ 🎱 🚗
Old country pub that has been comfortably modernised with

psuedo beams and woodwork. Slender bar area with loud music, popular with the young. No evening food Saturday and Sunday.

STAG & HOUNDS
The Broadway, Beaconsfield Road
☎ (01753) 647676
11am-3pm; 5.30pm-11pm
Fuller's London Pride; Greene King IPA; Rebellion Mutiny; Regular Guest Beer

Until recently a country-style pub, but modernised this year into one open plan bar.

VICTORIA
Victoria Road
☎ (01753) 643624
11am-3pm; 6pm-11pm
(Opens 7pm Saturday evening)
Morland Independent IPA, Original Bitter; Theakston's XB

Well kept village local opposite the church. Sports loving clientele provide four darts teams and a crib team.

YEW TREE
Collinswood Road
(One mile north of village)
☎ (01753) 643723
11am-11pm
Morland Independent IPA, Original Bitter, Old Speckled Hen

Friendly and relaxed roadside pub. The public bar has a true country atmosphere and is frequented by clay pigeon shooters and ferret fanciers. The saloon is given over to food which includes the unique 'stone cooking' in the evenings.

FARNHAM ROYAL

Map Reference: F10
Just to the north of Slough, a straggling suburb along the Beaconsfield road (A355). The 'Royal' refers to the bestowal of the manor by William the Conqueror on one of his court aides.

CROWN
Farnham Road
☎ (01753) 643935
11am-11pm
Courage Best Bitter; John Smith's Bitter

Alterations are due as guide goes to press. The bar and restaurant form part of the original building with the plush public bar being a thirties extension with pseudo beams to match the originals.

DUKES HEAD
Farnham Road
☎ (01753) 643138
11am-11pm
Courage Best Bitter; John Smith's Bitter; Marston's Pedigree; Wadworth 6X

Roadside Courage house.

P D Associates
DIRECT COMPUTER CONSULTANTS

INSTALLATIONS,
TRAINING
NETWORKING,
MAINTENANCE
BESPOKE SOFTWARE
D.T.P. SUPPORT

COMPAQ
HEWLETT PACKARD
SAGE
Microsoft
IBM Personal Computer
AST

TEL: (01296) 437601
FAX: (01296) 415476

Temple House, 10 Temple Square,
Aylesbury, Buckinghamshire HP20 2QH

EMPEROR OF INDIA
Black Pond Lane
☎ (01753) 643006
11am-3pm; 5.30pm-11pm
*Boddingtons Bitter;
Brakspear Bitter; Fuller's
London Pride; Flowers
Original*

Small single bar, low ceilinged 300 year old country inn with business clientele lunchtimes and local trade in the evening. A conservatory will be added to the rear. The old barn is weatherproofed and can be used for functions.

FARNHAM PUMP
Park Road
☎ (01753) 644380
11am-11pm
Boddingtons Bitter; Regular Guest Beers

Originally called 'The Jolly Butchers' as there was a butchers shop on the site. The tiled front is listed but hidden under a false exterior. The open plan single bar has a replica of the Farnham pump in the centre. Small games room to the left of the entrance. No food Sunday.

GREEN MAN
Beaconsfield Road
☎ (01753) 643812
11am-3pm; 5pm-11pm
*Boddingtons Bitter;
Butcombe Bitter; Fuller's
London Pride*

Recently refurbished old coaching

inn, reputedly haunted. Pleasant atmosphere with home cooked lunches a speciality.

FAWLEY

Map Reference: C9
A quiet spot high on the Chilterns, above the Thames near Henley. The nearby 17th century Fawley Court was built by Christopher Wren in 1684 and the grounds laid out by Capability Brown. The grounds and museum are open to the public.

WALNUT TREE
(O.S. Ref. 757872)
☎ (01491) 638360
11am-3pm; 6pm-11pm
Brakspear Bitter, Special

1950's country inn and restaurant set on top of the Chiltern Hills. Bar meals, specials and full à la carte menu. Adjoining restaurant and conservatory enables it to serve an intimate dinner for two or meals for parties up to 70.

FINGEST

Map Reference: C9
Marlow 6 miles SE. A tiny hamlet in a magnificent Chilterns setting. The church is Norman, the massive tower dwarfing the rest of it, and topped by a rare double-saddleback roof.

CHEQUERS
(O.S. Ref. 777911)
☎ (01491) 638335
11am-3pm; 6pm-11pm
Brakspear Bitter, Special, Old

Friendly 15th century pub opposite church. Emphasis on food with separate restaurant - closed Sunday evening. Large, level garden with furniture that greatly extends the eating/drinking area especially in summer.

FINMERE

Map Reference: B4

A chain of houses running away from the A421 about 3 miles W of Buckingham which benefit from a small aerodrome that doubles as a Sunday Market.

RED LION
Mere Lane
☎ (01280) 847836
Noon-3pm; 5.30pm-11pm
Fuller's Chiswick Bitter, London Pride, ESB, Seasonal Beers

A thatched and stone built 16th century village local with a turn of the century interior. Friendly and inviting, this roadside pub is run by an enthusiastic landlord and lady. One long slender bar with an inglenook fireplace and a small restaurant area. Aunt Sally played in garden.

FLACKWELL HEATH

*Map Reference: E9
High Wycombe 3 miles NW*

CHERRY TREE
5 Straight Bit
☎ (01628) 522299
11am-2.30pm; 5pm-11pm
(Opens 4.30pm Friday afternoon)
Benskins Best Bitter; Greene King IPA; Rebellion Mutiny; Occasional Guest Beer

Local village pub, previously called 'Heath's' and 'Valiant Trooper' and has reverted to its original name. Extensively refurbished in 1995 and specialising in home cooked food.

GREEN DRAGON
241 Blind Lane (O.S. Ref. 901892)
☎ (01628) 520764
11am-11pm
Brakspear Special; Fuller's Lonon Pride; Wethered Bitter

Medium sized community pub, mainly local, in suburb of Flackwell Heath. Runs a Sunday football team and weekly quiz night Thursday. Satellite TV.

GREEN MAN
16 Straight Bit
☎ (01628) 520845
11am-11pm
Wadworth 6X; Flowers IPA, Strong Country Bitter

Pub with mixed clientele at centre of Flackwell Heath. Separate pool room, restaurant and children's area. Very happy to supply take-away food.

MAGPIE
56 Heath End Road
☎ (01628) 523696
11am-11pm
Morland Independent IPA, Original Bitter; Regular Guest Beer

Victorian village pub next to Flackwell Heath FC. Horseshoe shaped bar with two differing areas. Large car park and garden with children's play area.

STAG
91 Heath End Road
☎ (01628) 521277
11am-2.30pm; 6pm-11pm
(Opens 5.30pm Saturday evening)
Boddingtons Bitter; Wadworth 6X; Whitbread Best Bitter

Large pub, part of which dates back to 1632, offering panoramic view of the Thames Valley. Restaurant offers varied international home cooked food both lunchtimes and evenings.

THREE HORSESHOES
The Common
☎ (01628) 520541
11am-2.30pm; 5.30pm-11pm
(11am-11pm Friday and Saturday)
Fuller's London Pride; Wethered Bitter; Regular

Chequers, Fingest   *AG, 1991*

Guest Beer
✕ ♣ 🚗

Impressive exterior but reverse Tardis effect. Beautiful, large garden allows grazing - no drinking! Lunches to order except Sunday. Pinball machine. who lived in a nearby cave whose history is displayed in the pub and Aylesbury Museum has one of his famous boots. Bookings taken in evening for meals in Saloon bar.

FORD

Map Reference: C7
Aylesbury 4 miles NE

DINTON HERMIT
Water Lane (O.S. Ref. 778095)
☎ (01296) 748379
11am-2.30pm; 6pm-11pm
(Closed Monday lunchtimes)
Draught Bass; ABC Best Bitter; Tetley Bitter
🏠 🍺 ✿ ✕ ✕ ♿ 🍻 ♣ 🚗
A friendly and cosy 15th century village inn. Named after a hermit

FORTY GREEN

Map Reference: E9
Beaconsfield 2 miles SE.

ROYAL STANDARD OF ENGLAND
Forty Green Road (O.S. Ref. 923919)
(Turn off B474 at Knotty Green Garage)
☎ (01494) 673382
11am-3pm; 5.30pm-11pm
Marston's Pedigree, Owd Rodger; Morland Old Speckled Hen; Rebellion IPA
🏠 🍺 ♿ ✿ ✕ ✕ 🚗

Ancient, rambling and historic pub in the same private ownership since 1961. Several bars of outstanding character. Difficult to find but popular at all times. Cold meals and cheeses a speciality.

teas in Summer. Home to Alvis and Aston Martin Owners Club.

FRIETH

Map Reference: D9
Marlow 5 miles SE

PRINCE ALBERT

Moors End (O.S. Ref. 798906)
(100 yds from Lane End to Frieth Road)
☎ (01494) 881683
11am-3pm; 5.30pm-11pm
Brakspear Mild, Bitter, Special, Old, OBJ
🏠 🍺 ❀ ✕ ♣

One of the best pubs in the Thames valley. Has appeared in the Good Beer Guide 21 times. Superb atmosphere, location and hospitality. Josie's platefuls are a bonus at lunchtime (Mon-Sat).

YEW TREE

(O.S. Ref. 798903)
☎ (01494) 882330
10.30am-2.30pm; 6pm-11pm
(Opens all day in summer)
Old Luxter's Barn Ale;
Ringwood Old Thumper;
Ruddles Best Bitter;
Webster's Yorkshire Bitter
🏠 🍺 ❀ ✕ ✕ 🅿 ♨ 🚗 🛏

Comfortable bar and recommended restaurant - Michelin and Good Food guides. Bar snacks till 10.30. Afternoon

FULMER

Map Reference: F10
Gerrards Cross 2m N. Tiny and attractive village nestling in a deep hollow.

BLACK HORSE

Windmill Road
☎ (01753) 663183
11am-11pm
Draught Bass; Boddingtons Bitter; Courage Best Bitter; Regular Guest Beers
🏠 🍺 ❀ ✕ ✕ ♨ ♣ 🚗

Early 17th century three-bar pub. Centre bar is smallest, plain and simple with parquet flooring. Comfortable saloon. Prior to becoming a pub it housed the workers who built the church next door. Shove Ha'penny in Fulmer bar, strictly no music or machines. No food Sunday lunchtime.

GAWCOTT

Map Reference: B4
Straggling village 1½ miles SW of Buckingham that was the birthplace of renowned architect, Sir Gilbert Scott, whose works include the restoration of Chester Cathedral, the design of Liverpool's Anglican Cathedral, the debating hall in the House of Commons and St Pancras Station.

CROWN
Hillesden Road
☎ (01280) 816267

Pub rarely if ever open. Expected refurbishment, sale or closure.

CUCKOO'S NEST
New Inn Lane
☎ (01280) 812092
11am-3pm; 6pm-11pm
Hook Norton Best Bitter; Morland Old Speckled Hen; Regular Guest Beer

Set back from the road this welcoming turn of the century two-bar village local is run by an enthusiastic landlord. Guest beers available during winter. A Good Beer Guide entry for 6 years. Eccentric characters in abundance should make any CAMRA member feel most at home! Closed Monday lunchtimes.

GAYHURST

Map Reference: D2
Scattering of houses 2 miles N of Newport Pagnell. The Francis Drake public house was the gatehouse to a large estate where the 'Gunpowder Plot' was hatched.

SIR FRANCIS DRAKE
Northampton Road (O.S. Ref. 851465)
☎ (01908) 551270
11am-2.30pm; 5.30pm-11pm
Charles Wells Eagle; Regular Guest Beer

Amongst the most unusual pub buildings in the country. It was originally the gatehouse to the manor given to Sir Francis Drake as a reward in the 16th century but the gatehouse didn't become a pub untill 1952. It now boasts a varied menu of very tasty home cooked meals and an ever changing range of real ales. Has been known to hold a beer festival from time to time.

GEORGE GREEN

Map Reference: F10
On the outskirts of Slough towards Uxbridge.

DOUBLE CENTURY
Uxbridge Road
☎ (01753) 528759
11am-11pm
Brakspear Bitter; Courage Best Bitter; Morland Old Speckled Hen

Basic pub set back from road. Built in 1960's to celebrate the bi-centenary of Uxbridge brewers Harman & Co. which was closed by Courage. Saloon and public bars, regular music nights including country & western and go-go dancers on Fridays. Large car park.

GEORGE
Uxbridge Road
☎ (01753) 550482
11am- 2.30pm; 5.30pm-11pm
(Opens 11am-11pm Friday &
Saturday)
*Draught Bass; Boddingtons
Bitter; Webster's Green
Label; Regular Guest Beer*
Spacious two-bar pub with
popular locals bar. The pine
finished saloon leads through to
the garden which has a clildrens
play area. Live music (country &
western or pop) on Friday nights
and discos on Saturday.

GERRARDS CROSS

Map Reference: F9
A small but superior commuter town on the A40.

APPLE TREE
Oxford Road
☎ (01753) 887335
11am-11pm
*Boddingtons Bitter;
Wadworth 6X; Flowers
Original*
Large 'Beefeater' roadhouse with
a mixed clientele.

ETHORPE HOTEL
Packhorse Road
☎ (01753) 882039
11am-11pm
*Courage Directors; Webster's
Yorkshire Bitter*
Hotel cum steakhouse which dates
back to Georgian times. Formerly
a nursing home then a family run
hotel it became a 'Berni Inn' in
the 70's and is now one of
Scottish and Newcastle's 'Country
Grills'. In addition to the
restaurant there is one large bar
where meals and snacks are also
available. Quiet on weekday
lunchtimes, the hotel attracts a
mixed clientele in the evenings.

FRENCH HORN
Oxford Road
☎ (01753) 883470
11am-11pm
*Benskins Best Bitter; Tetley
Bitter*
Large and loud one-bar pub, very
much a young persons venue.

PACK HORSE
West Common Road
☎ (01753) 883554
11am-11pm
*Benskins Best Bitter;
Marston's Pedigree; Tetley
Bitter*
Young persons pub with mixed
trade at lunchtimes. Loud in the
evening and occasional live
music. No lunches on Sunday.

THREE PIGEONS
Austenwood Lane
☎ (01753) 887291
11am-3pm; 4.30pm-11pm
(Opens 11am-11pm Friday &
Saturday)

Prince Albert, Frieth   *AG, 1991*

Courage Best Bitter, Directors; Wadworth 6X

Friendly one-bar, country pub with a restaurant, in a conservation area. A pleasant watering hole in an area with a shortage of traditional pubs.

GIBRALTAR

Map Reference: C6
Tiny hamlet of approximately 40 inhabitants, situated between Dinton and Cuddington. Originally known as Littleworth but called Gibraltar for the last 150 years or so. The hamlet is believed to be sited on limestone rock 'as firm as the Rock of Gibraltar'.

BOTTLE AND GLASS
(O.S. Ref. 758108)
☎ (01296) 748488
11.30am-2.30pm; 6pm-11pm
Morrells Dark, Bitter, Varsity

Delightful 15th century thatched house with wichert walls and flagstone floors. Extensive and varied menu (including vegetarian).

GRANBOROUGH

Map Reference: C5
Winslow 2 miles N. A handful of thatched cottages and a 14th century church grace this small village. The church is one of several hundred restored by the prolific Gilbert Scott and is worth a visit.

CROWN
7 Winslow Road
☎ (01296) 670216
11am-3pm; 5.30pm-11pm
John Smith's Bitter; Ruddles Best Bitter; Regular Guest Beer

Recently refurbished, neat village local with low ceilings, oak beams and a friendly atmosphere. One bar has been converted to a restaurant, hence emphasis on food, but worth a visit for the beer. No food Sunday evening.

GREAT BRICKHILL

Map Reference: E4
Long village extending between the old A5 and the A4146 Leighton Buzzard road. Many fine houses, an attractive church and some spectacular views.

DUNCOMBE ARMS
32 Lower Way
☎ (01525) 261226
11am-3pm; 5.30pm-11pm
Adnams Broadside; Charles Wells Eagle

A very large floodlit garden where it is possible to play 'adult games'! 9 hole putting green, 19 petanque rinks, full size skittles, American horseshoes (or pitch & toss if you prefer), croquet and giant chess. Reasonably priced single rooms and doubles en suite. Due to be refurbished in early 1995 which will add to the facilities and double the number of real ales.

OLD RED LION
Lower Way
☎ (01525) 261715
11.30am-2.30pm; 5.30pm-11pm
Boddingtons Bitter; Brakspear Bitter; Flowers Original; Young's Special

Traditional village pub with restaurant area. Booking advised at weekends. Occasional quiz nights. Barbecues in the summer, picturesque views from the tidy garden complete with childrens play area.

GREAT HAMPDEN

Map Reference: D7
Princes Risborough 4 miles NW. The body of John Hampden 'the patriot' was brought home for burial after his death at Chalgrove Field. The great Saxon earthwork of Grim's Ditch runs right across the front of Hampden House.

HAMPDEN ARMS
☎ (01494) 488255
Noon-2.30pm; 7pm-11pm
Eldridge Pope Hardy Country; Greene King Abbot; Morland Old Speckled Hen; Tetley Bitter; Wadworth 6X

🍺 ❀ 🍴 ✕ 🚗

Small two-bar country pub on land owned by Hampden Estate and surrounded by beech woods. Extensive and imaginative menu makes this a popular eating house at latter end of week although it does not always open Sunday evenings in the depths of winter.

GREAT HORWOOD

Map Reference: C4
Located 1 mile S of the A421 midway between Bletchley and Buckingham this pleasant village spreads out along the roads from the church at its centre.

CROWN INN
The Square (O.S. Ref. 771311)
☎ (01296) 712295
11am-3pm; 6pm-11pm
Tolly Cobbold Bitter
🍺 ❀ ⚓ ✕ 🍴 ♨ ⛺ 🚗 ♿

Small two-bar village pub with a ubiquitous collection of horse brasses. No food Wednesday.

SWAN
1 Winslow Road
☎ (01296) 712556
11am-2.30pm;
5.30pm-11pm
Jennings Bitter; Webster's Yorkshire Bitter
🍺 ✕ 🍴 ♨ 🚗

Almost lost to the cause but under a new owner, things are looking up. Building up a good food trade as well as a potentially interesting range of guest beers.

GREAT KIMBLE

Map Reference: D7
Wendover 3 miles NE. Great and Little Kimble form a triangle with Smokey Row, on the Lower Icknield Way, with a pub at each corner. There are two churches in the parish, both are worth a visit; All Saints has 14th century wall paintings, while St. Nicholas' displays the names of those (led by John Hampden) who refused to pay the illegal 'ship money' to King Charles.

BERNARD ARMS
Risborough Road
☎ (01844) 46173
11am-3pm; 6pm-11pm
(Closes 2.30pm Sunday lunchtime)
Benskins Best Bitter,
Ind Coope Burton Ale;
Tetley Bitter;
Wadworth 6X
❀ ⚓ ✕ 🍴 📷 ♨ ♣ ❽ 🚗

Prominent hotel and restaurant on ridge at rear of Chequers estate. Haunt of Prime Ministers. Lounge bar with separate games room in barn. International menu with French/Italian overtones and the beer is secondary to an extensive wine cellar. No meals Sunday evening.

SWAN
Lower Icknield Way
☎ (01844) 46175
Small converted cottage with two bars. Closed in August 1991 - future uncertain.

GREAT KINGSHILL

Map Reference: E8
High Wycombe 3 miles S.

RED LION
Missenden Road
☎ (01494) 711262
Noon-2.30pm; 6pm-11pm
Marston's Pedigree; Tetley Bitter; Tolly Cobbold Bitter
19th century brick and flint pub specialising in fish and shellfish. Drinkers still welcome.

ROYAL OAK
Missenden Road
☎ (01494) 711199
11am-3pm; 5pm-11pm
Draught Bass; Morrells Bitter, Varsity
Traditional brick and flint pub with games room. Note unusual bottle end figures on North wall. Happy hours 5.00-7.30 Monday - Friday. Large garden with extensive children's play area.

GREAT MISSENDEN

Map Reference: E8
A large village in the Misbourne Valley north-west of Amersham. An abbey was founded here in 1133; later buildings on the site accommodate an adult education centre. The main street has many interesting builings.

BLACK HORSE
Mobwell (O.S. Ref. 891021)
☎ (01494) 862537
11.30am-3pm; 6pm-11pm
Greene King IPA; Tetley Bitter; Wadworth 6X; Young's Bitter
Popular cosmopolitan pub situated at northern end of the village; famous for the local hot-air ballooners who operate from an adjoining field. Pub also adjoins a Caravan Club of Great Britain site. No food Sundays.

CROSS KEYS
40 High Street
☎ (01494) 865373
11am-3pm; 5.30pm-11pm
Fuller's Hock, London Pride, ESB
About 450 years old, this is the oldest pub in Great Missenden. No dining in the bar in the evening, so retains a good pub atmosphere. High backed settles and a large open fireplace dominate the comfortable bar. Fullers Country pub of year award for 1993 - a gem!

GEORGE
94 High Street
☎ (01494) 862084
11am-11pm
Adnams Bitter; Wadworth 6X; Regular Guest Beers

Interesting multi-level bar in extensive building with separate restaurant area and hotel accomodation. Beams and inglenooks abound in this 15th century coaching inn. Slow moving guest beers on blanket pressure.

NAGS HEAD
London Road
☎ (01494) 862945
11am-3pm; 6pm-11pm
Greene King IPA; Benskins Best Bitter; Marston's Pedigree

Interesting building, parts of which date back to the 16th century, at southern end of the village. Long low beamed bar with inglenook and raised dining area. Later extensions have a 1930's character. Home of Missenden Cricket Club whose pitch is opposite.

WAGGON AND HORSES
109 High Street
☎ (01494) 862934
11am-2.30pm; 5.30pm-11pm
(Opens 11am-11pm Saturdays)
Adnams Bitter; Thomas Greenall's Bitter; Regular Guest Beers

One-bar pub opposite the George.

WHITE LION
57 High Street
☎ (01494) 862114
11am-11pm
Draught Bass; Tetley Bitter

Large one-bar Victorian pub with emphasis on games. Pin table, pool, darts and cribbage teams. Several ante-rooms off bar area but no lobby. Small car park and garden at rear. Strong support by local artisans.

GRENDON UNDERWOOD

Map Reference: B5
Aylesbury 11 miles SE. Famous for its two prisons, the village was a resting place for Shakespeare when travelling from Stratford to London; allegedly he drew the comic characters Dogberry and Verges from an incident which took place here.

SWAN
Main Street
☎ (01296) 770242
Noon-2.30pm; 6pm-11pm
Hancock's HB; Brakspear Bitter; Regular Guest Beer

An attractive, thatched village pub (grade two listed building) with open fires. Garden with swings and Aunt Sally. Noted for good home cooking (no food Wednesday) and very friendly atmosphere.

HADDENHAM

Map Reference: C7
Aylesbury 7 miles NE. An enlarged mediaeval village, once important in the duck-rearing trade. Narrow streets connect groups of cottages built of wichert, a local material not unlike devon cob; one of the ponds is enclosed by a wichert wall with its overhanging thatch 'to keep the ducks dry'.

CROWN INN
19 Fort End
☎ (01844) 292042
11am-3pm; 6pm-11pm
Adnams Bitter; Ansells Bitter; Wadworth 6X

Large, 300 year old pub with definite pub games bias. Reputed to be haunted by a ghost called 'Henry'. Expresso and cappuccino coffees a speciality.

GREEN DRAGON
Churchend
(Follow signs for Churchend)
☎ (01844) 291403
11.30am-2.30pm; 6.30pm-11pm
(Closes 2.30pm Sunday lunchtime)
Marston's Pedigree; Flowers IPA

Attractive and substantial flint stone building, situated near the church and duckpond. The oldest pub in Haddenham, once used as the Courthouse. Boules piste in large attractive garden.

KING'S HEAD
High Street
☎ (01844) 291391
11am-3pm; 5.30pm-11pm
Draught Bass; Ansells Bitter; Tetley Bitter; Occasional Guest Beers

Superb traditional village pub dating back to the 16th century, with unusual hand-carved sign. Home cooked food available every day except Sunday. Approached from either High Street or Townside.

RED LION
Churchend
☎ (01844) 291606
11.30am-3pm; 5.30pm-11pm
(Opens 11am-11pm on Saturday)
Worthington Best Bitter; ABC Best Bitter; Marston's Pedigree; M&B Highgate Mild

Straightforward two-bar local overlooking the village duckpond. One of the longest serving landlords - 23 years.

RISING SUN
9 Thame Road
☎ (01844) 291744
11am-3pm; 6pm-11pm
(Opens 11am-11pm Friday & Saturday)
Charles Wells Eagle; Regular Guest Beers

A small and friendly one-bar village local. A free house since early 1993, having been purchased from Wells. Offers an interesting range of guest beers and occasionally runs mini-beer festivals. No lunches on Sunday. Real cider only in summer.

ROSE AND THISTLE
6 Station Road
☎ (01844) 291451
11.30am-2.30pm; 5.30pm-11pm
(Opens 6pm on Saturday)
Greene King IPA, Abbot
Rambling pub near Churchend Green with long lounge, cosy snug, function room and large garden. Wichert wall in car park.

HAMBLEDEN

Map Reference: D9
Henley-on-Thames 3 miles SW. A delightful brick-and-flint Chilterns village; the first Viscount Hambleden was better known as W.H.Smith. The manor house was the birthplace of the 7th Earl of Cardigan, who led the charge of the Light Brigade at Balaclava. Hambleden Mill on the Thames is much photographed.

STAG AND HUNTSMAN
(O.S. Ref. 785866)
(1 mile North of A4155)
☎ (01491) 571227
11am-2.30pm; 6pm-11pm
Brakspear Bitter, Special; Old Luxter's Barn Ale; Rebellion IPA; Wadworth 6X, Farmer's Glory, Old Timer

Unspoilt, three-bar pub in a picturesque National Trust village. Full à la carte menu in new restaurant. Small parties and weddings catered for.

HANDY CROSS

Map Reference: D9
Just south of Cressex industrial estate on outskirts of Wycombe, at Junction 4 on the M40. Mainly modern commercial development including superstores and the 'Wycombe Six' cinema complex.

BLACKSMITH'S ARMS
Old Marlow Road
☎ (01494) 525323
11am-11pm
Boddingtons Bitter; Wadworth 6X; Flowers Original
Long established pub transformed into Beefeater restaurant ten years ago and refurbished in September 1994. All day licence on Sunday for food.

BOULEVARD
Crest Road
☎ (01494) 461054
11am-2.30pm; 5.30pm-11pm
(Closed Sunday lunchtimes)
Long pseudo-Victorian bar with stained glass mirror wall behind and ceiling supports reminiscent of an old gin palace. Jazz on Thursdays and other live music Tuesday and Saturday.

CREST HOTEL
Crest Road
☎ (01494) 442100
11am-11pm
Courage Directors

Smart hotel for business clientele. Plush, spacious and comfortable bar area. Pool table in separate area with glass walls. Jelly babies available from dispenser on bar.

FLATFOOT SAM'S
Cressex Road
☎ (01494) 450067
11am-11pm
(Closes midnight Friday & Saturday)
Boddingtons Bitter; Flowers Original

Fun, theme venue bar with two ten-pin bowling alleys. Discos or live music five nights a week. Children welcome in large games area.

HANSLOPE

Map Reference: D2
Large village on the Northants border with a church famous for its tall tower that can be seen for miles.

COCK INN
High Street (O.S. Ref. 468805)
☎ (01908) 510553
11am-2.30pm; 6pm-11pm
(Opens till 4pm Saturday afternoon)
John Smith's Bitter;
Wadworth 6X; Webster's Green Label

1920's red brick reconstruction of a 16th century property that burnt down. A clear watershed between the mature customer earlier on and the youngster later.

GLOBE
50 Hartwell Road, Long Street (O.S. Ref. 805468)
☎ (01908) 510336
Noon-2.30pm; 6pm-11pm
(Opens Noon-Midnight on Saturdays)
Banks's Mild, Bitter;
Marston's Pedigree

A two bar 'Olde Worlde' style roadside inn though certainly authentic in parts. One bar with separate games room, the other with an eating area. The new tenant is trying to build up the food trade by getting away from the ordinary pub grub image hence the Sunday all day opening. Large car park and garden replete with a childrens zoo. Opens till midnight on Friday. Banks' beers served by electric dispense.

WATTS ARMS
Castlethorpe Road (O.S. Ref. 805468)
☎ (01908) 510246
Noon-3pm; 6pm-11pm
(Opens 11am-11pm Saturdays)
Charles Wells Eagle, Bombardier

Detached brick built pub standing in the centre of the village. Served

**Thame Road
Haddenham
Buckinghamshire
HP17 8BY**

Using only the *best quality malted barley* and *whole hops*, plus a *traditional brewing method that complies with the stringent German Purity laws* to produce **"The Finest Ale in the Vale"**

Trade & Retail Sales (01844) 290008

---

by two bars, the lounge bar has a dining area set off in an alcove whilst games can be enjoyed in the public bar. A pleasant and friendly atmosphere inside or a large garden and play area if you prefer the open air. Good pub grub and special senior citizens meals Monday to Friday, likewise a happy hour from 6.00 till 7.00 Mondays to Fridays.

HARDWICK

*Map Reference: D5
A hilltop village with an impressive church; there is a monument to Sir Thomas Lee, ancestor of the American Confederate leader.*

BELL
Lower Road
☎ (01296) 641303
Noon-3pm; 6.30pm-11pm
(Opens 11.30am on Saturday)
Draught Bass; Tetley Bitter; Flowers Original; Regular Guest Beers

Friendly two-bar 17th century local which is a listed building. No food Sundays or Monday evening.

HARTWELL

*Map Reference: D6
The Jacobean Hartwell House, was the home of Louis XVIII in*

the early nineteenth century while Napoleon held sway in France. Until a few years ago it was a finishing school for young ladies and is now an expensive hotel, restaurant and conference centre.

BUGLE HORN

Oxford Road
☎ (01296) 748209
11.30am-2.30pm; 6pm-11pm
Ind Coope Burton Ale; Tetley Bitter; Wadworth 6X; Regular Guest Beer

Attractive 17th century inn on the Oxford Road. Conservatory opens onto large garden with excellent children's play area. Open all day Saturday in Summer. No food Monday or Tuesday evening.

HAVERSHAM

*Map Reference: D2
Quiet village about 1 mile NW of Wolverton set on a back road almost on the banks of the River Great Ouse.*

GREYHOUND

2 High Street (O.S. Ref. 829429)
☎ (01908) 313487
11.30am-2.30pm; 5.30pm-11pm
(Opens Noon-3pm; 6.30pm-11pm Saturdays)
Greene King XX Dark Mild, IPA, Abbot

The doomsday book mentions a pub on this site and the current building is at least 400 years old. Today it is noted for a wide range of good value food (no food available on Sundays or Tuesday and Wednesday evenings) Children are welcome in the bar at lunchtimes and until 8.30 at night and there are 17 different pub games available. If that isn't enough amusement there is live music on Tuesday evenings.

HAWRIDGE

*Map Reference: F7
Chesham 4 miles South.
Acres of Commonland high on the Chilterns with a few cottages, pubs and a windmill. Hawridge Court, once the manor farm, is built on the rampart of a prehistoric encampment.*

FULL MOON

(O.S. Ref. 936069)
☎ (01494) 758262
Noon-3pm; 6pm-11pm
Courage Best Bitter; Morrells Bitter, Graduate; Ruddles Best Bitter; Regular Guest Beer

Fine old country pub which has been licensed for over 300 years and was once a 'house of dubious repute'! The pub has been tastefully and radically extended in recent years. No evening meals on Sunday.

ROSE AND CROWN

☎ (01494) 758386
11am-3pm; 6pm-11pm
Courage Best Bitter; Morrells Bitter, Graduate; Ruddles

Best Bitter; Usher's Best Bitter
🍺 ❀ 🗡 ✕ 🚗

Large, recently refurbished pub with two car parks! Owned by the Old English Pub Company. One long bar with dining area at end.

HAZLEMERE

Map Reference: E8
A mainly modern development around a crossroads north of High Wycombe. From a seat in the churchyard it is possible to see almost as far as the other Haslemere in Surrey.
The nearby Beech Tree at Terriers is listed under High Wycombe.

CEDARS
Cedar Avenue
☎ (01494) 716777
11am-11pm
Boddingtons Bitter
♣ 🎱 🚗

Young persons' suburban pub but with recently refurbished lounge area with piano. Features two-lane bowling alley. The future of the pub is in some doubt. Used to be called 'Ninepins'.

CROWN
277 Amersham Road (O.S. Ref. 886953)
☎ (01494) 530188
11.30am-2.30pm; 5.30pm-11pm
(Open 11.30am-11pm Saturday)
Draught Bass; Boddingtons Bitter; Courage Best Bitter
❀ 🗡 🎱 🚗

Large long roomed pub set back off main road, (opposite church). Flint building with attractive floral display at front. Note appropriate slogan across road. Separate pool table area.

MAYFLOWER
193 Penn Road
☎ (01494) 813341
11am-11pm
Boddingtons Bitter; Fuller's London Pride; Flowers Original
❀ 🗡 ✕ ♣ 🚗

Corner pub on main Hazlemere/Penn road. Large room with games area and comfortable lounge. Built in 1953 and rebuilt in 1982. No food Sunday evening.

QUEEN'S HEAD
352 Amersham Road
☎ (01494) 711980
11.30am-2.30pm; 5.30pm-11pm
Morland Independent IPA, Original Bitter, Old Masters
❀ 🗡 ♣ ✓ 🚗

300 year old pub, ex-coaching inn. Stable converted into darts area annexe off public bar. Family crest on wall in lounge. Friendly locals' pub.

THREE HORSESHOES
329 Amersham Road
☎ (01494) 711793
11am-2.30pm; 5.30pm-11pm
(Open 11am-11pm on Friday)
Greene King IPA; Marston's Pedigree
❀ 🗡 🍴

Quiet traditional locals' pub built in the 1760's. Near the parade of shops at Hazlemere crossroads. No food Sunday lunchtime.

HEDGERLEY

Map Reference: F9
Beaconsfield 3m NW.
Hidden in a wooded dell south of the M40, and largely unspoilt by virtue of the narrowness of the surrounding lanes. The church has a pulpit made from satinwood, rescued from a 17th century church in Antigua destroyed by an earthquake.

BRICKMOLD

Village Lane
☎ (01753) 642716
11am-2.30pm; 5.30pm-11pm
(Opens 11am-11pm Saturdays)
Hook Norton Best Bitter; Morland Old Speckled Hen; Theakston's Old Peculier; Wadworth 6X; Regular Guest Beers

Lively village local popular with young people. The pub naturally splits into public and saloon sides. The name originates from the former village brickmaking industry. Garden to side of pub, quite suitable for children. All food home-cooked.

ONE PIN

One Pin Lane
☎ (01753) 643035
11am-3.30pm; 5.30pm-11pm
Courage Best Bitter, Directors

Traditional two-bar pub with an air of class in the saloon. Bar billiards table in the public bar. The landlord has been in residence for thirty years. No food Sunday.

WHITE HORSE

Village Lane
☎ (01753) 643225
11am-3pm; 5.30pm-11pm
Regular Guest Beers

Usually seven beers available, all served by gravity. Picturesque village pub over 500 years old. Wonderful public bar with flagstone floor and inglenook fireplace. Saloon has small bar and open rafters. All food home-cooked. Beer festival in marquee on Whitsun bank holiday.

HIGH WYCOMBE

Map Reference: E9
Halfway from London to Oxford, Wycombe is situated in a long valley surrounded by hills. Industrially, the town is best known for furniture manufacture, which developed from chairmaking using the local beech; the 'bodgers' who produced the legs and rails are immortalised in the Chair Museum on Castle Hill.
Being situated on a coaching route, Wycombe once possessed a considerable number of inns. The Red Lion Hotel in the High Street, where Disraeli made his first political speech, has like many of the older buildings (not least pubs), given way to shops and

offices. There was once a local brewing industry but Wheelers, the last remaining brewery, closed in 1929.

Some parts of the old town remain despite the urban sprawl; Wycombe Abbey (once owned by the Carringtons and now a famous school for girls), the attractive open common along the London Road known as the Rye, the Market Hall (nicknamed 'Pepper Pot') and the 18th century Guildhall which still presents an impressive sight for visitors entering the town from the East. The 13th century church is the largest in Buckinghamshire and features include two remarkable 18th century monuments, a 17th century Jacobean memorial tablet and a colourful 20th century window commemorating seventeen famous women.

There are two shopping centres but little sign of the River Wye as the planners decided to bury it under a car park. The opening of the Swan Theatre in 1992 has significantly increased the range of entertainment available in the town.

The Buckinghamshire College continues its expansion in the university sector, with new degrees combining Criminology, Sociology and Psychology in the Social Sciences faculty, and Tourism, Music Industry Management and Leisure management with Sports Studies degrees in the new Leisure and Tourism faculty.

Today, Wycombe is probably best known for its football club and is the only town in Buckinghamshire to have a league team. Pubs situated in Wycombe's many suburbs (eg. Totteridge, Terriers, Micklefield, Desborough, Sands) are included here but there is a separate entry for Wycombe Marsh.

ANCHOR
7 Crown Lane
☎ (01494) 436000
11am-11pm
Morland Old Speckled Hen; Regular Guest Beers

Working class pub near The Buckinghamshire College. No juke box. Traditional games very popular.

ANGEL
Pauls Road
☎ (01494) 520180
11am-11pm
(Closes 4pm-7pm Saturdays)
Tetley Bitter; Occasional Guest Beers

Popular young persons pub in town centre. Attractions include two pool tables in separate room, video juke box and a large selection of games machines. Karaoke Wednesdays and disco Thursdays. No food Sunday.

ANTELOPE
Church Square
☎ (01494) 471407
11am-11pm
Courage Best Bitter, Directors; Morland Old Speckled Hen; Rebellion IPA; Wadworth 6X; Young's Special

Beams, bricks, steps and low ceilings. Students and young

HIGH WYCOMBE – town centre

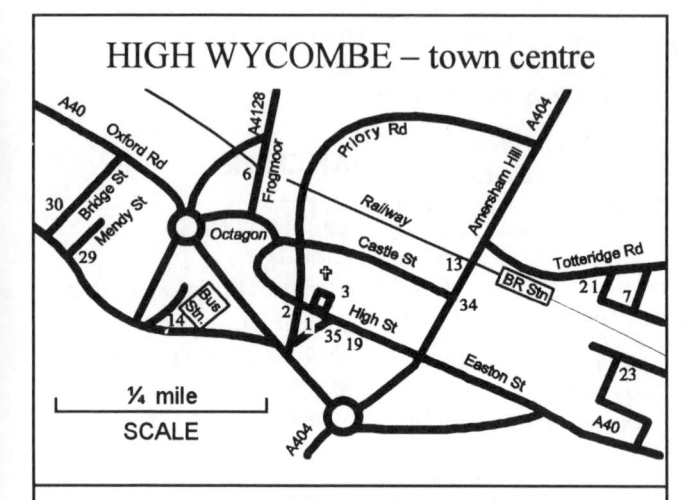

Key to both High Wycombe maps

1. ANCHOR
2. ANGEL
3. ANTELOPE
4. BEACONSFIELD ARMS
5. BEECH TREE
6. BELL
7. BELLE VUE
8. BIRD IN HAND
9. BLACK BOY
10. CENTRE SPOT
11. DESBOROUGH ARMS
12. DOLPHIN
35. FALCON
13. FLINT COTTAGE
14. GATE
15. GOLDEN FLEECE
16. GORDON ARMS
17. HALF MOON
18. HAPPY WANDERER
19. HOBGOBLIN
20. HOUR GLASS
21. IRON DUKE
22. JOLLY BODGER
23. MASON'S ARMS
24. MICKLEFIELD INN
25. MORNING STAR
26. NAG'S HEAD
27. PHEASANT
28. QUEEN
29. ROSE AND CROWN
30. ROUNDABOUT
31. SARACEN'S HEAD
32. WENDOVER ARMS
33. WHITE HORSE
34. WHITE LION

clientele. Oldest pub in Wycombe (14th century) - HQ of Wycombe Militia, forerunner of Sandhurst. Listed building rumoured to have been used by Oliver Cromwell during the Civil War. No food Sunday lunchtimes in summer.

BEACONSFIELD ARMS

110 Hughenden Road
☎ (01494) 522820

11am-11pm

Benskins Best Bitter, Ind Coope Burton Ale

Friendly two-bar local with wide ranging clientele. Regular disco Sunday nights and quizzes on Tuesdays. Golf society organises regular golfing days. Morning breakfast available between 6.30am and 9am weekdays.

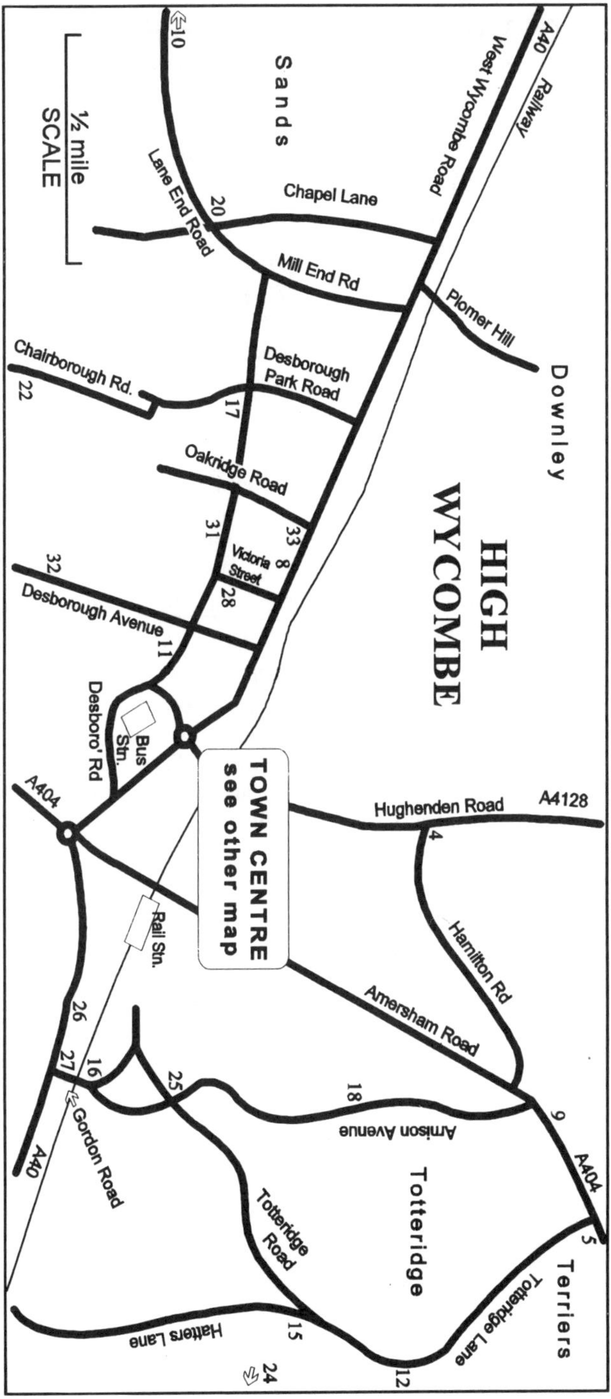
HIGH WYCOMBE
Sands
Downley
Totteridge
Terriers
½ mile
SCALE
A40
Railway
West Wycombe Road
Chapel Lane
Lane End Road
Mill End Rd
Plomer Hill
Chairborough Rd.
Desborough Park Road
Oakridge Road
Victoria Street
Desborough Avenue
Desboro' Rd
Bus Stn.
A404
TOWN CENTRE see other map
Hughenden Road
A4128
Hamilton Rd
Rail Stn.
Amersham Road
Amison Avenue
A404
Totteridge Road
Gordon Road
A40
Hatters Lane
Totteridge Lane
10
20
22
17
31
33
8
32
28
11
4
26
27
16
25
18
9
5
15
24
12

BEECH TREE
Amersham Road, Terriers (O.S. Ref. 882949)
☎ (01494) 528573
11am-11pm
Courage Best Bitter, Directors; Wadworth 6X

The 1988 renovation removed the small rooms that were the key to the character of the pub. Special children's play facilities in garden. Beautiful setting. Emphasis on food, with restaurant extension opening in February. Directors only available in winter.

BELL
Frogmoor
☎ (01494) 521317
11am-3pm; 5.30pm-11pm
(Opens 7pm Saturday evening)
Fuller's Chiswick Bitter, London Pride, ESB; Seasonal Beers

Cosy pub on edge of town centre. Popular lunchtime venue transforms to night club/disco at weekends (closes 2am Friday & Saturday). Large fresh fish menu evenings Monday to Saturday lunchtimes and Monday to Thursday evenings.

BELLE VUE
45 Gordon Road
☎ (01494) 524728
11am-11pm
John Smith's Bitter

Small 140 year old pub, catering mainly for a regular locals' trade. Handy for railway station.

BIRD IN HAND
81 West Wycombe Road
☎ (01494) 523502
11.30am-3pm; 5.30pm-11pm
Courage Best Bitter, Directors; Marston's Pedigree; Wadworth 6X; Young's Special

Refurbished with restaurant attached, but some character still remains. No food Sunday evening.

BLACK BOY
133 Amersham Road, Terriers
☎ (01494) 523827
11am-11pm
Morland Original Bitter, Old Speckled Hen; Regular Guest Beer

Two-bar locals' pub at top of Amersham Hill. Children's play area in garden and small car park at front. No bar food on Sundays.

CENTRE SPOT
Adams Park, Hillbottom Road (O.S. Ref. 832933)
☎ (01494) 473689
11am-3pm; 6pm-11pm
Fuller's London Pride; Morland Independent IPA, Old Speckled Hen

Bright modern pub forming part of Wycombe Wanderers ground and near Loakes Park Nature Reserve. Members only when Wycombe are playing at home.

DESBOROUGH ARMS
199 Desborough Road
☎ (01494) 522055
11am-11pm
Courage Best Bitter; John Smith's Bitter

Simple but cosy pub, handy for launderette. Lounge and public totally separate on split levels. A mecca for bar billiards players - this pub fields two teams.

DOLPHIN
56 Totteridge Lane (O.S. Ref. 885942)
☎ (01494) 524517
11am-3pm; 5pm-11pm
(Opens 11am-11pm Thursday to Saturday)
Greene King IPA, Abbot

Well placed on main link road on edge of town. Renovated in August 1991 as two room family pub. Own football team. No food Sunday lunchtime.

FALCON
Cornmarket
11am-11pm
Theakston's Best Bitter, XB; Younger's Scotch; Regular Guest Beers

J.D. Wetherspoon conversion of a long closed hotel which reopened in December 1994.

FLINT COTTAGE
Amersham Hill
☎ (01494) 526600
11am-11pm
Courage Best Bitter

Urban pub by railway station. Discos three nights a week. No Sunday lunches.

GATE
Newlands
☎ (01494) 528644
11am-11pm
Benskins Best Bitter; Tetley Bitter; Wadworth 6X; Regular Guest Beer

Large corner pub near bus station and college, popular with students. Cheap lunches for pensioners on Thursday. County bar billiards championships played here. Supports own football team and provides bars for outside functions. No lunches at weekends.

GOLDEN FLEECE
Hatters Lane
☎ (01494) 442776
11.30am-2.30pm; 5pm-11pm
(Opens 11am-11pm Friday & Saturday)
Benskins Best Bitter; Tetley Bitter

Recently refurbished and extended, this "Big Steak" pub offers good value food (with children's menu) in a comfortable relaxed atmosphere. Secluded patio/garden with adjacent children's play area. Open all day Sunday for meals.

Gordon Arms, High Wycombe *GG, 1993*

GORDON ARMS
Gordon Road
☎ (01494) 522977
11am-11pm
Everards Tiger; Morland Independent IPA, Old Masters, Old Speckled Hen; Charles Wells Bombardier

Large Victorian building with imposing frontage catering mainly for local's trade. Live music on Saturday. No meals on Sunday.

HALF MOON
103 Dashwood Avenue
☎ (01494) 529465
11am-3pm; 5.30pm-11pm
(Opens 11am-11pm Friday & Saturday)
Courage Best Bitter, Directors; Rebellion IPA

Corner pub decorated with posters of cinema memorabilia. All food home cooked and take-away food available. Popular with students and home football fans. Free pool table Wednesday and state of the art pinball machine. Discos Thursday and Sunday nights.

HAPPY WANDERER
143 Arnison Avenue
☎ (01494) 523903
11am-11pm
Boddingtons Bitter; Brakspear Special; Wethered Winter Royal

Prominently placed suburban pub with a large garden which caters extensively for children. The play area has traditional equipment plus a cabin with nets. There is also a family room and a disabled toilet. The pool area also contains an air hockey table.

HOBGOBLIN
High Street
☎ (01494) 526533
11am-11pm
Courage Best Bitter, Directors; Wychwood Best,

Hobgoblin; Regular Guest Beer

Town centre pub, a listed building dating back to 18/19th century. Business at lunchtime; students evening. Recently refurbished, busy and noisy. Lunches Sunday - Friday; evening meals Monday - Thursday.

HOUR GLASS

144 Chapel Lane, Sands
☎ (01494) 525094
11am-11pm
Benskins Best Bitter; Tetley Bitter

Friendly two-bar games oriented locals pub. No food Sundays.

IRON DUKE

Duke Street, Totteridge Road
☎ (01494) 529644
11am-2.30pm; 5.30pm-11pm (Opens 11am-3pm, 6pm-11pm Saturdays)
Courage Best Bitter, Directors; Regular Guest Beer

Clean, family-run street corner pub with lounge, public bar and pool room following curve of bar. Good value food (not available Sunday). Many games teams.

JOLLY BODGER

Chairborough Road
☎ (01494) 528229
Noon-2.30pm; 6.30pm-11pm (Opens 12am-11pm on Saturday)
Brakspear Bitter; Wadworth 6X; Regular Guest Beer

Split-level estate pub built around 1968 with covered patio and barbecue adjoining the bar. Ladies and Gents darts teams. No food Sundays.

MASONS ARMS

Saffron Road
☎ (01494) 452204
11am-11pm
John Smith's Bitter; Ruddles Best Bitter

Comfortable, airy town pub (accessible on foot from station or via tunnel under railway line) containing a long rectangular bar with plenty of seating and standing room. Small platform in corner for discos. Pleasant patio garden.

MICKLEFIELD INN

Micklefield Road
☎ (01494) 522896
11am-11pm
John Smith's Bitter

Basic local watering hole in large housing estate.

MORNING STAR

Totteridge Road
☎ (01494) 522038
11am-11pm
Courage Directors; John Smith's Bitter

Recently tastefully refurbished large town pub with one bar used as a pool room or for meetings when required. Saturday evening bands or discos. No food Sundays.

NAG'S HEAD
63 London Road
☎ (01494) 521758
11.30am-3pm; 6pm-11pm
(Opens 11am-11pm Saturday)
Courage Best Bitter; Ruddles County; Wadworth 6X
❀ ✕ 🎲 ❽ ♪

Wycombe's permanent rock festival with live groups Friday and Sunday in bar, Thursday and Saturday in upstairs room.

PHEASANT
99 London Road
☎ (01494) 527138
11am-3pm; 6pm-11pm
(Opens 11am-11pm Friday & Saturday)
Courage Best Bitter; John Smith's Bitter; Wadworth 6X
❀ ✕ ✕ 🎲 ♣ ❽ 🚗

Recently refurbished locals' pub catering for a wide age range. Many resident games teams. No evening meals Sunday or Monday.

QUEEN
2 Victoria Street
☎ (01494) 521747
11am-11pm
Fuller's Chiswick Bitter, London Pride, ESB
🏠 ❀ ✕ ✕ 🍺 ♣

Smart, cosy, friendly corner locals' pub with designer tudor interior decor. Superbly decorated at Christmas. Quiz nights popular on Wednesdays. Meat raffle Sundays. Balti meals available.

ROSE AND CROWN
Desborough Road
☎ (01494) 527982
11am-3pm; 5pm-11pm
(Opens 11am-11pm Friday & Saturday)
Courage Best Bitter; Gales HSB; Marston's Pedigree; Usher's Best Bitter; Wadworth 6X; Regular Guest Beers
🏠 ✕ 🎲 ♣ ☺ ♿

Wycombe's most interesting selection of beers in an L-shaped, corner pub with busy office lunchtime trade.

ROUNDABOUT
Bridge Street
☎ (01494) 520227
11am-11pm
Courage Directors; Wychwood Fiddlers Elbow, Best, Dr Thirsty's Draught, Hobgoblin
❀ ✕ 🎲 ❽ ♪

Former Watney house, now run by the Wychwood Brewery with their full range of beers. Large town centre pub with one main bar and two through bars. Popular with college students. Live bands on Friday and Saturday evenings.

SARACEN'S HEAD
Green Street
☎ (01494) 525918
11am-11pm
Courage Directors
❀ ❽ ♿

Recently converted to one bar pub with new beer garden and function hall in converted coach house. Regular Sunday barbecues. Rehearsal point for local steel band with occasional concerts. Proposing to do food in near future.

Iron Duke, High Wycombe *AG, 1994*

WENDOVER ARMS
Desborough Avenue
☎ (01494) 526476
11am-11pm
Brakspear Mild, Bitter, Special, OBJ

Large local, catering for a varied clientele, with a games area consisting of three pool tables and video machines for the younger drinker. Only constant real mild outlet in town. Large garden with barbecue in summer.

WHITE HORSE
95 West Wycombe Road
☎ (01494) 527672
11am-11pm
Tetley Bitter

Popular football supporters pub with Sky sports on TV. Live music Thursday, Friday and Saturday, Disco Sunday, karaoke Tuesday and exotic dancers Friday, Saturday and Sunday afternoons. Happy hour 6pm - 7pm.

WHITE LION
34 Crendon Street
☎ (01494) 524110
11am-11pm
Adnams Bitter; Greenalls Cask Bitter

Large town centre pub with mixed clientele. Happy hour 5.30 - 6.30pm weekdays. Regular raffle every Sunday lunchtime. Live music most weekends.

HOLMER GREEN

Map Reference: E8
Christina Rossetti, possibly the greatest British poetess, lived here for many years in a house which formerly stood behind the present site of the 'Old Oak'.

BAT AND BALL
Penfold Lane
☎ (01494) 716218

Noon-2.30pm; 5pm-11pm
(Opens Noon-11pm Friday &
Saturday)
Draught Bass; Tetley Bitter
Typical village local overlooking green. Piano available for budding Liberaces.

EARL HOWE
Earl Howe Road
☎ (01494) 713261
Noon-3pm; 5.30pm-11pm
(Opens 11am Friday & Saturday)
Courage Best Bitter; Regular Guest Beers
Clean and friendly, 18th century pub, with good garden offering barbecues in summer. Bar snacks Friday and Saturday and no Sunday lunches.

OLD OAK
New Pond Road
☎ (01494) 715947
Noon-11pm
John Smith's Bitter; Ruddles Best Bitter; Wadworth 6X; Webster's Yorkshire Bitter; Regular Guest Beers
Owned by Old English Pub Company. Formerly 'The Valiant Trooper' but now tastefully and comfortably refurbished. Single bar with dining area.

HOLTSPUR

*Map Reference: E9
Beaconsfield 2 miles East.*

KINGS HEAD
London Road
☎ (01494) 673337
11am-3pm; 5pm-11pm
(Opens 11am - 11pm on Saturdays)
Draught Bass; Courage Best Bitter; Ruddles County
Forte restaurant by mini roundabout on A40.

HUGHENDEN VALLEY

*Map Reference: E8
Attractive and largely unspoiled, it extends northwards from High Wycombe towards Hampden. At the southern end is Hughenden Park, owned by the National Trust and Wycombe Council; the interesting Manor House is a Disraeli museum.*

HARROW
Warrendene Road (O.S. Ref. 861975)
☎ (01494) 564105
Noon-11pm
Courage Best Bitter; Wadworth 6X; Regular Guest Beer
Traditional country pub recently refurbished but retaining flagstoned public bar with gravity dispense of real ales from barrels on stillage at rear of serving area (handpumps used in summer). The large garden contains children's play equipment and a

Harrow, Hughenden Valley   *GG, 1993*

barbecue. Vegetarian food also served. Occasional real cider and live music.

HYDE END

Map Reference: E8
About a mile east of Great Missenden, on the B485.

BARLEY MOW

Chesham Road (O.S. Ref. 912012)
☎ (01494) 865625
11am-3pm; 6pm-11pm
(Opens 11am-11pm Saturday & in summer)

Brakspear Bitter; Courage Best Bitter; Marston's Pedigree; Regular Guest Beers

Isolated pub on hill above Great Missenden. One large L-shaped bar with an attached dining room which is bookable for parties.

HYDE HEATH

Map Reference: E8
Equidistant from Great Missenden, Chesham and Amersham.

PLOUGH

The Common (O.S. Ref. 929004)
☎ (01494) 783163
Noon-3pm; 5.30pm-11pm
(Opens 6pm Saturday evening)

Courage Directors; ABC Best Bitter; Tetley Bitter

Popular and friendly, one-bar country pub opposite village cricket field. Dogs allowed. No evening meals on Monday or on Sunday in winter.

IBSTONE

Map Reference: C9
Stokenchurch 2 miles North. A stretch of common land high above Turville and the Hambleden valley.

FOX
The Common (O.S. Ref. 752940)
(Off Junction 5 of M40)
☎ (01491) 638289
11am-3pm; 6pm-11pm
Brakspear Bitter; Fuller's London Pride; Greene King Abbot; Regular Guest Beers

A popular pub offering high quality hotel accommodation and food in both bar and restaurant; also a large garden in superb countryside.

Best Bitter; Morland Old Speckled Hen

Very attractive 15th century timber framed thatched coaching inn. Special Kiddies and Toddlers play area and special children's menu. Varied menu with 'Eat as much as you like' buffet lunchtimes. German food a speciality. Aunt Sally and petanque played.

ROYAL OAK
2 Bridge Road (O.S. Ref. 648075)
☎ (01844) 339633
11.30am-4pm; 6pm-11pm
(Opens 11am-11pm in Summer)
Morrells Bitter

Genuine one-bar village local with good atmosphere and a friendly welcome. Popular with walkers and at the start of the Otmoor Walk. Aunt Sally in garden. Lunches available in summer.

ICKFORD

Map Reference: B7
Thame 4 miles East. A pleasant village in the meadows by the Thame, with a three-arch bridge over the river. A windowsill in the church is marked out for the game of Nine Men's Morris.

RISING SUN
Worminghall Road
☎ (01844) 339238
Noon-3pm; 6pm-11pm
Hancock's HB, Worthington

IVER

Map Reference: G10
Slough 4m W. Despite its proximity to Greater London, the village retains the right sort of atmosphere; there is an interesting church with Roman bricks in Saxon walls, Norman arches, mediaeval art and Tudor monuments. Not far away is Coppins, the former home of Princesses Marina and Alexandra.

BULL

7 High Street
☎ (01753) 651115
11am-3pm; 5pm-11pm
Ind Coope Burton Ale; Flowers IPA; Regular Guest Beer

Welcoming traditional Victorian pub. Look out for the decorative leaded windows, miniature car collection and tankards. Plush saloon bar. Food highly recommended (not available Sundays).

CHEQUERS

64 High Street
☎ (01753) 653869
11am-11pm
Courage Best Bitter; Fuller's London Pride

Small cosy pub on main street dating from beginning of the century. Single bar split into two distinct areas. Collection of artistic wood carvings relating to Norman conquest. No food at weekends.

FOX & PHEASANT

22 Thorney Lane North
☎ (01753) 653175
11am-11pm
Courage Best Bitter; Ind Coope Burton Ale; Morland Old Speckled Hen; Wadworth 6X; Regular Guest Beer

Turn of the century pub built to cater for the workforce of the local brick works. The Finnegan boxing brothers were locals. Live folk/blues on Fridays and old-time piano singalongs Sunday lunchtimes. Saturday pool knockout for cash prizes. Happy hour on Tuesdays.

GURKHA

Langley Park Road
☎ (01753) 654257
11am-11pm
Courage Best Bitter, Directors; Ruddles Best Bitter; Wadworth 6X; Regular Guest Beer

Pub dates from 19th century and was originally called 'The Red Lion'. The present owner took over the tenancy in 1964. The name was changed in 1971 to commemorate the Gurkha Regiment Welfare Appeal which the locals were connected with. The bar areas are half-panelled with a treasure of Gurkha memorabilia. Frequented by business customers at lunchtime, and locals in the evening, especially in the summer, there being a large garden. Imperial Russian Stout available at time of survey. No food Sunday evening.

SWAN

2 High Street
☎ (01753) 655776
11am-3.30pm; 6pm-11pm
Brakspear Bitter; Courage Best Bitter; Regular Guest Beers

Originally a 16th century coaching inn. A tunnel, a remnant of the Civil War, connects the pub to the church. Alterations over the years have been kind to this historic building, a lot of the open beams remaining. The bar fronting the main road is the public, with the cosy saloon leading through to the stables and restaurant, part of which comprises the original archway entrance to the court yard.

IVER HEATH

Map Reference: G10
The Irish Free State Treaty was signed at Heatherwood Hall, an elegant Georgian mansion, in 1921. The house and its 100-acre estate became Pinewood Studios in 1936.

BLACK HORSE
95 Slough Road
☎ (01753) 653044
11am-3pm; 5pm-11pm
(Opens 7pm Saturday evening)
Fuller's London Pride; Tetley Bitter; Regular Guest Beers

Present building dates from the 1920's and originally had three bars. Now a single bar which still has some of its original character. Two restaurant areas with upmarket atmosphere appeals to a wide range of customers. No food Sunday evening.

CROOKED BILLET
Five Points
☎ (01753) 651159
11am-11pm
Boddingtons Bitter; Tetley Bitter

'Beefeater' steakhouse. Very large single bar with Victorian style partitions, painted stained glass etc. No really big expanses, but distinct seating areas. Former 1930's roadside inn with Art-Deco patio. Upstairs function room can be booked for private use.

ODDFELLOWS ARMS
146 Swallow Street
☎ (01753) 653684
11am-11pm
Courage Best Bitter; Rebellion IPA; Ruddles Best Bitter; Webster's Yorkshire Bitter; Young's Bitter, Special

A 19th century building which was originally a barbers shop. The name originate from the pub being a meeting place for the 'Oddfellows Society' and is one of six pubs allowed to use the name and coat of arms. It has a large single bar in a traditional style. You can clock in on the early 1990's clock to play darts. Some beers may be on a cask breather.

PRINCE OF WALES
75 Slough Road
☎ (01753) 651378
11am-11pm
Courage Best Bitter; Regular Guest Beer

Small pub fronted by fenced patio area. Single bar with modern interior. Due for renovation at time of survey. No food Sunday.

STAG & HOUNDS
Church Road
☎ (01753) 655144
11am-11pm
Courage Best Bitter; Wadworth 6X; Regular Guest Beers

At time of going to press alterations are imminent. The bar is to be divided into two distinct areas, finished in a traditional style to match the pub's 160 years.

WHIP & COLLAR
135 Swallow Street
☎ (01753) 653455
11am-2.30pm; 5.30pm-11pm
Courage Best Bitter

The building dates from around 1820, a single small bar with a traditional country feel. The modern interior gives the impression of an old building constructed from ships timbers. Popular with locals. No food Sunday.

IVINGHOE

Map Reference: F6
Cramped village below the Chilterns where the Lower and Upper Icknield Ways converge. The former Roberts and Wilson brewery closed in the 1920's. Ivinghoe Beacon is the start of the Ridgeway Path and offers superb views.

ROSE AND CROWN
Vicarage Lane (O.S. Ref. 945163)
(Take turning opposite church, then first right)
☎ (01296) 668472
Noon-2.30pm; 6pm-11pm
Adnams Bitter; Greene King IPA; Morrells Dark; Regular Guest Beer

Hard to find, but very much worth the effort, this street corner local has a comfortable lounge and a lively public bar on different levels.

IVINGHOE ASTON

Map Reference: F5
Straggling village with a Bedfordshire look, in the shadow of the beacon, immortalised in the tales of Sir Bernard Miles.

SWAN
☎ (01525) 220544
Noon-3pm; 5.30pm-11pm
(Opens Noon-11pm Saturday)
Greene King IPA, Abbot; Regular Guest Beers

Rural pub in quiet village near to Ivinghoe Beacon and worth a detour. The pub has a games room to the rear and offers a choice of four beers. Live music every fortnight.

Swan, Iver   *GG, 1994*

KINGSWOOD

Map Reference: B5
On A41 midway between Aylesbury and Bicester.

CROOKED BILLET

Ham Green
☎ (01296) 770239
11am-11pm
(Closes 3pm-5pm Monday and Thursday)
Draught Bass; Hook Norton Best Bitter; Wadworth 6X; Regular Guest Beers

Deceptively large 17th Century single storey pub on A41 with spacious garden, restaurant and function room. Popular with ramblers, car clubs and hot air balloonists. Occasional jazz nights.

PLOUGH AND ANCHOR

Bicester Road
☎ (01296) 770251
11am-11pm
Boddingtons Bitter; Theakston's XB; Regular Guest Beer

Pleasant, roomy 16th century village inn, now a free house (since 1992) catering for all ages. Happy hour during the week between 5.30 and 7pm. Sky Sports, live music every Friday night, Bingo every second Sunday and Karaoke every month.

KNOTTY GREEN

Map Reference: E9
Beaconsfield 2 miles South.

RED LION
Penn Road
☎ (01494) 674702
11am-11pm
Brakspear Bitter; Greene King IPA; Marston's Pedigree; Tetley Bitter
Just outside Beaconsfield New Town, this pub has an adjoining room which can be used for functions.

LACEY GREEN

Map Reference: D8
A breezy village above Princes Risborough with fine views of the Vale of Aylesbury. The 17th century smock mill is one of the few surviving examples in England, and has been carefully restored by the Chiltern Society, and is open to the public on Sunday afternoons.

BLACK HORSE
Main Road
☎ (01844) 345195
11.30am-3pm; 5.30pm-11pm
(Opens 11am on Saturday)
Wadworth 6X; Wethered Bitter; Regular Guest Beers
Traditional village pub although beer under cask breather. Friendly welcome to all including dogs and families. Holds regular special events. Children's play area in garden. No meals Tuesday evening.

PINK & LILY
Pink Rd, Parslows Hillock (O.S. Ref. 828019)
☎ (01494) 488308
11.45am-3pm; 6pm-11pm
Boddingtons Bitter; Brakspear Bitter; Chiltern Beechwood; Courage Directors; Wychwood Hobgoblin; Flowers Original
Lively and popular country pub noted for choice of beers and food (no chips!). The snug bar is original and unaltered and is dedicated to the poet Rupert Brooke.

WHIP
Main Road
☎ (01844) 344060
11am-2.30pm; 5.30pm-11pm
Regular Guest Beers
Lively country pub with strong repartee and backchat; man-sized meals and good cellar.

LANE END

Map Reference: D9
Marlow 3 miles SE A large and rambling village at the end of a good half-dozen lanes. The Chairmaker's Arms is redolent of the former local industry, now superseded by various more modern pursuits.

105

CHAIRMAKERS ARMS
40 The Row
☎ (01494) 881593
11am-3pm; 6pm-11pm
(Opens all day Saturday)
Morland Independent IPA, Original Bitter
❀ ✕ ♣

Terraced pub with cosy bar and local atmosphere. Round corner from lesser village pond.

CLAYTON ARMS
High Street
☎ (01494) 881269
11am-11pm
(Closes 3pm-5.30pm on Saturdays)
John Smith's Bitter; Old Luxter's Barn Ale; Ruddles County; Wadworth 6X; Webster's Yorkshire Bitter
🅟 ⌂ ❀ ✕ ✕ 🅞 🚗 Ⓢ ♨

Pub built around a busy restaurant business. Happy hours 11am-noon; 5.30pm-7pm. Next to main village pond. 17th century building with family room.

JOLLY BLACKSMITH
Ditchfield Common (O.S. Ref. 805916)
☎ (01494) 881899
11am-2.30pm; 6pm-11pm
Wethered Bitter
🅟 🅘 ❀ ♣ 🚗

Small, old fashioned local with a friendly welcome. The same family has run the pub and adjacent blacksmiths/ironwork business for 134 years. Two real fires, one with unusual 19th century French fireplace. Fine views over locality.

OLD SUN
Church Road
☎ (01494) 881235
11.30am-2.30pm; 5.30pm-11pm
(11am-3pm, 6pm-11pm Saturday)
Brakspear Bitter; Wadworth 6X; Wethered Bitter
🅟 ❀ ✕ ✕ 🅞 ♨ ♣ 🚗

Traditional village pub providing comfortable seating with tables and an adjacent drinking area plus games. No food Tuesday evening.

OSBORNE ARMS
High Street
☎ (01494) 882358
11am-2.30pm; 6pm-11pm
(Opens till 3pm on Saturday)
Brakspear Bitter; Rebellion IPA; Tetley Bitter; Webster's Yorkshire Bitter
❀ ✕ ✕ ✓

Friendly, well appointed brick and beam free house with local drinkers bar and separate family dining area. No food Sunday or Monday evenings.

LAVENDON

Map Reference: E1
Large village on the Bedfordshire border. A mix of limestone cottages and red brick houses scattered along the A428.

GREEN MAN
High Street (O.S. Ref. 916537)
☎ (01234) 712611
11am-2.30pm; 5.30pm-11pm
Draught Bass; Greene King

IPA, Abbot; Marston's Pedigree

An ambient setting for this large pub with friendly staff. Suitably quiet if you want to enjoy a relaxed pint. Smart casual dress preferred. Restaurant where families are welcome. Food is available at the bar at all times. A really nice pub where the customers can feel at ease.

HORSESHOES
High Street (O.S. Ref. 916537)
☎ (01234) 712648
11am-2.30pm; 5.30pm-11pm
Hall & Woodhouse Tanglefoot; Charles Wells Eagle; Regular Guest Beer

Reputedly haunted old coaching inn offering the mixed local clientelle a relaxing and friendly atmosphere. Shirts or top must be worn. A cosy public bar with a fire, beams and cheese skittles and a well appointed lounge with dining area, no food on Sundays Mondays or Tuesdays. Always at least one guest beer available.

LEDBURN

Map Reference: E5
Leighton Buzzard 2 miles NE.

HARE AND HOUNDS
(O.S. Ref. 905222)
☎ (01525) 373484
Noon-3pm; 6pm-11pm
Ruddles Best Bitter, County; Wadworth 6X; Webster's Yorkshire Bitter; Regular Guest Beers

Built in 1902 as part of the Mentmore Estate. Exterior architecture in Dutch style, and fine views across the Rothschild's Ascott Estate (National Trust). Large central bar and separate dining area. Wooden floor and pine furniture. Train robbers memorabilia.

LEE COMMON

Map Reference: E7

BUGLE
(O.S. Ref. 906043)

LENT RISE

Map Reference: E10
Burnham 1m N.

BRICKMAKERS ARMS
170 Lent Rise Road
☎ (01628) 602840
11am-3pm; 5.30pm-11pm
Courage Best Bitter; Wadworth 6X; Regular Guest Beer

Small single-bar pub.

MAYPOLE
82 Hitcham Road
☎ (01628) 604457
Noon-11pm
Courage Best Bitter; John Smith's Bitter; Regular Guest Beer
♣ ❽ 🚗

Large single-bar pub with separate area for pool, and at opposite end a separate area for darts with large TV screen in corner.

PHEASANT
205 Lent Rise Road
☎ (01628) 605843
11am-11pm
Courage Best Bitter, Directors
❀ ✕ 🍴 🎮 ♣ 🚗

Old roadside pub with large porch entrance. Single bar but with three separate drinking areas. Varied clientele. Garden to side of building.

LEY HILL

Map Reference: F8
Chesham 2 miles SW
A popular and attractive common and golf course.

CROWN
☎ (01494) 783910
11am-11pm
Adnams Extra; Greene King IPA; Marston's Pedigree; Tetley Bitter; Regular Guest Beer
❀ ✕ 🍴 ♣ 🚗

1920's country pub with one bar opposite the village common and cricket ground. Mixed clientele but supports both darts and crib teams. Carpet bowls and trips often organised.

SWAN
Ley Hill
☎ (01494) 783075
11am-2.30pm; 5.30pm-11pm
(Closes 3pm Saturday lunchtime)
Benskins Best Bitter, Ind Coope Burton Ale; Tetley Bitter; Regular Guest Beers
🏠 ❀ ✕ 🍴 📺 🛏 ♣ 🚗 🛌

15th century country pub overlooking the village common. No food Sunday evening.

LITTLE BRICKHILL

Map Reference: E4
Standing on the old A5 this small cluster of houses runs into its Great Brickhill brother.

GEORGE & DRAGON
Watling Street (O.S. Ref. 912325)
☎ (01525) 261298
11am-2.30pm; 5.30pm-11pm
John Smith's Bitter; Webster's Green Label
🏠 ❀ ✕ 🍴 📺 ❽ 🚗 ♪

Friendly locals pub with games in the public bar and television in the quiet lounge. Garden with slide and swings.

OLDE GREEN MAN

Watling Street (O.S. Ref. 910325)
☎ (01525) 261253
11am-2.30pm; 5.30pm-11pm
(Opens 11am-3pm; 6pm-11pm Saturdays)

Courage Directors; Elgood's Bitter; John Smith's Magnet; Morrells Varsity; Ruddles Best Bitter

One of three Old English Pub Company houses this interesting 17th century roadside Inn with a real log fire, exposed brick and wood panelled walls, beamed ceiling and flagstoned floors, offers a friendly atmosphere. Enjoy a pint from one of the unusual variety of cask only ales. Bar snacks always available (try the cheese board). The restaurant is closed on Mondays.

LITTLE CHALFONT

Map Reference: F8
Metroland's last gasp, incongruously located above the beautiful Chess Valley, and dominated by Amersham International, the area's largest employer.

PINEAPPLE

White Lion Road
☎ (01494) 762153
11am-11pm

Benskins Best Bitter, Ind Coope Burton Ale; Marston's Pedigree; Tetley Bitter; Regular Guest Beer

Friendly one-bar pub which has been recently refurbished to a very high standard, now offering excellent family and disabled facilities. Large garden with safe and well organised childrens play area. One end of the bar has been tastefully laid out like a public bar with high backed settles and a flagstoned floor.

SUGAR LOAVES

Station Road
☎ (01494) 765579
11am-11pm

Adnams Bitter; Morland Old Speckled Hen; Wadworth 6X; Young's Bitter

Busy two-bar town pub near underground station. Many sports teams are based at the pub which has regular live music and quiz nights. No food Sunday evening.

WHITE LION

White Lion Road
☎ (01494) 763346
11.30am-2.30pm; 5pm-11pm
(Opens 11am-11pm on Saturday)

Courage Best Bitter, Directors; Webster's Green Label; Regular Guest Beer

Much extended village boozer parts of which date back to 1750. At the rear of the pub is a large meeting room. Webster's Green Label is rare in this area and is excellent value. Live music in evening at weekends.

LITTLE HAMPDEN

Map Reference: E7
Great Missenden 3 miles SE. Off the road leading to Chequers and Princes Risborough, a tiny hamlet in marvellous walking country; whilst welcoming ramblers, a notice warns them to remove their boots before entering the pub! The primitive-looking Norman church has striking 13th century wall paintings only rediscovered in 1907.

RISING SUN
(O.S. Ref. 857040)
☏ (01494) 488393
11.30am-2.30pm; 6.30pm-11pm
(Closed Sunday Evening and all day Monday)
Adnams Bitter; Brakspear Bitter; Marston's Pedigree
✿ ✗ ✗ ▢ ♞ 🚗

Extensive, well maintained pub in the heart of beech woods at the far end of a long no through road. Popular with walkers at weekend lunchtimes whilst evening trade focuses on home cooked food.

OLD CROWN
11 Mursley Road
☏ (01296) 713062
11.45am-11pm
Ansells Bitter; Tetley Bitter
✿ ✗ ✗ ♞ ♣ 🚗 ♪

Two-bar village local. Live music once a month.

SHOULDER OF MUTTON
Church Street
☏ (01296) 712514
11am-2.30pm; 6.30pm-11pm
(Closed Monday lunchtime)
ABC Best Bitter; Flowers Original
🏠 ✿ ✗ ✗ ▢ ♞ 🚗

A Grade 1 thatched and white washed building dating in the most part from the 14th century. A compact L shaped bar with inglenook fireplace, a wealth of beams, a former flagstoned but now tiled floor. Separate dining area where you can enjoy a range of high quality home cooked meals. Note the very appropriate collection of china and porcelain swans in the display cabinet. Advice to the tall, mind your head.

LITTLE HORWOOD

Map Reference: D4
A church overlooks this humble village about 6 miles W of Bletchley and S off the A421

LITTLE KIMBLE

Map Reference: D7
On the Icknield Way near Chequers Estate and the curious hill known as Cymbalines's Mount.

CROWN
Risborough Road
☎ (01296) 613230
11am-11pm
(Opens 7am for breakfasts)
Ruddles Best Bitter; Tetley Bitter

Under enthusiastic new management. Small restaurant area (also serving breakfasts and cream teas) and verandah.

LITTLE KINGSHILL

Map Reference: E8
Great Missenden 2 miles N

FULL MOON
Hare Lane
☎ (01494) 862397
11.30am-3pm; 6pm-11pm
Adnams Bitter; Greenalls Cask Bitter; Wadworth 6X

300 year old pub with one bar aimed towards diners and the other, with a large inglenook fireplace, for drinkers.

PRINCE OF WALES
Windsor Lane
☎ (01494) 862172
Noon-2.30pm; 6pm-11pm
(Opens Noon-11pm Saturday)
Marston's Pedigree; Flowers IPA

Busy, one-bar, village local with bar-billiards table.

LITTLE MARLOW

Map Reference: E9
On A4155; Marlow 2 miles W. A tiny village opposite Winter Hill, the famous Thames-side beauty spot, and a convenient lunch halt for riverside walkers. The novelist, Edgar Wallace was buried here in 1932.

CROOKED BILLET
Sheepridge Lane (O.S. Ref. 883895)
☎ (01628) 521216
11am-3pm; 5.30pm-11pm
Brakspear Bitter; Flowers Original, Wethered Winter Royal

Cosy, friendly, smart, low-beamed pub between Flackwell Heath and Little Marlow. Bar concealed behind wooden and brick pillars and customers. Famous in 1950's for locally made cider.

KING'S HEAD
Church Road (O.S. Ref. 872882)
☎ (01628) 484407
11am-3pm; 5.30pm-11pm
Boddingtons Bitter; Brakspear Bitter; Marston's Pedigree; Wadworth 6X; Young's Special; Regular Guest Beer

One-bar village local with much character. Varied, home-cooked meals are always available. New separate dining room. Families very welcome.

QUEEN'S HEAD
Pound Lane, off Church Road (O.S. Ref. 873880)
☎ (01628) 482927
Noon-3pm; 5.30pm-11pm
(Opens 6pm Saturday evening)
Worthington Best Bitter; Benskins Best Bitter; Flowers Original

Tucked away at end of cul-de-sac just off main road. Refreshingly traditional layout. Mini cricket bats in public bar. Near 12th century church. Specials cooked to order lunchtimes (not Sunday). Perfect atmosphere for rapidly disappearing art of conversation.

LITTLE MISSENDEN

Map Reference: E8
An idyllic village in the Misbourne Valley. The tiny church has mediaeval wall paintings and is the focus for an annual arts festival. Unlike many other fine villages, the pubs really do live up to their location.

CROWN
(O.S. Ref. 926989)
☎ (01494) 862571
11am-2.30pm; 6pm-11pm
(Closes 2.30pm Sunday lunchtime)
Draught Bass; Hook Norton Best Bitter; Morrells Varsity; Regular Guest Beer

Authentic old village pub with a genuine welcome. The single small bar manages to combine a two-bar atmosphere. Comfortable and warm the bar is decorated with much brasswork and many farm implements. No food on Sundays.

RED LION
(O.S. Ref. 923989)
☎ (01494) 862876
11am-2.30pm; 5.30pm-11pm
(Opens 6pm Saturday evening)
Hook Norton Old Hooky; Benskins Best Bitter; Wadworth 6X; Regular Guest Beer

Ancient fireplace, dated 1649, dominates the bar of this classic village local, which remains totally unspoilt. All are welcomed and families with children are allowed in the separate games room. Occasional weekend sing-songs.

LITTLEWORTH COMMON

Map Reference: E9
Beaconsfield 3m N.
Based upon a triangle of lanes and sporting three pubs, it is thickly wooded and noted for the nearby country estates of Dropmore and Dorneywood. The latter has been the official country retreat of the Foreign Secretary.

BEECH TREE

Dorney Wood Road
☎ (0175) 642169
11am-11pm
Boddingtons Mild; Brakspear Bitter; Flowers IPA; Occasional Guest Beers

Small traditional country inn on the south west corner of the green. A single bar with comfortable seating around the walls. Note the crib tables made by a previous landlord. The food (not available Sunday) is standard pub fare at very reasonable prices.

BLACKWOOD ARMS

Common Lane
☎ (01753) 642169
11am-2.30pm; 5.30pm-11pm
(Opens 11am-11pm Friday & Saturday)
Regular Guest Beers

Outstanding free house in idyllic woodland surroundings, with the fastest changing range of beers in the country - over 900 in 1994 all from independent breweries. Good value food from this small but very popular country pub. Not to be missed.

JOLLY WOODMAN

☎ (01753) 644350
11am-11pm
Boddingtons Bitter; Flowers Original; Regular Guest Beers

Originally three 16th century woodland cottages, considerably extended at the rear. A rowing scull hangs in the rafters.

LONG CRENDON

Map Reference: B7
Thame 2 miles SE. An

Blackwood Arms, Littleworth Common   *NH, 1994*

113

exceptionally fine village in which a remarkable number of old cottages survive more or less intact, together with three great houses. The Court House, given by Henry V to Catherine after Agincourt, was at one time used by the wool merchants of Crendon, and was the first acquisition of the National Trust in 1900. The chief local industry was needlemaking, until eclipsed by Redditch.

ANGEL INN

Bicester Road
☎ (01844) 208268
Noon-3pm; 6pm-11pm
(Closed Sunday evening)
Brakspear Bitter; Flowers IPA

Outward appearances suggest a pub, but to all intents and purposes this is a restaurant. Originally a 16th Century inn, now decorated and furnished in 'Country Living' style. Interesting menu available in various rooms including the rear conservatory.

CHANDOS ARMS

83 Bicester Road
☎ (01844) 208659
Noon-3pm; 6pm-11pm
Brakspear Bitter; Wethered Bitter; Regular Guest Beer

Attractive thatched village inn, dating back to 1690 though only a pub from early this century. Friendly atmosphere with mixed clientele. Low beamed interior that was once two separate bars. No evening meals on Sunday or Monday. Slight blanket pressure on draught ales.

CHURCHILL ARMS

1 High Street
☎ (01844) 208344
Noon-3pm; 6pm-11pm
Fuller's London Pride; Tetley Bitter; Regular Guest Beer

Named after the Churchill family who were landowners in the area. The interior contains many Churchill mementoes and an inglenook fireplace. Apart from the restaurant there are two distinct drinking areas and a back room used for either pool or special functions. Aunt Sally played. Occasional live music in winter.

EIGHT BELLS

51 High Street
(Near church)
☎ (01844) 208244
Noon-3pm; 5.30pm-11pm
(Opens 6pm Saturday evening)
Draught Bass; Tetley Bitter; Flowers IPA

A clean and friendly village local. Built c.1625 and claimed to be the oldest Long Crendon pub; the name recalls the existence of nearby Notley Abbey which was dissolved by Henry VIII, and is linked to the number of bells in the church tower of which there are now ten! Aunt Sally played and the home of Long Crendon Morris Men.

STAR

5 Bicester Road
☎ (01844) 208388
11am-2.30pm; 5.30pm-11pm
(Opens 11am-11pm Friday &

Saturday)
Worthington Best Bitter; ABC Best Bitter
✕ ♨ ♣ ❽

Very popular one-bar village local with pool tables situated behind partition at one end. Cooked lunches on weekdays. Closes 2.30pm on Sunday lunchtimes. Off sales department at rear entrance on back road off Market Square.

LONGWICK

Map Reference: D7
Princes Risborough 1½ miles SE.

RED LION
Thame Road
☎ (01844) 344980
Noon-2.30pm; 6pm-11pm
(Opens 6.45pm on Saturday)
Fuller's London Pride; Hook Norton Best Bitter; Tetley Bitter
⋈ ✕ ✕ 🚗

Substantial roadside inn with split level dining area and rear bar. A long established family-run free house. Beware of Theakstons on keg tall font.

WHITE HORSE
Thame Road
☎ (01844) 344008
Noon-3pm; 6pm-11pm
Marston's Pedigree; Tetley Bitter; Flowers Original
♣ ✕ ✕ ♨ ♣ 🚗

L-shaped basic pub with a friendly welcome. Popular with the locals, but food trade not established at present and not always available evenings.

LOUDWATER

Map Reference: E9
On A40 between Wycombe and Beaconsfield.

DEREHAMS INN
5 Derehams Lane (O.S. Ref. 903907)
☎ (01494) 530965
11am-3pm; 5.30pm-11pm
Boddingtons Bitter; Brakspear Bitter; Fuller's London Pride; Taylor's Landlord; Wadworth 6X; Young's Bitter
🏠 ♣ ✕ ♣ 🚗

Cosy pub, originally known as the Bricklayers Arms. Hard to find so mainly geared to local trade. Beer range varies. Small car park. Lunches weekdays only.

HAPPY UNION
Boundary Road (O.S. Ref. 900905)
☎ (01628) 620972
11am-3pm; 5.30pm-11pm
Boddingtons Bitter; Wethered Bitter
♣ ✕ ✕ ❽ 🚗 ♪

Open plan pub with interesting interior. Next to a busy road junction. Occasional live music on Friday.

WHITE BLACKBIRD
London Road

☎ (01494) 524455
11am-2.30pm; 5.30pm-11pm
(Opens 11am-11pm Saturday)
*Courage Best Bitter,
Directors; John Smith's
Bitter; Regular Guest Beer*
A one-time coaching inn with
several small bars. Now has a
large open-plan lounge and a
public bar with two pool tables.
Very "sporty" pub having its own
football team. No food Sundays.

WYCOMBE HEIGHTS
Rayners Avenue
(½ mile north of A40)
☎ (01494) 816686
11am-11pm
Greene King IPA, Abbot
Three year old Greene King pub
at end of Rayners Lane, with two
eighteen hole golf courses,
floodlit driving range and
restaurant attached. Smart and
comfortable bar and separate
family area. Open Sunday
afternoon for meals. A reasonable
standard of dress is expected.

LUDGERSHALL

*Map Reference: B6
Off A41; Aylesbury 10 miles SE.
An unusually scattered village
around a common. The mainly
14th century church has some fine
memorials, and there are some
splendid old farmhouses,
including Small Farm which was
once the Five Bells pub.*

BULL & BUTCHER
The Green (O.S. Ref. 662178)
☎ (01844) 238094
11.30am-2.30pm; 6.30pm-11pm
(Closed all day Monday)
*Tetley Bitter; Regular Guest
Beer*
Small but very pleasant country
pub. Good value steaks are a
speciality (the landlord was once
a butcher). No intrusive music or
pub games.

MAIDS MORETON

*Map Reference: B3
Pleasant sprawling village set
around and beyond the village
green 1 mile N of Buckingham on
the A413.*

BUCKINGHAM ARMS
Duck Lane (O.S. Ref. 703354)
☎ (01280) 813085
12.10pm-3pm; 7pm-11pm
*Draught Bass; Worthington
Best Bitter; Charrington IPA*
Pub due to have change of
landlord at time of survey.

WHEATSHEAF
Main Street (O.S. Ref. 703354)
☎ (01280) 815433
12.10pm-3pm; 6pm-11pm
Flowers IPA

116

Enjoying a new lease of life since fire damage took this grade 2 listed building out of service. With a newly thatched roof and a freshly painted inside it is hard to believe the true age of this little gem. In the past it has been a bakers and a butchers and now succeeds in pleasing the drinking public. An unobtrusive conservatory has been added for the benefit of diners and the garden has a childrens play area, much to the delight of parents. Only Flowers I.P.A at the time of the survey so who knows what you'll find on your visit.

MARLOW

Map Reference: D9
An attractive, popular and lively town set in fine surroundings, with a splendid suspension bridge close to All Saints church - both are much photographed. The poet Shelley lived here with his wife Mary in 1817, when she wrote Frankenstein. It was also notable as the home of Thomas Wethered's brewery in the High Street which ceased brewing in 1988.

BANK OF ENGLAND

Dean Street
(On B482)
☎ (01628) 890648
11am-2.30pm; 5pm-11pm
(Opens 11am-11pm Friday & Saturday)

Greene King IPA, Rayments Special, Abbot

Suburban pub, now a Greene King managed house. No food Sunday lunchtime.

BRITANNIA

Little Marlow Road
☎ (01628) 483852
11am-11pm

Boddingtons Bitter; Flowers Original; Regular Guest Beers

Large and cosmopolitan with emphasis on games, families and six regularly changing real ales. Full meals and extensive snacks menu always available. Wide range of live music on alternate Friday evenings. Families very welcome in dining area and garden.

CARPENTERS ARMS

15 Spittal Street
☎ (01628) 473649
11am-11pm

Morrells Bitter, Varsity

Thriving working-man's local of considerable character. Acquired by Morrell's of Oxford in 1992. Variety of fresh home-made sandwiches always available.

CHEQUERS

High Street
☎ (01628) 482053
11am-11pm

Brakspear Bitter, Special

17th century inn with two bars and a restaurant. Opposite site of Wethered's Brewery. Breakfast from 7.30am (8am Friday & Saturday), morning coffee and afternoon teas. Families welcome in eating areas.

MARLOW

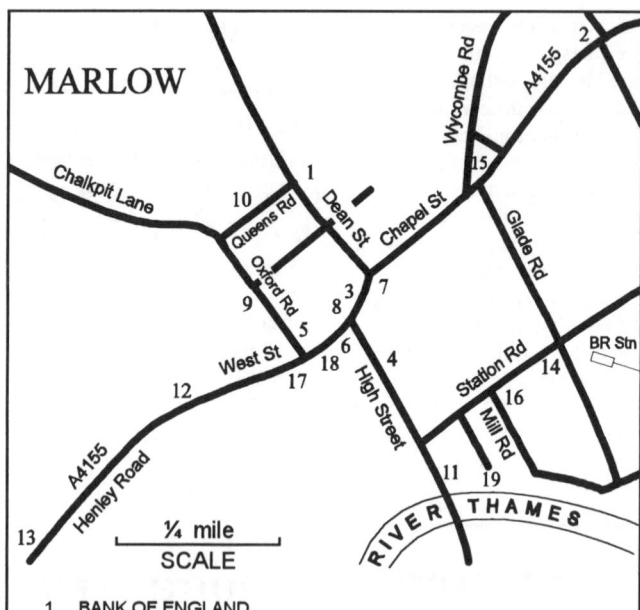

1. BANK OF ENGLAND
2. BRITANNIA
3. CARPENTERS ARMS
4. CHEQUERS
5. CLAYTON ARMS
6. COACH AND HORSES
7. CROSS KEYS
8. CROWN
9. CROWN AND ANCHOR
10. DUKE OF CAMBRIDGE
11. GEORGE AND DRAGON
12. HAND AND FLOWERS
13. HARE AND HOUNDS
14. MARLOW DONKEY
15. PLOUGH
16. PRINCE OF WALES
17. RED LION
18. SHIP
19. TWO BREWERS

CLAYTON ARMS

Quoiting Square

☎ (01628) 478620

11am-2.30pm; 5.30pm-11pm
(Opens 11am-3pm, 6pm-11pm Saturdays)

Brakspear Mild, Bitter, Special, Old

Town centre gem with two small bars, the original and genuine local. Pigeon Club and Fishermen's Club meet regularly in meeting room. Planning permission now passed for new kitchen and outside patio drinking area.

COACH AND HORSES

West Street

☎ (01628) 483013

11am-2.30pm; 5.30pm-11pm
(Opens 6pm on Saturdays)

Boddingtons Bitter; Courage Best Bitter, Directors; Wadworth 6X

Comfortable pub with display of copper and brasses. Courtyard garden has won floral decorations competitions. Sunday roasts a speciality from noon to 9pm.

CROSS KEYS
46 Spittal Street
☎ (01628) 482522
11am-11pm
Courage Best Bitter; John Smith's Bitter; Regular Guest Beer

One room pub with pool table at far end. Landlord's idea of a good pub is one where the bitter and the Guinness are looked after. Meals and snacks not available on Sunday evenings or after 6pm on Fridays and Saturdays. Live modern jazz every Monday evening.

CROWN
Market Square
☎ (01628) 483010
Noon-3pm; 6pm-11pm
(Opens 7.30pm Friday & Saturday evenings)
Courage Best Bitter

Large, prominently located old stone pub with clock tower. Caters for young evening lager drinkers. Napoleonic POWs were kept here. Indoor beer garden in interior conservatory. Coffee shop open 8am - 3pm Monday to Friday for breakfasts and home cooked lunches. Live bands on Tuesday evenings, karaoke Sunday and discos Friday and Saturday evenings.

CROWN AND ANCHOR
45 Oxford Road
☎ (01628) 472247
Noon-3pm; 7pm-11pm
(Opens Noon-11pm Friday & Saturday)
Draught Bass; Fuller's London Pride; Morland Independent IPA; Theakston's XB; Regular Guest Beers

Male ghost in the Ladies or the cellar, various strange noises. Recently changed interior, now a free house with up to six real ales and pies a speciality. Enthusiastic licensees converted a tied house into one of Marlow's best selection of real ales. Families welcome and petanque and barbecues in garden. Live music and discos on Friday & Saturday evenings.

DUKE OF CAMBRIDGE
19 Queens Road
☎ (01628) 484994
11am-2.30pm; 5.30pm-11pm
(Opens 11am-11pm on Saturday)
Regular Guest Beers

Comfortable and friendly one-bar local within 5 minutes walk from town centre. Constantly changing choice of four real ales from the Whitbread portfolio. Keen following for darts matches and pub quizzes. Garden lantern lit summer evenings. Petanque piste available. No food Sundays.

GEORGE AND DRAGON
The Causeway
☎ (01628) 483887
11am-11pm
Boddingtons Bitter; Brakspear Special; Marston's Pedigree; Flowers Original

Very large Beefeater restaurant beside Marlow bridge. Open all day Sunday for diners. Over 21s only for drinking at the bar. Beers range may vary.

HAND AND FLOWERS
West Street
☎ (01628) 482277
11am-3pm; 6pm-11pm
Morland Independent IPA, Original Bitter, Old Speckled Hen; Regular Guest Beer

Originally several cottages but now joined into smart long bar with low ceilings and games area at one end. Food not available Sunday or Monday evenings.

HARE AND HOUNDS
Henley Road (O.S. Ref. 838857)
☎ (01628) 483343
11am-3pm; 5.30pm-11pm
Boddingtons Bitter; Brakspear Bitter; Rebellion IPA

Large roadside pub, serving restaurant quality food in a pub atmosphere. Children's menu available.

MARLOW DONKEY
Station Road
☎ (01628) 482022
11am-11pm
Boddingtons Bitter; Fuller's London Pride; Wethered Bitter, Flowers Original

Comfortable split-level pub opposite station and named after local train. Families welcome in conservatory. No food Sunday evening.

PLOUGH
Little Marlow Road
☎ (01628) 482857
11.30am-3pm; 5.30pm-11pm
Brakspear Special; Fuller's Chiswick Bitter; Rebellion IPA; Wadworth 6X; Wethered Bitter, Flowers IPA

Two-bar local accessed from Wycombe Road or Little Marlow Road. Recently refurbished and very comfortable. Large collection of jugs. Live folk/contemporary duos on Sunday evenings.

PRINCE OF WALES
Mill Road
☎ (01628) 482970
11am-11pm
Beer Range Varies

Friendly back street local with two connecting bars - a comfortable public and a lounge with a dining area (families welcome). No food Sunday evening. Constantly changing range of four real ales from the Whitbread stable.

RED LION
West Street
☎ (01628) 482957
11am-11pm
Ansells Bitter, Ind Coope Burton Ale; Tetley Bitter

Allied Breweries theme pub, much extended and refurbished. Occasional live music and quiz evenings. Landlord is in the guild of Master Cellarmen for Burton Ale.

SHIP
West Street
☎ (01628) 484360
11am-11pm
Boddingtons Bitter; Brakspear Bitter; Wadworth 6X; Wethered Bitter, Pompey Royal

Cosy low-beamed pub with nautical theme enhanced by the large number of prints adorning the walls. Can get very busy. Petanque played in garden.

TWO BREWERS
St Peter Street
☎ (01628) 484140
11am-3pm; 5.30pm-11pm
(Opens 11am-11pm Saturday)
Brakspear Bitter; Wadworth 6X; Flowers IPA

Comfortably furnished pub with beamed ceiling. A few yards away from Thames. Food available (not Sunday evening) in bar or small upstairs restaurant. Much of "Three Men In A Boat" was written here.

MARLOW BOTTOM

Map Reference: D9
The Rebellion Beer Company brews here.

PEGASUS
61 Marlow Bottom Road
☎ (01628) 484926
11am-2.30pm; 5.30pm-11pm
Worthington Best Bitter; Rebellion IPA; Wadworth 6X; Regular Guest Beers

Carpenters Arms, Marlow   *AG, 1994*

Extensive free house and restaurant. Large function room caters for a variety of events; live music on Sunday and Wednesday evenings. No food on Sunday evenings.

MARSH

Map Reference: D7
Isolated hamlet 3 miles south of Aylesbury.

PRINCE OF WALES
(O.S. Ref. 814088)
☎ (01296) 612276
11am-2.30pm; 6pm-11pm
ABC Best Bitter; Tetley Bitter

One-bar country drinking house, a meeting place for a variety of local activities ranging from pigeon racing and beagles to the cricket club. Mine host has been in residence for over 30 years. Juke box removed in 1993. A rare gem.

MARSH GIBBON

Map Reference: B5
A few miles from Bicester, this Bucks village has an Oxfordshire feel and an undeniably marshy landscape. The Gibbon family occupied the Manor in the 13th century; it was also owned by the Duke of Suffolk, Joan of Arc's prisoner at Orleans. The Phillips Brewery operated from the Greyhound from 1981-85.

GREYHOUND
West Edge
☎ (01869) 277365
Noon-3.30pm; 6pm-11pm
Fuller's London Pride; Greene King IPA, Abbot; Hook Norton Best Bitter

Listed building, probably of Tudor origin, with 17th century brickwork. Rebuilt after a fire in 1740, it still has the fire plaque of Sun Insurance. Specialising in Thai cuisine and popular for steaks and quick business lunches.

PLOUGH
Church Street
☎ (01869) 277305
Noon-2.30pm; 6pm-11pm
Morrells Bitter, Varsity; Regular Guest Beer

16th century pub with separate dining room. Occasional live music. No food on Mondays or Sunday evening.

MARSWORTH

Map Reference: E6
Tring 2 miles S
A canalside village on the southern edge of the Vale. It is close to the Tring reservoirs, a famous bird sanctuary.

ANGLERS RETREAT
Startops End
☎ (01442) 822250
11am-2.30pm; 6pm-11pm
Fuller's London Pride; Theakston's XB; Wadworth 6X

Friendly unspoilt village local opposite Tring Reservoir.

RED LION
90 Vicarage Road (O.S. Ref. 919147)
(Off B489, near Grand Union canal bridge 130)
☎ (01296) 668366
11am-3pm; 6pm-11pm
Draught Bass; Hook Norton Best Bitter; Wadworth 6X; Regular Guest Beers

Idyllic, canalside, village pub with three contrasting bars on two levels. The comfortable lounge bar has recently been extended into what was part of the old stables. No food Sunday evening.

WHITE LION
Startops End
☎ (01442) 822325
Noon-11pm
Courage Best Bitter, Directors; John Smith's Bitter; Wadworth 6X; Regular Guest Beer

Totally refurbished old canalside pub with restaurant and bars on two levels. Large canalside patio and garden. Beware the fake handpump dispensing keg 'Scrumpy Jack' cider.

MEDMENHAM

Map Reference: D10
Marlow 3 miles NE. A largely Edwardian village on A4155 by the Thames. The Abbey was 'revived' by Sir Francis Dashwood and his lurid cronies masquerading as monks. Harleyford Manor, visible only from the river, is a Grade 1 listed building.

DOG AND BADGER
Henley Road (O.S. Ref. 804846)
☎ (01491) 571362
11am-3pm; 5.30pm-11pm
Boddingtons Bitter; Brakspear Bitter; Wadworth 6X; Flowers Original; Occasional Guest Beers

Old roadside inn of great character dating back to 1390. Many exposed beams and lots of brass. Originally three cottages, now one long bar with restaurant area at far end. Large car park.

MENTMORE

Map Reference: E5
The stately home, Mentmore Towers, once the family seat of the Rosebery's, is now a base for the Maharishi's adherents (of yogic flying fame).

Dog and Badger, Medmenham   *AG, 1994*

STAG INN
The Green
☎ (01296) 668146/668423
11am-3pm; 6pm-11pm
Charles Wells Eagle, Bombardier; Regular Guest Beer

Smart country inn with high class restaurant. Excellent traditional public bar. Evening meals only in restaurant. No food Saturday lunch, Sunday evening or Monday.

MILTON KEYNES

Map Reference: E3
The new city is much the biggest centre of population in the county and is a place genuinely unlike any other. Its open spaces and American-style-and-quality road network merge beautifully with the new housing of the highest standard and also complement the small towns and numerous villages which provided the framework on which the new city was built. The result is a captivating blend of old and new, offering an infinite variety, obvious to all but those who will not see.

BARGE
Newport Road, Woolstone
☎ (01908) 679596
11am-2.30pm; 5.30pm-11pm
(Opens 11.30am-3pm; 6pm-11pm Saturdays)
Adnams Bitter; Draught Bass

A recently refurbished and extended 16th century country inn with a restaurant and conservatory. At one time a spur from the Grand Union canal served a wharf close by and this pub served the canal workers, hence the name.

BEACON

Bond Avenue, Mount Farm
☎ (01908) 649025
11am-11pm
Ind Coope Burton Ale; Tetley Bitter
🍺 ❀ ✕ ♿ ♣ ❽ 🚗 👶 ♪
One of the first pubs to be built in the new city of Milton Keynes and built in the style of the first lighthouses to grace our coastline. It stands almost appropriately next to a series of small lakes. Red brick walls with a semi circular bar split into two, plus an upstairs gallery. On the outside there is a veranda overlooking the lake. Loud live music at weekends.

BLACK HORSE

Wolverton Road, Great Linford (O.S. Ref. 847424)
☎ (01908) 605939
11am-2.30pm; 5.30pm-11pm
ABC Best Bitter, Ind Coope Burton Ale; Tetley Bitter
❀ ✕ ✕ 🅾 🚗
Much extended canalside pub now changed out of all recognition. A split level open plan bar with an island servery and raised dining area. What were once four small bars full of character and a separate dining room have been completely destroyed by being knocked into one. The decor, wooden screens augmentd by farm implements and old bottles etc which can be purchased very cheaply by the skip load may do much to impress tourists but are poor imitations of how an old pub should be and what could have been Carlsberg Tetley's flagship locally is now just another pub turned restaurant.

BLACKSMITHS ARMS

Percheron Place, Downs Barn
11am-2.30pm; 5.30pm-11pm
☠
Fizz then, fizz now and forever more. Amen.

BRADWELL MONK

Brookside, Hodge Lea
☎ (01908) 315958
12.01pm-3pm; 5.30pm-11pm (Opens Noon-11pm Fridays & Saturdays)
Draught Bass
❀ ❽ 🚗 ♪
Estate pub overlooking sports field. Built in the 70's with a games bar and lounge both upstairs. Can get crowded on Saturday nights.

BROUGHTON HOTEL

Milton Road, Broughton Village (O.S. Ref. 897399)
☎ (01908) 667726
11am-11pm
Charles Wells Eagle, Bombardier
❀ 🛏 ✕ ✕ 🅾 🚗 👶
Completed in the 80's to catch the motoring businessmen, this building makes much of its brick and wooden architecture. It has a single but very plush bar offering a good list of lunchtime bar food.

CALDECOTTE ARMS

Bletcham Way, Caldecotte
☎ (01908) 366188
11am-2.30pm; 5.30pm-11pm

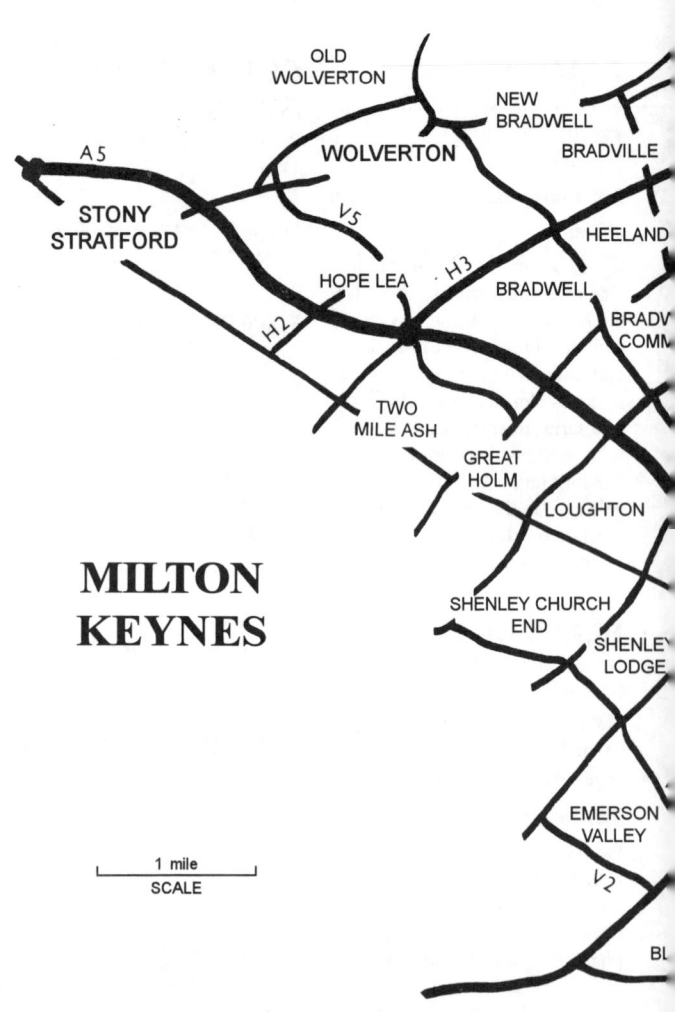

Shipstones Bitter; Tetley Bitter; Thomas Greenall's Bitter

Ideally situated in Milton Keynes very own green belt. Built on the site of Caldecote Farm from old bricks this mock windmill complete with sails, overlooks Caldecote Lake and looks like it has always been here. Its cavernous inside has a farming theme naturally enough. On the whole it caters for families and is complemented by a huge childrens play area within an easy stroll of the bar.

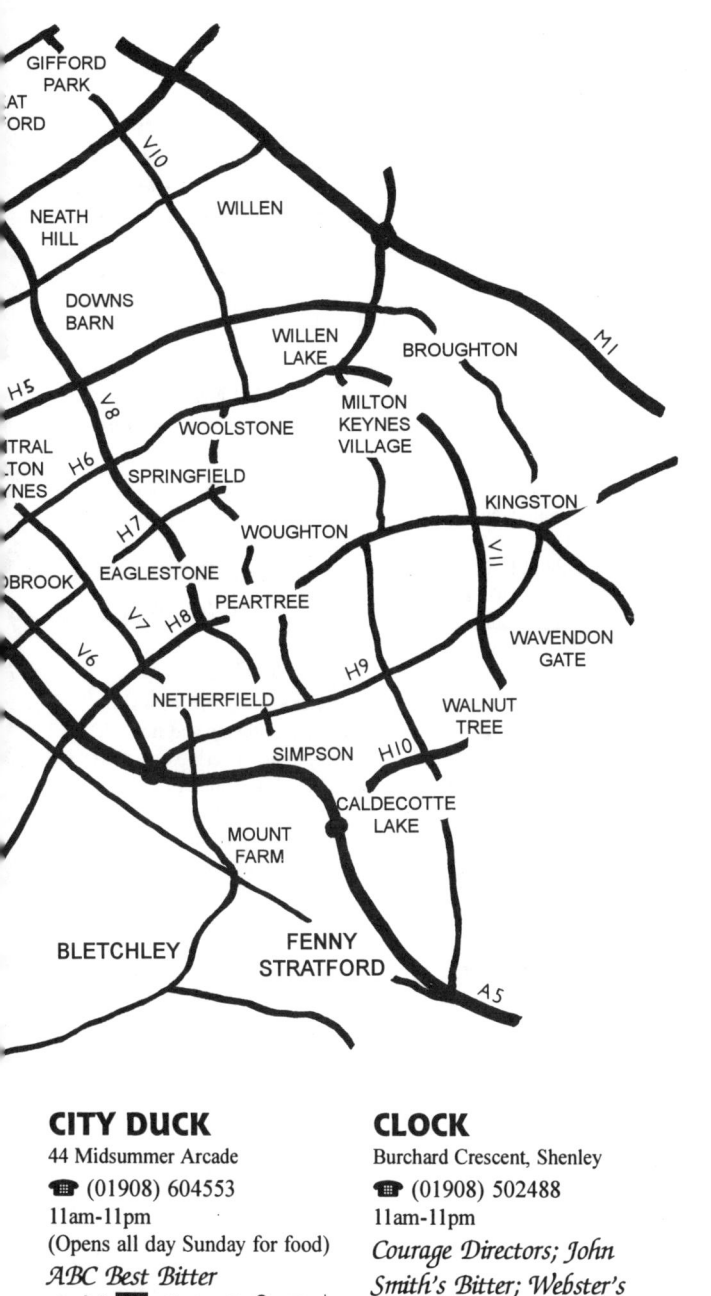

CITY DUCK
44 Midsummer Arcade
☎ (01908) 604553
11am-11pm
(Opens all day Sunday for food)
ABC Best Bitter
✿ ✕ 🆗 🍴 ♿ 🏨 ♣ 🚗 ♪
City centre pub with 'City Fayre' restaurant adjacent.

CLOCK
Burchard Crescent, Shenley
☎ (01908) 502488
11am-11pm
Courage Directors; John Smith's Bitter; Webster's Yorkshire Bitter; Regular Guest Beer

Opened in 1991 this one-bar public house is part of a sports complex. Sunday night is comedy night and Monday nights are quiz nights. Coffee and tea available from 9am every day.

CLOCK TOWER

White Horse Drive, Emerson Valley
☎ (01908) 503153
11am-2.30pm; 5.30pm-11pm
(Opens 11am-11pm on Saturdays)
Tetley Bitter

Opened in the late 1980's to serve the Emerson Valley and Furzton area. Currently in something of a decline and about to undergo a much needed refurbishment. Only one real ale at present but the manager is hoping to change that. We shall see.

COUNTRYMAN

Bradwell Common Boulevard
☎ (01908) 676346
11am-11pm
Courage Directors; John Smith's Bitter; Webster's Yorkshire Bitter

Busy and often crowded this modern split level pub near the centre of Bradwell Common's housing estate is a little over half a mile from Central Milton Keynes railway station. The beers listed are always supplemented to a total of eight and sometimes twelve real ales. Regular beer festivals are held.

COUNTY ARMS

Newport Road, New Bradwell
☎ (01908) 313840
Noon-11pm
Ruddles Best Bitter; Webster's Yorkshire Bitter

Opened on 7th December 1866 and during the early part of this century was known locally as the Corner Pin. The present landlord has been here for 28 years and you may wish to ask him about it's history.

CRICKETERS

Oldbrook Boulevard, Oldbrook
☎ (01908) 678844
11am-3pm; 4.50pm-11pm
(Opens 11am-11pm Fridays & Saturdays)
Greene King XX Dark Mild, IPA, Rayments Special, Abbot

Modern estate pub with a cricketing theme and not surprisingly overlooking a cricket pitch. Close enough to the city centre for lunchtime visits and ideal on warm summer evenings for spectating as the players work up a thirst. No meals Saturday lunchtime or Sunday evening.

CROSS KEYS

34 Newport Road, Woolstone
☎ (01908) 679404
11am-2.30pm; 7pm-11pm
Charles Wells Eagle, Bombardier

Thatched and whitewashed 16th or 17th century exterior with old and new extensions. Surrounded by a modern but unobtrusive housing development this busy popular two-bar pub enjoys its original village setting.

CUBA
81 Newport Road, New Bradwell
☎ (01908) 313904
11am-11pm
Charles Wells Eagle

Strangely named and even more strangely angled corner pub with stained glass above the bar in the saloon.

EAGER POET
2 Tower Crescent, Neath Hill
☎ (01908) 663053
11am-11pm
Boddingtons Bitter; Whitbread Best Bitter, Flowers Original

Set beneath a clock tower in the local centre this modern pub has a separate games room and family room. Disco at the weekend.

EAGLE
Harrier Court, Eaglestone
Modern estate pub closed since 1991.

FORESTERS
21 Newport Road, New Bradwell
☎ (01908) 312348
10.30am-11pm
Charles Wells Eagle, Eagle, Bombardier

Popular two-bar local on busy main road. Architecturally an Edwardian building though possibly earlier. Recent decoration has thankfully done little to change the character of this down to earth frequently very crowded boozer. Essentially, the beer is never less than excellent.

FORTE CREST HOTEL
500 Saxon Gate West
☎ (01908) 667722
11am-11pm
Courage Directors

Just three minutes walk from the main shopping centre this hotel has a large and roomy cafe bar that is modern, continental in style yet quiet and relaxing. In fact an ideal place to wind down after the day's shopping.

FOUNTAIN
Watling Street, Loughton
☎ (01908) 666203
11am-3pm; 5pm-11pm
(Opens 11am-11pm Saturdays)
Draught Bass; Courage Best Bitter, Directors; John Smith's Bitter

Just off the old A5 so probably an old coaching inn dating in part from the 16th century. Low ceilings and beams abound though not all genuine. Now run as a Harvester pub/restaurant but a warm and cosy place to be on a cold damp winter evening.

GIFFARD PARK
Broadway Avenue, Giffard Park
☎ (01908) 210025
11am-11pm
(Opens all day Sunday for diners)
Boddingtons Bitter; Marston's Pedigree; Flowers Original

Modern canalside pub with something for everyone. Childrens

playroom and outside a bouncy castle. Restaurant area serving all day. Drinks with meals only on Sundays between 3.00 and 7.00. For the canal boat owner there are towpath moorings, water and elsan points and local shops nearby.

GREBE

Kensington Drive, Great Holm
☎ (01908) 260320
11am-2.30pm; 5.30pm-11pm
(Opens 11am-11pm Saturdays)
Greene King IPA, Rayments Special, Abbot

Opened in the late eighties this popular pub is situated towards the edge of the housing estate. It has a main bar and a second bar for families but only serving non alcoholic drinks. In the main bar there is a book case from which you can take a book to read whilst enjoying a pint or two. Dimmed lighting gives a warm and friendly atmosphere.

GREEN'S CAFE BAR

Abbey Hill Golf Course, Monks Way, Two Mile Ash
☎ (01908) 562566
11am-11pm
Greene King IPA

Despite being beside the golf course, this is not the clubhouse, although it is used by golfers and general public alike. Nor is it a café; it's a pub (once known at the Golden Eagle). No meals served on Sundays.

HUNGRY HORSE

101 Bradwell Road, Bradville
☎ (01908) 312987
11am-2.30pm; 6pm-11pm
(Opens Noon-11pm Saturdays)
Draught Bass; Boddingtons Bitter; Webster's Green Label

Formerly a three-bar pub called The Jovial Priest, it changed hands and likewise its name to The Bradville, later Halley's. The one large bar now offers real ales to accompany the regular discos.

KINGSTON

40 Winchester Circle, Kingston Centre
☎ (01908) 584371
11am-11pm
Boddingtons Bitter; Marston's Pedigree; Castle Eden Ale; Flowers Original

A new public house cum restaurant which is geared mainly for families and food rather than beer. Built in a pseudo coaching inn style but more imaginatively with a large play area safely inside. Called the Kids Fun Factory this area includes a climbing frame cum maze, slides and ball pool and all manner of things for your budding Tarzan or Jane. Open for food on Sunday from 12.00 noon until 10.00pm.

LEATHERN BOTTLE

Newport Road, Wavendon (O.S. Ref. 915374)
☎ (01908) 582027
11am-2.30pm; 6pm-11pm
Charles Wells Eagle, Bombardier

Snug and friendly pub on the edge of the village overlooking the countryside. Photographic evidence of support for sporting and charitable activities. Aroma of good food permeates throughout.

NAGS HEAD
High Street, Great Linford
☎ (01908) 670146
Noon-2.30pm; 5.30pm-11pm
(Opens Noon-11pm Saturdays)
ABC Best Bitter; Tetley Bitter
🏠 ✿ ✕ ✕ 🍴 ♣ 🚗

Thatch and whitewashed village pub with two bars, under new and temporary management. Capable of a lot more, only time will tell.

NETHERFIELD
Farthing Grove, Netherfield
☎ (01908) 667072
11am-11pm
Greene King IPA
🍴 ❽ 🚗 🅿

Built in the early seventies next to the local shops on a council house estate this one-roomed bar is furnished with dark wood tables and ornamental partitions. Just a short stagger to Milton Keynes General Hospital.

NEW INN
2 Bradwell Road, New Bradwell
☎ (01908) 312094
11am-11pm
Adnams Broadside; Charles Wells Eagle, Bombardier
🏠 🍺 ✿ ✕ ✕ 📷 🍴 🛏 ♣ ❽ ☺ 🚗 🅿

Nicknamed the War Office prior to the Great War this two-bar pub with good value food stands between the bridges of the canal and the old railway. It has a separate pool room and serves good value food either in the bar or in the upstairs restaurant. It has a fenced garden to the rear with childrens play area, a menagerie with cavies, rabbits and a goat. It also has a canalside drinking area with moorings for passing boats.

Clayton Arms, Marlow   AG, 1994

OLD BARN
Secklow Gate
☎ (01908) 663388
11am-11pm
Boddingtons Bitter; Flowers Original; Regular Guest Beers

Beefeater restaurant and bar; also 38 room Travel Inn. Two regular and two changing beers, all from the Whitbread range. Childrens play areas both inside and outside. Live jazz on Thursdays.

OLD BEAMS
Paxton Crescent, Shenley Lodge
☎ (01908) 201054
11am-11pm
Adnams Bitter; Fuller's London Pride; Marston's Burton Best Bitter, Pedigree

Refreshingly reversing the trend of pubs becoming private dwellings, this grade 2 listed farmhouse has become a public house! Sympathetically restored, featuring real old beams, this owner occupied business is in an idyllic setting. Enjoy this facility.

OLDE SWAN TAVERN
Newport Road, Woughton on the Green
☎ (01908) 679489
11am-2.30pm; 6pm-11pm
Courage Directors; John Smith's Bitter; Theakston's Best Bitter

An extended and much altered pub, in parts 600 years old. Close associations with Dick Turpin along with several hundred other pubs that claim that distinction, although there is some evidence to suggest that this connection is genuine.

PEARTREE BRIDGE INN
Waterside, Peartree Bridge
☎ (01908) 691515
11am-2.30pm; 5.30pm-11pm
Draught Bass

Modern hotel and pub complex on the side of the Grand Union and overlooking a marina.

PILGRIMS BOTTLE
Linford Local Centre, St Ledger Drive, Great Linford
☎ (01908) 679616
11am-11pm
M & B Brew XI; Greene King IPA

Opened in the seventies this two-bar estate pub had a reputation for being a bit of a rough house, but thankfully, under the influence of the present landlord it is somewhat quieter though no less popular.

PLOUGH
Simpson Road, Simpson Village
☎ (01908) 670015
Noon-3pm; 5.30pm-11pm
(Opens Noon-11pm Saturdays)
Morland Old Speckled Hen; Charles Wells Eagle, Bombardier; Regular Guest Beers

Backing onto the canal this pub is ideally situated. It has two bars, one a plush L shaped lounge bar with a separate dining area. The other with linoleum and formica tables where all the games can be found.

PLOUGH

Walton Road, Wavendon
☎ (01908) 584447
11am-2.30pm; 6pm-11pm
Adnams Bitter; Tetley Bitter; Regular Guest Beers

Traditional village local, recently refurbished, with 40 seater restaurant. Food is genuinely home cooked with frequently changing specials; some recipes include real ale!

PRINCE ALBERT

Vicarage Road, Bradwell
☎ (01908) 312080
11am-2.30pm; 5.30pm-11pm
(Opens all day Saturday & Sunday)
Charles Wells Eagle, Bombardier; Regular Guest Beers

A popular pub with a friendly village atmosphere. Regular guest beers and quiz nights. Very near the YHA hostel.

QUEEN VICTORIA

Vicarage Road, Bradwell
☎ (01908) 316355
11am-2.30pm; 5.30pm-11pm
(Opens 11am-11pm Fridays & Saturdays)
Ruddles Best Bitter; Webster's Yorkshire Bitter;
Regular Guest Beers

Almost two-bar pub with YHA hostel near by.

ROSE & CASTLE

122 Midsummer Arcade
☎ (01908) 664785
9am-7pm
(Opens lunchtimes only on Sundays)
Theakston's Best Bitter, XB, Old Peculier

Shopping centre pub with food and family theme, yet no childrens room or families welcomed? Shopping centre location influences opening time. Landlord will open after 7 pm for special bookings, such as Christmas or business parties.

SHENLEY CHURCH INN

Burchard Crescent, Shenley Church End
☎ (01908) 505467
11am-11pm
Draught Bass; Worthington Best Bitter; Charrington IPA

Standing in its own grounds just off of Watling Street this hotel bar is furnished mostly in wood, with partitioned and split level seating areas affording some measure of privacy. Very popular so can be crowded.

SHIP ASHORE

Beaufort Drive, Willen
☎ (01908) 609998
11am-2.30pm; 5pm-11pm
(Opens 11am-3pm; 6pm-11pm Saturdays)

Real Ale

We pride ourselves on offering a more varied choice of ales for our customers to enjoy, and we achieve this by regularly changing our stock of ales, which can vary from Thomas Hardy Country Bitter to Thomas Greenall's Original.

Visit any one of our houses listed below, to experience an exciting range of traditional cask conditioned ales, in a warm and friendly atmosphere.

Black Horse, Chesham - Bull & Butcher, Fenny Stratford
Chequers, Weston Turville - Churchill Arms, Long Crendon
Crown, Colnbrook - Eagle, Amersham
George and Dragon, Chesham - Griffin, Chesham
Jolly Farmer, Chalfont St Peter - Nags Head, Great Linford
Pheasant, Chesham - Pineapple, Amersham Common
Ship Inn, Aylesbury - Wayfarer, Willen Lake
White Hart, Chalfont St Peter - Woolpack, Stoke Mandeville

Draught Bass; Fuller's London Pride

Excellently designed modern pub on a tastefully nautical theme using ships timbers. Split level bar with flagstone floors. Modest no smoking area. Fenced childrens play area and spacious conservatory for families. Good food though not available on Sunday evenings.

SPRINGFIELD

Springfield Boulevard
☎ (01908) 679092
5.30pm-11pm
(Opens 11am-3.30pm; 7pm-11pm Saturdays)

John Smith's Bitter; Ruddles Best Bitter

15 year old pub on housing estate with pleasant views over Woolstone, the Grand Union canal, the M1 and the Bedfordshire countryside.

SUFFOLK PUNCH

1 Langcliffe Drive, Heelands
☎ (01908) 311166
11am-11pm

Boddingtons Bitter; Morland Old Speckled Hen; Wadworth 6X; Flowers IPA, Original; Regular Guest Beer

Formerly a Tolly Cobbold house this modern three-bar pub has something for all tastes. Popular with business people at lunchtimes and a regular evening trade.

SWAN

Broughton Road, Milton Keynes Village
☎ (01908) 665240
Noon-3pm; 6pm-11pm

Boddingtons Bitter; Courage Best Bitter; Marston's Pedigree

Thatched village pub with main building dating back to 1490. Sympathetically extended to include a non smoking reataurant area serving excellent food. Features include inglenook fireplaces (with seating) in both bars.

TALBOT

London Road, Loughton
☎ (01908) 666420
11am-2.30pm; 5.30pm-11pm
(Opens 11.30am-11pm Saturdays)

Courage Directors; Theakston's Best Bitter; Webster's Yorkshire Bitter

Though at least 200 years old and probably a coaching inn originally, this building with its male orientated bar has been extended to accommodate a carvery with a pay and go drinks area.

TAWNY OWL

Fyfield Barrow, Tongwell Street, Walnut Tree
☎ (01908) 232490
11am-3pm; 5.30pm-11pm

Greene King IPA, Rayments Special, Abbot

Spacious modern town pub with an art deco interior and a no smokers area. Lively cosmopolitan clientele.

WAYFARER
Brickhill Street, Willen Lake
☎ (01908) 675222
11am-11pm
Ind Coope Burton Ale; Tetley Bitter

Modern hotel, pub and water sports complex in a picturesque setting overlooking Willen Lake. Good family pub.

WOUGHTON HOUSE HOTEL
Woughton on the Green
☎ (01908) 661919
11am-2.30pm; 6pm-11pm
Courage Best Bitter, Directors; John Smith's Bitter

A modernised Georgian building with a quiet atmosphere. Regular special events.

Milton Keynes
BLETCHLEY

Map Reference: E3
Until the arrival of the railways in the late 19th century Bletchley was a small rural village. In the 1880's Sir Henry Leon bought and renovated Bletchley Park and during WW II the house and grounds were used for intelligence work and it was here that the ENIGMA code was cracked. The site was used as a training ground for telecom engineers but is now vacated, there are plans to turn the park into a museum.

BLETCHLEY ARMS
Queensway
11am-11pm

No real ale.

DOLPHIN
Whaddon Way
☎ (01908) 371381
11am-11pm
Charles Wells Eagle, Bombardier, Fargo

A very popular estate pub built in the late 1960's with two well lit but cosy bars that are frequently crowded on Friday and Saturday nights.

EIGHT BELLS
Buckingham Road
11am-2.30pm; 5.30pm-11pm
(Opens 11am-11pm Saturdays)
Boddingtons Bitter; Wadworth 6X; Castle Eden Ale; Flowers Original

Large one bar pub on busy main road. Separate darts area and table football machine.

ENIGMA TAVERN
Princes Way
☎ (01908) 645523
11am-11pm
Banks's Mild, Bitter; Camerons Strongarm

❀ ✂ ✕ ♜ ♿ 🍺 🚗

Name inspired by Bletchley Parks code cracking activity this is a purpose built 'niche' pub for couples and business men and women lunching. One bar split into three areas. A small WW2 theme area, a stand, eat and drink area close to the bar and a modestly screened, seated dining area, decorated with puzzles etc.

GEORGE

16 Buckingham Road
☎ (01908) 372365
11am-2.30pm; 5.30pm-11pm
(Opens 11am-11pm Saturdays)
Greenalls Cask Bitter,
Thomas Greenall's Bitter
✂ ✕ ♜ ♿ 🍺 🚗 ♪

Recently refurbished, this main road pub has an off white painted brick exterior and a smart and bright interior with a two-tone wooden bar, a mix of floor tiles and carpeting. Very near the famous Bletchley Park.

LONDON PRIDE

Serpentine Court
11am-2.30pm; 5.30pm-11pm
☠

Keg pub - little to recommend it.

OLD SWAN

Shenley Road
☎ (01908) 372926
Noon-3pm; 6pm-11pm
(Opens 11am-11pm Saturdays)
Draught Bass; Boddingtons
Bitter
✂ ✕ 🍺 🚗

A drab and uninviting place which could be transformed if promised improvements ever materialize.

PARK BARREL HOUSE

4 Chandos Place
☎ (01908) 684069
11am-2.30pm; 5.30pm-11pm
(Opens 11am-11pm Saturdays)
Boddingtons Bitter; Castle
Eden Ale; Flowers IPA;
Regular Guest Beers
❀ ✂ ✕ 🅾 🍺 🚗

As its name would suggest, this is a large smart comfortable pub with a circular bar, various drinking areas tastefully decorated with memorabilia and always has an extensive range of guest ales. Good value food in separate restaurant. No food Sunday evenings.

PLOUGH

Manor Road, Water Eaton
☎ (01908) 373118
11am-2.30pm; 5.30pm-11pm
(Opens 11am-11pm Saturdays)
Tetley Bitter
♜ ♿ 🍺 ❀ ⑧ 🚗 ♪

Modern pub serving a large residential area. Separate games room. Live music.

SHENLEY HOTEL

2-6 Shenley Road
☎ (01908) 372485
11am-11pm
Courage Directors; Tetley
Bitter; Young's Bitter
🍺 ❀ 🛏 ✂ ✕ 🅾 ♜ ♿ 🍺
⑧ 🚗 ④ ♪

A large Victorian dwelling that has been a succesful hotel for a number of years. One very large bar with numerous entertainments. Good meals available all day with a pleasant dining room, should it be required. Whilst there are not any outstanding beers, all are well kept.

THREE TREES
Buckingham Road
11am-11pm
Boddingtons Bitter

Large modern open-plan bar with separate games/family area.

WISHING WELL
Tattenhoe Lane, Far Bletchley
☎ (01908) 372573
Noon-11pm
Tetley Bitter

Large one-bar pub built in the late 1960's. Has recently become a Mr Q's pool bar.

Milton Keynes
FENNY STRATFORD

Map Reference: E3
Located on the A5 Watling Street and the Grand Union canal and probably well established before Bletchley. Bletchley Brewery was here until 1896. No doubt as prosperity shifted to railway oriented Bletchley, so did Fenny's identity.

BRIDGE INN
12 Watling Street
☎ (01908) 373107
11am-11pm
Banks & Taylor Shefford Bitter; Boddingtons Bitter; Theakston's XB; Charles Wells Eagle, Bombardier; Regular Guest Beer

Re-opened in May 1995 after an expensive refurbishment as a free house (previously owned by Grand Metropolitan). Comfortable open-plan lounge style bar area - live music three nights a week.

BULL
15 Watling Street
☎ (01908) 373018
11am-2.30pm; 5.30pm-11pm

BULL & BUTCHER
30 Aylesbury Street
☎ (01908) 372964
11am-2.30pm; 5.30pm-11pm
(Opens 11am-11pm Saturdays)
Benskins Best Bitter, Ind Coope Burton Ale; Tetley Bitter; Regular Guest Beer

Situated on the busy A4146 Leighton Buzzard to Bletchley Road this smart and comfortable two-bar pub has a separate eating area and alongside the three standard choice beers has a regular guest ale.

CHEQUERS
11am-11pm

No real ale.

FOUNDRY ARMS
Victoria Road
☎ (01908) 377621

Formerly North & Randall established 1851

DAYLA GROUP

Still the original family firm

THE GREAT DAYLA ALE TRAIL

DAYLA is privileged to be associated with many of the country's leading Regional Brewers as their appointed agents supplying their ales to the same high quality standards upon which they have built their own strong reputations.

DAYLA'S association with Brewing is much longer than most would ever have imagined. Joesph Holland Senior, great Grandfather of today's Managing Director ran two Ale Houses, a Coaching Inn and a Brewery in the village of Wendover at the foot of the Chiltern Hills.

Having bought the Brewery from his father, Joseph the Younger continued brewing until the First World War after which he joined North & Randall Ltd. Mineral Water Manufacturers of Aylesbury.

DAYLA is still very much the FAMILY business with the 3rd generation of the family at the helm.

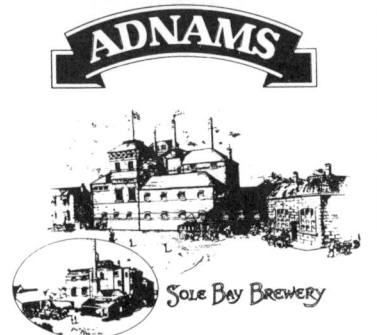

TETLEY BITTER

FULLER'S

ADNAMS — Sole Bay Brewery

WADWORTH & CO. LTD. 6X *Traditional Draught Bitter* — ALCOHOL 4.3% VOL.

BATEMANS — GOOD HONEST ALES

Total Refreshment **Dayla**

BUTCOMBE BITTER — *Your Traditional Beer*

DAYLA HOUSE : 80-100 HIGH STREET : AYLESBURY : BUCKS
TELEPHONE: 01296 20261   FACSIMILE: 01296 397012

11am-2.30pm; 5.30pm-11pm
(Opens 11am-11pm Saturdays)
Charles Wells Eagle

Small and basic one bar local.

KILRUSH
2 Watling Street
☎ (01908) 372599
11am-2.30pm; 5.30pm-11pm

Irish club.

MALTSTERS
45 Aylesbury Street
☎ (01908) 372801
11am-2.30pm; 5.30pm-11pm
(Opens 11am-11pm Saturdays)
Wadworth 6X; Flowers IPA

Large two-bar local on busy main road.

RED LION
11 Lockview Lane (O.S. Ref. 343883)
☎ (01908) 372317
Noon-3pm; 5.30pm-11pm
(Opens Noon-4pm; 6pm-11pm Saturdays)
Draught Bass; Greene King IPA

Pleasant two-bar pub situated beside Fenny Lock on the Grand Union canal. No childrens room but families are welcome.

SWAN HOTEL
36 Watling Street
☎ (01908) 370100
11am-2.30pm; 5.30pm-11pm
(Opens 11am-11pm Saturdays)
Adnams Bitter; Marston's Pedigree; Tetley Bitter

Large one-bar well appointed roadhouse. Discos and karaoke a regular feature.

Milton Keynes
STONY STRATFORD

Map Reference: D3
Now a development within greater Milton Keynes this well healed town on famous Watling Street, is situated just south of the Bucks / Northants natural border, the River Great Ouse. Stony Stratford is steeped in Roman, Elizabethan and Cromwellian history. Though many buildings were destroyed in the 18th century by fire, the two coaching inns the 'Cock' and the 'Bull' were undamaged. Tall tales were told by employees of these inns to attract and entertain customers and has given rise to the phrase cock and bull stories, and that's the truth.

BULL HOTEL & VAULTS BAR
64 High Street
☎ (01908) 567104
Noon-11pm
Draught Bass; Fuller's London Pride; Hook Norton Best Bitter; ABC Best Bitter; Theakston's Old Peculier; Wadworth 6X

Ever popular beer drinkers pub with a welcoming atmosphere, serving a varied cross section clientele. This stone flagged long narrow bar is attached to the Bull Hotel (a former coaching inn) which also has its own bar (ABC and Tetley on last visit). Victoriana and breweriana in abundance and the cellar stillage in full view. Regular darts and cards played and a Sunday lunchtime folk workshop. Bar snacks at lunchtimes and full meals in the evening.

COCK HOTEL
High Street
☎ (01908) 567733
11am-3pm; 5pm-11pm
Hook Norton Best Bitter; Jennings Bitter; Morland Old Speckled Hen

Large hotel fronting the High Street with a public bar to the left side and small restaurant down the mews. The other half of the Cock and Bull story.

CROWN
9 Market Square
☎ (01908) 563263
11am-3pm; 6pm-11pm
(Opens 11am-11pm Saturdays)
Ruddles Best Bitter, County; Webster's Yorkshire Bitter

Attractive grade 2 listed 17th century pub with large oak beams. A reputation for good food with a 50 seater restaurant offering a full English menu, Sunday roast specials and pub grub in the bar. Strong darts and quiz teams, folk nights on Tuesday evenings, bring & buy sales on Sunday A.M and discos in the evening.

DUKE OF WELLINGTON
61 Wolverton Road
☎ (01908) 563383
Noon-11pm
Draught Bass; Webster's Yorkshire Bitter

Being refurbished at time of survey. Currently pool, darts, Sky TV and live bands on Thursday evenings. Only bar snacks available and bed and breakfast during the week only.

FORESTERS ARMS
Wolverton Road
☎ (01908) 567115
11am-2.30pm; 5.30pm-11pm

Reopened after having been closed due to loss of licence at end of 1994.

FOX & HOUNDS
87 High Street
☎ (01908) 563307
11am-2.30pm; 5.30pm-11pm
(Opens 11am-11pm Saturdays)
Marston's Pedigree; Webster's Yorkshire Bitter; Regular Guest Beers

17th century two bar pub in prime High Street position with a nice west facing garden (sun trap). Friendly and welcoming atmosphere. Pub teams represented in darts, skittles, cricket and quizzes. Food lunchtimes and evenings except Sundays. Occasional exotic food nights, blues nights and treasure hunts. For the 'Knotties' this is the H.Q of Ballards parliamentary regiment.

OLD GEORGE
41 High Street
☎ (01908) 562181
11am-11pm
Boddingtons Bitter; Hook Norton Best Bitter; Ind Coope Burton Ale; Regular Guest Beer

Standing in the High Street with its bar entrance set slightly below the current street level this hotel, caters for all tastes though with two restaurants, more so for the diner than the drinker.

PLOUGH
London Road
☎ (01908) 561936
11am-3pm; 5.30pm-11pm
(Opens 11am-11pm Fridays & Saturdays)
Charles Wells Eagle, Bombardier, Fargo

19th century school house built of local limestone and brick. Converted to a pub in the 1930s. Refurbished about two years ago it has a well appointed and comfortable lounge and is family oriented. Bar meals at lunchtimes and evening main meals and two course roast dinner on Sundays.

WHITE HORSE
49 High Street
☎ (01908) 567082
11am-11pm
Boddingtons Bitter; Whitbread Best Bitter

There has been a pub on this site since 1546 but the current building is not that old. Basic two roomed pub fronting historic High Street.

WHITE SWAN
34 High Street
☎ (01908) 261471
11am-2.30pm; 5.30pm-11pm
(Opens Noon-2.30pm; 7pm-11pm Saturdays)
John Smith's Bitter; Ruddles Best Bitter, County; Webster's Yorkshire Bitter

High Street town pub formerly the White Swan then refurbished and called the Stratford Arms and now the White Swan again. Beer range small and frequently changing, a bit like the name.

Milton Keynes
WOLVERTON

Map Reference: D2
Victorian railway town that grew out of the success of the railways. This one-time mecca for railway historians is now part of the greater connurbation of Milton Keynes. It is no longer dominated by the carriage works which are virtually closed and the site is being cleared for development.

CRAUFURD ARMS
59 Stratford Road
☎ (01908) 313864

Noon-11pm
Draught Bass; Worthington Best Bitter
🌼 ⋈ ✕ ✕ 🎰 ♣ ❽ 🚗 🏨 ♪

A large and imposing pub built in 1908 and still retaining many original features. A well apointed L-shaped lounge in a Victorian style provides comfort whilst the more austere public bar doubles as a games room. Live bands most Sunday lunchtimes. Regular well kept and good priced guest beers alongside those from Bass.

GALLEON
Old Wolverton Road
☎ (01908) 313176
Noon-2.30pm; 5.30pm-11pm
(Open Noon-3pm; 6pm-11pm Saturdays)
Ansells Mild, Ind Coope Burton Ale; Tetley Bitter
🏠 🌼 ✕ ✕ 🎰 🚗

Known now as the The Galleon but as Wharf House c1865 and The Locomotive Hotel. This spacious canalside pub has its emphasis on food. Meals from a large and varied menu are available at all times.

NORTH WESTERN
11 Stratford Road
☎ (01908) 312200
11am-11pm
Charles Wells Eagle
🎰 🎰 ❽ 🚗

Basic Victorian town local much altered inside with a large lounge and small public bar.

QUEEN VICTORIA
44 Church Street
☎ (01908) 315447
11am-11pm
☠
A sad case, former Midsummer Inn, reopened and now run down.

MOULSOE

Map Reference: E2
Set on the Bedford side of the M1 junction 14, this village is part of the Carrington estate, hence the name of the pub.

CARRINGTON ARMS
Cranfield Road
☎ (01908) 615721
11am-2.30pm; 5.30pm-11pm
Adnams Bitter; Theakston's Old Peculier; Charles Wells Eagle; Regular Guest Beers
🌼 ✕ ✕ ♿ 🚗

A fine building, once the estate manager's house, this free house has been a pub since between the wars. It now specialises in food - steaks and fish etc are cooked at a special stove in the middle of the (well ventilated) room for all the customers to see. The gents' loos are incredibly posh!

MURSLEY

Map Reference: D4
Pretty village with many old and thatched properties. 1 Mile S of the A421, mid way between Bletchley and Buckingham. Up until the early part of this century the village held cattle markets, hence the width of the road.

BREWED FOR THOSE WITH TASTE! –

the original and unique flavour of the Chilterns from Buckinghamshire's oldest working brewery.

Our own prized draught and bottled beers, trade and retail from our extensive BREWERY SHOP

Plus the Chiltern Brewery Chandlery range of beer-related foods (selected for the opening of CAMRA's new Headquarters in St Albans, July 1995)

Don't forget our newly opened small BREWERY MUSEUM and never-to-be forgotten BREWERY TOURS

THE CHILTERN BREWERY
Nash Lee Road (B4009 Opposite Worlds End Nursery)
Terrick, Aylesbury, Buckinghamshire HP17 0TQ
Tel: 01296 613647 Fax: 01296 612419

Chequers, Marlow *AG, 1994*

GREEN MAN
22 Main Street (O.S. Ref. 818285)
☎ (01296) 720389
11am-3pm; 6pm-11pm
Worthington Best Bitter;
ABC Best Bitter; Tetley
Bitter

This flower strewn red brick pub dates only from the 30's but stands almost on the site of the former Green Man as the photograph in the very comfortable and friendly public bar will prove. A collection of pewter pots, bottle openers and china plates adorn the walls of both bars. Trophies of Mursley United F.C. fill the remaining gaps so this would appear to be their alternative H.Q.

NAPHILL

Map Reference: D8
High Wycombe 3 miles S.

BLACK LION
Woodlands Drive
☎ (01494) 563176
11am-11pm
Courage Best Bitter; Ruddles

Best Bitter, County; Webster's Yorkshire Bitter

Two distinct seating areas. Close to Air Force Station. Substantial menu with several homemade dishes. Large pleasant garden and new conservatory. No food Sunday evening.

WHEEL
100 Main Road
☎ (01494) 562210
11am-3pm; 6pm-11pm
Morland Independent IPA, Original Bitter, Old Speckled Hen; Regular Guest Beer

Compact two-bar pub with good car parking and large gardens including children's adventure play area. Pensioners discounts on food. Good area for walkers.

NASH

Map Reference: C3
Hamlet nestled in Whaddon Chase about 4 miles SW of Stony Stratford

OLD ENGLISH GENTLEMAN
2 Stratford Road (O.S. Ref. 783340)
☎ (01908) 610325
Noon-3pm; 6.30pm-11pm
Boddingtons Bitter; Ruddles Best Bitter; Webster's Yorkshire Bitter

Much altered old pub dating from the 17th century, that could have had a great deal more character as the remaining inglenook fireplace would prove. Nonetheless pleasant. Note the heavy wooden beams and the out of place porthole? Reputedly haunted by female ghost whose predelection is to move things around. If the ghost doesn't get you then the serious cup winning dominoes team will.

NEW DENHAM

Map Reference: G10

DOG AND DUCK
74 Oxford Road
☎ (01895) 237241
Noon-3pm; 5pm-11pm
(Opens Noon-11pm Friday & Saturday)
Boddingtons Bitter; Greene King Abbot; Wadworth 6X

450 years old and formerly a slaughterhouse. A quiet two-bar local.

LAMBERT ARMS
96 Oxford Road
☎ (01895) 255613
11am-11pm
(7am (8am Sat, 9am Sun) for breakfast)
Regular Guest Beers

Large one-bar pub with three ghosts and four ever changing real ales. Formerly a Harman's of Uxbridge pub. No food Sunday evening.

NINE STILES

Newtown Road
☎ (01895) 232432
11am-3pm; 5pm-11pm
(Opens 11am-11pm Friday & Saturday)
Morland Old Speckled Hen; Webster's Yorkshire Bitter
❀ ✕ ✕ 🍺 ♣ 🚗

Originally, two cottages and a barn, then an alehouse with a brewery. Now the barn is the restaurant and the two cottages form the bar area. Everything from dining to darts is catered for.

WAGGON AND HORSES

37 Oxford Road
☎ (01895) 233168
11am-11pm
Ind Coope Burton Ale; Tetley Bitter
🏠 ❀ 🍺 ♣ ⑧ 🚗

Recently refurbished roadside pub.

NEWPORT PAGNELL

Map Reference: E2
Bustling town in its own right whose claims to fame was its allegiance to Oliver Cromwell in the Civil War, Taylors Mustard and nationally, a motorway service station.

BULL

33 Tickford Street
☎ (01908) 610325
11am-2.30pm; 5.30pm-11pm
(Opens 11.30am-3pm; 6.30pm-11pm Saturday)
Boddingtons Bitter; Marston's Pedigree; Regular Guest Beers
🍺 ❀ ✕ ✕ 🍴 ⛺ ♣ ⑧ 🚗 🛏 ♪

A small friendly pub about 200 yards off the High St and dating from the 17th century when it was called the Bull & Bitch. A dog fighting pit was found when the toilets were refitted. There is also a ghost of a nun from nearby Tickford Abbey. There are no less than three darts teams and it's also a popular meeting place for various clubs and societies. Six other handpumps offer an ever changing range of beers and the food is good value with huge portions.

CANNON

50 High Street
☎ (01908) 211495
11am-3pm; 4.30pm-11pm
Draught Bass; Fuller's London Pride
🏠 ✕ 📷 ♣ 🚗 🛏 ♪

The former Cannon Brewery of Newport Pagnell used to be on this site. There may be some photographic or architectural evidence to support that. Much of the 18th century grade 2 listed building remains, i.e beams that actually hold the roof up and under the guidance of a new and enterprising owner, our hopes are held high too.

COACHMAKERS ARMS

117 High Street
☎ (01908) 610163

147

NEWPORT PAGNELL

Map locations:
1. BULL
2. CANNON
3. COACHMAKERS ARMS
4. DOLPHIN
5. DOVE
6. GREEN MAN
7. KING'S ARMS
8. KINGFISHER
9. PLOUGH
10. RED HOUSE
11. ROSE AND CROWN
12. SWAN REVIVED

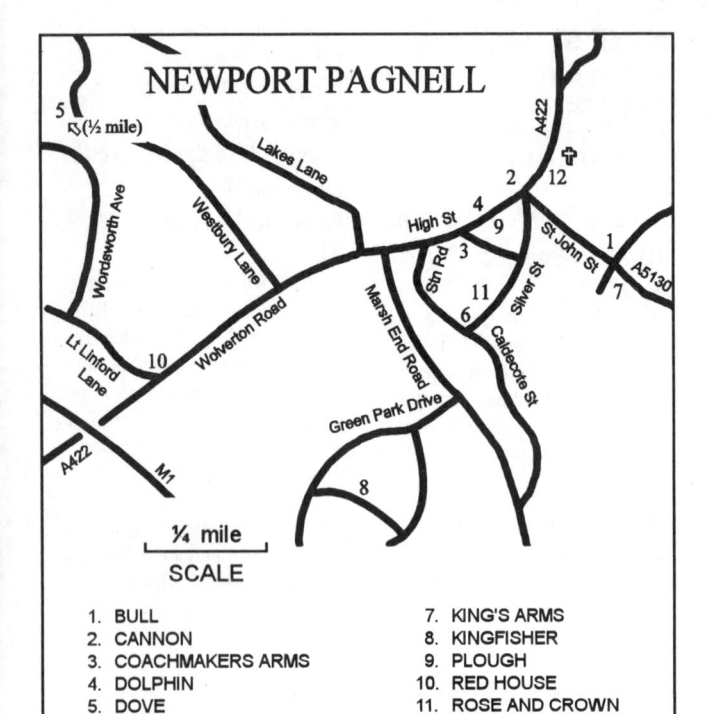

Noon-11pm
Courage Directors; John Smith's Bitter; Theakston's Best Bitter

Pub set back from the High Street and very popular with the younger members of the community.

DOLPHIN
82 High Street
☎ (01908) 611370
11am-3pm; 6pm-11pm
Charles Wells Eagle, Bombardier

Popular High Street pub with two bars and a warm welcome.

DOVE
Wordsworth Avenue
☎ (01908) 615343
11am-3pm; 5.30pm-11pm
(Opens 11am-11.00pm Saturdays)
Tetley Bitter

Typical estate pub in an open plan style. Plenty of sports trophies on shelves, a big screen T.V for televised sports and several darts boards combine to give this pub a very sporty feel.

GREEN MAN
Silver Street
☎ (01908) 611914
Noon-3pm; 6pm-11pm
(Opens noon-11pm Saturday)
Banks's Mild, Bitter;

Camerons Strongarm; Marston's Pedigree; Regular Guest Beers

Very friendly and welcoming back street pub, one of the few pubs selling mild. Reasonable prices too for an ever increasing range of beers. Lively public bar houses the pub games including Northampton skittles. A well in the centre of the public bar is all that remains from an old brewery.

KINGFISHER

Kingfisher Centre, Elthorne Way
☎ (01908) 618390
11am-3pm; 6pm-11pm
(Opens 11am-11pm Friday & Saturday)

Greene King IPA, Abbot

Refurbished at the end of 1994, this nine year old modern single bar public house is situated on the Green Park Estate.

KINGS ARMS

122 Tickford St
☎ (01908) 610033
Noon-3pm; 5.30pm-11pm
(Opens Noon-3pm; 7pm-11pm Saturdays)

Adnams Extra; Charles Wells Eagle, Bombardier

Once an 18th century private house; now a sports orientated pub with just the one bar decorated with key rings.

PLOUGH

57 High Street
☎ (01908) 210751
11am-11pm

Charles Wells Eagle

A light weight contender in the arena of pubs.

RED HOUSE

Wolverton Road
☎ (01908) 611193
11am-3pm; 5.30pm-11pm
(Open Noon-11pm Saturdays)

John Smith's Bitter; Theakston's XB

Standing on a corner next to the roundabout this pub has one large and one small bar. Good food at all times but frequently noisy.

ROSE & CROWN

Silver Street
☎ (01908) 611685
11am-2pm; 5.30pm-11pm

Charles Wells Eagle, Bombardier

Two-bar back street local with a quiet lounge bar and a lively public bar. Rock and blues music at weekends featuring the best local talent and singalongs.

SWAN REVIVED HOTEL

High Street
☎ (01908) 610565
11am-11pm

Ruddles Best Bitter

16th century coaching inn with a large lounge and a horseshoe shaped bar near the main reception. A restful atmosphere for those wishing to relax.

NEWTON BLOSSOMVILLE

Map Reference: E1
Sleepy village on the banks of the River Great Ouse and a stone's throw from the Beds border.

OLD MILL BURNT DOWN

☎ (01234) 881768
Noon-3pm; 5.30pm-11pm (Thursday, Friday and Saturday in Winter)
Courage Best Bitter, Directors; John Smith's Bitter; Marston's Pedigree

Traditional village pub with olde worlde feel, although it was rebuilt after the fire of some 12 years ago, hence the name.

NEWTON LONGVILLE

Map Reference: D4
Peninsula of far Bletchley and former chimneyed landmark of the London Brick Company. The chimneys have now all gone.

CROOKED BILLET

2 Westbrook End (O.S. Ref. 848315)
☎ (01908) 373936
11am-2.30pm; 5.30pm-11pm
(Opens 11am-11pm on Saturday)
Hook Norton Best Bitter; Wadworth 6X; Regular Guest Beers

A medieval pub which has recently been refurbished sympathetically. Large open fires. Warm and inviting decor. No fruit machines or juke boxes, just the odd click of dominoes. The home cooked food is superb (no food Sunday evening). The landlord keeps a good cellar with an ever changing range of beers. A great summer pub with a childrens play area in the garden.

RED LION

18 Church End (O.S. Ref. 848315)
☎ (01908) 373522
11am-3.30pm; 6pm-11pm
Ruddles Best Bitter, County

A twin bar pub with 200 years of mixed history. Known to have had a bad reputation at one time but that is no longer a problem. Very friendly, very straight forward - drop in and be a local. The public bar attracts a young clientele, but a firm control is maintained. The hours are more flexible than those shown and there are guest beers from time to time too depending on the landlord's mood.

NORTH CRAWLEY

Map Reference: E2
Pleasant village about 3 miles E of Newport Pagnell

Hunting for Perfection~
MORLAND
"OLD SPECKLED HEN"
Strong Pale Ale
"OLD SPECKLED HEN"
When you've a thirst
for tradition
MORLAND OF ABINGDON. BREWERS SINCE 1711.

CHEQUERS
24 High Street (O.S. Ref. 929448)
☎ (01234) 391224
11am-2.30pm; 6pm-11pm
(Opens 11am-11pm Friday & Saturday)
Greene King XX Dark Mild, IPA, Abbot

Typical homely traditional village pub dating from the 18th century. A reputation for excellent food and in addition a take away food service up until 10pm. Barbecues feature in the summer.

COCK
High Street (O.S. Ref. 929448)
☎ (01234) 391222
11am-2.30pm; 6pm-11pm
Adnams Broadside; Theakston's Best Bitter; Charles Wells Eagle, Bombardier

Olde worlde, rambling two-bar pub with separate restaurant area as well as designated food area in lounge bar. Collection of old bottles.

NORTH MARSTON

Map Reference: C5
Winslow 4 miles N. A quiet village in the vale, with a really outstanding church. For many years a centre of pilgrimage in honour of Sir John Schorne, rector in 1290, who reputedly conjured the devil into a boot thereby giving rise to Jack-in-a-box toys (and lots of Boot inns).

BELL
25 High Street
☎ (01296) 670635
11am-3pm; 6pm-11pm
Draught Bass; Worthington Best Bitter; Flowers Original

Excellent example of brick built and bay windowed Bucks village pub. Friendly and comfortable split-level bar with original fireplace and much timber. Large and varied menu but no food Sunday evening.

NORTHALL

Map Reference: F5
Leighton Buzzard 3 miles NW

NORTHALL INN
Leighton Road
☎ (01525) 221979
11am-3pm; 6pm-11pm
Boddingtons Bitter; Flowers IPA

Authentic and unspoilt 16th century, two-bar pub which is set back from the road. Large food trade at weekends means that the front bar becomes more of a restaurant.

SWAN
Leighton Road
☎ (01525) 220444

11am-11pm
*Fuller's Chiswick Bitter;
Flowers Original; Regular
Guest Beer*

Solid friendly, two-bar local catering for everyone.

NORTHEND

*Map Reference: C9
Henley-on-Thames 9 miles S.*

WHITE HART
(O.S. Ref. 735924)
☎ (01491) 638353
11am-2.30pm; 6pm-11pm
Brakspear Mild, Bitter, Special, Old

Attractive, friendly unspoilt pub in beautiful surroundings. Noted for good food, log fires and large well-kept garden with children's play area. Children welcome in separate room. No food Sunday evening.

OAKLEY

*Map Reference: B6
Thame 6 miles SE. Nestling in water meadows below Brill Hill, and close to what remains of the ancient Bernewood Forest.*

CHANDOS ARMS
8 Turnpike
☎ (01844) 238296
Noon-3pm; 5pm-11pm
*Boddingtons Bitter;
Worthington Best Bitter;
Regular Guest Beer*

Small, old fashioned low-beamed local; fine for a drink and good conversation. Aunt Sally played in summer.

ROYAL OAK
Worminghall Road
☎ (01844) 238242
11.30am-2.30pm; 5.30pm-11pm
(Open all day at weekends)
Regular Guest Beers

17th century village local which attracts the younger set.

OLNEY

*Map Reference: E1
Yes, the pancake capital of the western world! The William Cowper Museum is here but he actually lived outside of Olney, preferring the countryside (perhaps, some might say, due to his morbid fear of pancakes?).*

BULL
9 Market Place
☎ (01234) 711470
11am-2.30pm; 5.30pm-11pm
Charles Wells Eagle, Bombardier, Fargo; Regular Guest Beers

🍺 ❀ ✕ ✘ ♟ 🛏

Warm, comfortable and welcoming old town pub run by friendly landlord and landlady. Various nooks and crannies for small or large groups and a corner with a TV and a games machine. Some music but background only. Excellent range of beers with guest beers on rotation.

CASTLE
Yardley Road
☏ (01234) 711570
11am-3pm; 5.30pm-11pm

Courage Directors; Ruddles Best Bitter; Wadworth 6X; Webster's Yorkshire Bitter

✕ ♟ ♪

Two-bar pub at the north end of High Street. Currently the public bar is being refurbished. Emphasis on play rather than beer with a games machine and a pool table as the key attractions.

SWAN
12 High Street
☏ (01234) 711111
11am-2.30pm; 5.30pm-11pm

Morrells Bitter; Samuel Smith's OBB; Regular Guest Beer

✕ ✘ ♟ 🛏

Attractive old town pub of stone construction with low ceilings and a warm welcoming feel. Offering bistro style food eaten in the bar.

TWO BREWERS
34 High Street
☏ (01234) 711393
11am-2.30pm; 5.30pm-11pm

Boddingtons Bitter; John Smith's Bitter; Marston's Pedigree; Webster's Yorkshire Bitter

❀ ✕ ✘ 🛏

Stone built pub in keeping with the feel of the town. Two bars; lounge and snug with background music. Games machine in the snug. Meals from a good menu.

OVING

Map Reference: C5
Between Whitchurch and North Marston, 'Ooving' is a compact hilltop village.

BLACK BOY
Church Road
☏ (01296) 641258
Noon-2.30pm; 6pm-11pm
(Closed all day Tuesday)

Greene King IPA; Marston's Pedigree

🏠 🍺 ❀ ✕ ✘ 🅿 ♟ 🚗

Original 17th century building with attached restaurant. Fine views over the Vale of Aylesbury. Notable antique cash register. Nearly 200 spirit jugs over bar. Closes 2pm Sunday afternoon.

OWLSWICK

Map Reference: D7
Princes Risborough 3 miles SE. A tiny hamlet outside the Green Belt which is itself protected; a distinguished resident was Bruce Bairns father, the celebrated comic artist of World War I.

Black Boy, Oving   *AG, 1991*

SHOULDER OF MUTTON
☎ (01844) 344304
Not generally trading - appears to operate as a conference/function centre only.

Extended 16th century popular village pub due for further extension. Stage in the saloon bar is very busy on Friday and Saturday nights with local bands on Friday nights and a disco on Saturday nights. Restaurant facility to be provided soon

PADBURY

Map Reference: C4
Slender village about 3 miles SW of Buckingham, running down hill from the A413 and overlooked by the church.

BLACKBIRD
Main Street
☎ (01280) 813017
11am-11pm
Boddingtons Bitter; Ruddles Best Bitter; Charles Wells Eagle; Castle Eden Ale

NEW INN & PETROL STATION
Winslow Road
☎ (01280) 813137
10am-3pm; 5pm-10.30pm
Hook Norton Best Bitter, Old Hooky; Morrells Bitter; Tetley Bitter

16th century roadside pub of considerable character featuring three bars. Hand pumps in each bar to cater for the discerning drinker. Welcoming landlord and landlady. Petrol is also available but not in the public bar. Pub doubles as the village community post office and grocers shop.

PENN

Map Reference: E9
High Wycombe 3 miles SW. 600 ft high in the Chilterns, it is said to have a view of several counties. In the church lie four grandsons of William Penn, the founder of Pennsylvania. A famous local industry in mediaeval times supplied glazed tiles to the Royal houses.

CROWN

Witheridge Lane
☎ (01494) 812640
11.30am-2.30pm; 6pm-11pm
(Opens 11am-11pm in summer)
Courage Directors; Theakston's XB; Webster's Yorkshire Bitter

Very large Chef & Brewer pub/restaurant with attractive garden. Old (c.1400) pub with lots of character not spoilt by modernisation.

RED LION

Elm Road
☎ (01494) 813107
11am-2.30pm; 5.30pm-11pm
(Opens 11am-11pm on Saturdays)
Boddingtons Bitter; Brakspear Special; Fuller's London Pride; Marston's Pedigree; Wadworth 6X; Flowers Original

Old pub facing Penn common. Spacious, decorative and popular for food.

PENN STREET

Map Reference: E8
Amersham 3 miles NE. A neat village with an attractive green opposite the 'Squirrel'. There are associations with the Earls Howe and the Curzons of Mayfair.

HIT OR MISS

☎ (01494) 713109
11am-3pm; 5.30pm-11pm
Brakspear Bitter; Fuller's Chiswick Bitter, London Pride; Hook Norton Old Hooky

Old pub with three bars, much exposed woodwork and a separate restaurant with an extensive, high quality menu.

SQUIRREL

☎ (01494) 711291
11am-3pm; 5.30pm-11pm
Adnams Bitter; Greenalls Cask Bitter; Regular Guest Beer

Friendly village local catering for all ages. Pub faces the village cricket pitch and is approached via a pleasant, crescent shaped drive. Evening meals on Fridays.

PIDDINGTON

Map Reference: D9
Incongruous furniture village near West Wycombe.

DASHWOOD ARMS
Old Oxford Road
☎ (01494) 881330
11am-2.30pm; 5.30pm-11pm
Courage Best Bitter, Directors; Wadworth 6X; Flowers Original; Regular Guest Beers
❀ ✕ ✕ ♣ 🚗

One large comfortable bar with a small games area. Food available, including vegetarian dishes, all sessions except Sunday evening.

PITSTONE

Map Reference: F6
An uninspiring village adjoining the more interesting Ivinghoe and dominated by the vast, now defunct, cement works. The impressive windmill (NT) is one of the oldest post mills in Britain and is open to the public.

BELL
80 Marsworth Road
☎ (01296) 668078
11am-11pm
Tetley Bitter; Regular Guest Beers
🏠 ❀ ✕ ✕ ♨ 🍺 ⛺ ♣ ❽ 🚗 ♪

Two bar village pub close to the cement works, usually offering three or four beers. Live music every fortnight.

DUKE OF WELLINGTON
Cook's Wharf (O.S. Ref. 927161)
(Opposite Pitstone Wharf)
☎ (01296) 661402
Noon-2.30pm; 6pm-11pm
(Closes 3pm Saturday lunchtime)
Butcombe Bitter; Fuller's London Pride; Marston's Pedigree
🏠 ❀ ✕ ✕ ♨ ♣ 🚗

Friendly, one bar, country pub half way between Pitstone and Cheddington. The Grand Union

Old Hat, Preston Bissett   *AG, 1991*

canal passes immediately behind the pub. Special rates for meals for senior citizens.

POUNDON

Map Reference: B5
Bicester 7 miles SW.

SOW AND PIGS
Main Street
☎ (01869) 277728
11am-3pm; 5.30pm-11pm
Charles Wells Eagle; Regular Guest Beer

Comfortable village pub with huge display of bottled beers from all over the world. Large pretty garden. Pub runs a successful clay pigeon team. Afternoon closing may vary. No food Sunday.

PRESTON BISSETT

Map Reference: B4
A Saxon village about 4 miles SW of Buckingham with an interesting Norman church.

OLD HAT
Main Street
☎ (01280) 848335
11am-2.30pm; 7pm-11pm
(Opens 6pm-11pm on Saturdays)
Hook Norton Best Bitter

Thatched village local unchanged for many years. Visit while you may and enjoy the warmth of the the fire and marvelous welcome.

WHITE HART
Pound Lane
☎ (01280) 847969
Noon-2.30pm; 6pm-11pm
ABC Best Bitter; Flowers Original

17th century thatched village local with varied seating areas. Good value home cooked food. Beer range changes.

PRESTWOOD

Map Reference: E8
Great Missenden 2 miles E.
A sprawling development with a fine 19th century church. Formerly known for its orchards of Bucks black cherries, it was the home for many years of Clement Attlee, the post-war Labour Prime Minister.

CHEQUERS INN
High Street
☎ (01494) 862218
11am-3pm; 6pm-11pm
(Saturday 11am to 4pm;7pm to 11pm)
Morland Original Bitter

Large village pub with small lounge bar and separate games room. In 1979 the chequered pub sign was replaced by a painting of Chequers House and unveiled by Harold Wilson.

Kings Head, Prestwood *AG, 1994*

GREEN MAN
2 High Street
☎ (01494) 890074
11.30am-3pm; 6pm-11pm
Draught Bass; Worthington Best Bitter; ABC Best Bitter; Tetley Bitter

Small friendly two bar pub with emphasis on traditional games. Resident ghost allegedly to be found in saloon bar. No snacks on Sunday.

KINGS HEAD
188 Wycombe Road
☎ (01494) 862392
11am-11pm
Adnams Broadside; Brakspear Mild, Bitter, Special, Old; Tring Old Icknield Ale

The ultimate antidote to the modern pub: traditional decor and atmosphere - no machines, no music, no draught lager, no meals (snacks only).

POLECAT
170 Wycombe Road
☎ (01494) 862253
11.30am-2.30pm; 6pm-11pm
Marston's Pedigree; Morland Old Speckled Hen; Ruddles Best Bitter, County; Webster's Yorkshire Bitter

Emphasis mainly on food, however, drinkers are actively encouraged. Extensive and attractive garden. No bar food on Sunday evening.

TRAVELLERS REST
54 High Street
☎ (01494) 862106
11am-3pm; 6pm-11pm
(Open 11am - 11pm Saturdays)
Greene King IPA; Marston's Pedigree; Tetley Bitter; Regular Guest Beer

Pub at centre of village with an emphasis on sports, catering for sports and social events. Karaoke on Thursday nights.

Kings Head, Prestwood (Cellar) *AG, 1991*

PRINCES RISBOROUGH

Map Reference: D7
A pleasant little mediaeval market town, it has fared less well than some of its Chilterns neighbours. The Market Square and Church Street remain almost intact, however, and there is a semblance of the old town in Bell Street also. The 17th century manor (NT) survives, together with an attractive Norman church. The name 'Princes' derives from its association with the Duchy of Cornwall.

BELL
Bell Street
☎ (01844) 274702
11am-11pm
Smiles Best Bitter; Tetley Bitter
Small, friendly village-style pub just off the High Street. Now opened out into one bar with games area at one end. Large garden with childrens play equipment.

BIRD IN HAND
Station Road
☎ (01844) 345602
11am-2.30pm; 5.30pm-11pm
(Closes 3pm on Saturday lunchtimes)
Greene King IPA, Abbot
Cosy cottage pub - a real local, with accent on games. Immaculate collection of brass trinkets and darts trophies. No food on Sunday. Dark mild and Rayments sometimes available.

BLACK PRINCE
Wycombe Road
☎ (01844) 345569
11am-11pm
Courage Best Bitter, Directors; Occasional Guest Beers

Small urban hotel/free house with an imposing frontage which has been recently re-decorated. Meals available at all times.

BUCKINGHAM ARMS

Longwick Road
☎ (01844) 345058
11am-11pm

Tetley Bitter; Regular Guest Beer

Substantial town hostelry with several large rooms. May be replaced by Tesco's soon.

GEORGE AND DRAGON

74 High Street
☎ (01844) 343087
10.30am-2.30pm; 5.30pm-11pm
(Open until later Fri/Sat afternoons)

Draught Bass; Benskins Best Bitter; Marston's Pedigree

Old (possibly 16th century) coaching inn with cobbled yard and restaurant. Decor typical of its type.

WHITELEAF CROSS

Market Square
☎ (01844) 346834
10.30am-2.30pm; 5.30pm-11pm
(Opens 10am-3pm; 6pm-11pm on Saturday)

Morland Independent IPA, Original Bitter, Old Speckled Hen

Immaculate town tavern overlooking the recently restored Market House with its arcades and surmounted clock. A popular and well run establishment. The new pub sign depicts the chalk cross on the hillside nearby. There is a small rear patio garden. No meals on Sundays.

QUAINTON

Map Reference: C5
Aylesbury 7 miles SE. A large attractive village with a tall brick windmill, and a green. There are 17th century almshouses and a fine 14th century church. The summit of Quainton Hill affords splendid views to the north-west, while to the south on the old Metropolitan Railway line, the local railway society actively preserves the age of steam.

GEORGE & DRAGON

32 The Green
☎ (01296) 655436
Noon-2.30pm; 6pm-11pm

Worthington Best Bitter; ABC Best Bitter, Benskins Best Bitter; Tetley Bitter

Split-level, two-bar pub overlooking sloping village green, close to Quainton Windmill. No food Mondays. Beer selection varies.

SWAN & CASTLE

52 Lower Street
☎ (01296) 655276

Noon-2pm; 7pm-11pm
(Opens 11am - 11pm on Saturday)
Greene King IPA, Abbot

Welcoming 19th century Rothschild-style building with open plan bar and emphasis on pub games. Decorative lettering below the gable end states '1888 - Fine Malt and Hop Ales'.

WHITE HART

4 The Strand
☎ (01296) 655234
11.30am-2.30pm; 7pm-11pm
Courage Best Bitter; ABC Best Bitter

Two-bar village local built in 'Chesham and Brackley' 1930's style. No food Monday or Tuesday evenings.

RADNAGE

Map Reference: D8
High Wycombe 6 miles SE. A scattered group of hamlets or 'ends' including Town End and The City! Church End is the prettiest tucked away in a Chiltern fold.

CROWN

City Road (O.S. Ref. 784967)
☎ (01494) 482301
11.30am-3pm; 6pm-11pm
Draught Bass; Fuller's London Pride; Morland Independent IPA

Pleasant country pub refurbished into one long bar. No food Sunday evening.

RICHINGS PARK

Map Reference: G10
About 1 mile South of Iver.

NORTH STAR

65 Thorney Mill Road
☎ (01895) 442128
11am-3pm; 5.30pm-11pm
(11am-11pm Friday & Saturday)
Courage Best Bitter; John Smith's Bitter; Regular Guest Beer

Originally a beer house in a row of cottages, the pub was extended to take in a further two cottages as well as having a modern day extension. The inside of the pub is light and airy, split into two bar areas. The original beams are exposed, but the bars are of a more recent date.

TOWER ARMS

Thorney Lane South
☎ (01753) 652624
11am-11pm
Draught Bass; M & B Brew XI; Fuller's London Pride; Tetley Bitter; Regular Guest Beer

Coaching inn on the main road from Staines to Colnbrook to Uxbridge. Now extensively opened up to a single bar with the original internal walls and beams. Note the 1925 hand drawn fire engine in the foyer. Generally a lively pub popular with younger clientele.

Well appointed country hotel with popular bar, restaurant and large garden. Greatly extended from original Wheelers/Courage pub.

SAUNDERTON

Map Reference: D8
A long thin parish extending along the Wycombe road almost from Risborough to Bradenham. Much of the original hamlet has disappeared, apart from a few buildings around the church.

GOLDEN CROSS

Wycombe Road
☎ (01494) 562293
11am-11pm
Ind Coope Burton Ale; Tetley Bitter

Well-appointed roadside pub in attractive surroundings with secluded garden. Varied menu of home-cooked dishes caters for vegetarians. Petanque facilities available.

ROSE AND CROWN

Wycombe Road
☎ (01844) 345299
11am-2.30pm; 6pm-11pm
Brakspear Bitter; Morrells Varsity; Morland Original Bitter; Regular Guest Beer

SEER GREEN

Map Reference: F9
Beaconsfield 2 miles SW
Unexceptional place amid wooded South Bucks countryside. The Quaker settlement of Jordans, where Penn is buried, is a delightful spot, with a barn supposedly built from the timbers of the Mayflower.

JOLLY CRICKETERS

24 Chalfont Road (O.S. Ref. 966920)
☎ (01494) 676308
11am-3pm; 5.15pm-11pm
Brakspear Bitter; Castle Eden Ale; Wethered Bitter; Occasional Guest Beers

Excellent, friendly village local with two bars. The pub supports four darts teams and a golf society and is involved in much charity work including an annual horticultural show. No lunches on Sunday.

THREE HORSESHOES

22 Orchard Road (O.S. Ref. 965920)
☎ (01494) 677522
11am-3.30pm; 5pm-11pm
(Opens 11am-11pm Saturday)

Bull, Stony Stratford   *NH, 1994*

Courage Best Bitter; John Smith's Bitter; Ruddles County

🍺 ❀ ✕ ✕ 🛏 🍻 ⛺ 🎲 ♣ 🚗

Two-bar country village pub adjacent to the church. Lounge bar is food orientated. No food Sunday evening.

SHABBINGTON

Map Reference: B7
Thame 3 miles East. A tiny riverside village in a bit of Bucks improbably to the West of Oxfordshire.

OLD FISHERMAN

(O.S. Ref. 667065)
☎ (01844) 201247
11am-3pm; 5.30pm-11pm
(Opens 11am-11pm on Saturday)

Morrells Bitter, Varsity

🍺 ❀ ✕ ✕ 🛏 ⛺ 🚗

Country local just out of village on the bank of the river Thame, very popular with fishermen and families. Theme events such as Caribbean or French evenings are held fairly regularly.

SHERINGTON

Map Reference: E2
Slowly expanding cottaged village 2 miles NE of Newport Pagnell. The 13th century church is dedicated to the little known French bishop, St Laud and is therefore unique.

SWAN

10 High Street (O.S. Ref. 891468)
☎ (01908) 610992
11am-3pm; 6pm-11pm
Charles Wells Eagle

Prominent two-bar village pub of whitewashed stone. The comfortable lounge is wood panelled and the public bar is basic but friendly. You can enjoy a game of darts, cards or dominoes and increasingly rare these days are the Northants skittles which you can try your hand at too.

WHITE HART

1 Gun Lane (O.S. Ref. 891468)
☎ (01908) 617591
Noon-3pm; 6.30pm-11pm
Exmoor Ale; Hook Norton Best Bitter

Run by an enterprising landlord, this pub has great potential with eight letting rooms, former stabling and outbuildings. Enjoying a slightly remote spot through the back of the village this three storey building dates from the early 17th century. Meals are served during opening hours except Wednesday evenings and Sundays all day. There is a walled drinking area to the rear that is a regular sun trap. Well worth the visit.

SKIRMETT

Map Reference: D9
Marlow 6 miles SE.
A tiny hamlet in glorious country along the Hambleden valley. The Old Crown is one of a number of attractive cottages at the lower end.

FROG AT SKIRMETT

☎ (01491) 638996
11am-2.30pm; 6pm-11pm
Brakspear Bitter; Old Luxter's Barn Ale; Occasional Guest Beers

Village laneside pub (previously the 'King's Arms'), reputedly 400 years old. Old Luxters brewery is only two miles away. The daily menu on beam above bar offers a good variety of restaurant and bar meals (Sunday lunch a speciality).

OLD CROWN

☎ (01491) 638435
10.30am-2.30pm; 6pm-11pm
Brakspear Bitter, Special

Totally restaurant oriented and does not encourage drinkers. No food Monday.

SLAPTON

Map Reference: E5
Leighton Buzzard 3 miles N. Small village in the water-meadows between the Ouzel and the Grand Union Canal

CARPENTER'S ARMS

1 Horton Road (O.S. Ref. 935207)
☎ (01525) 220563
Noon-3.30pm; 7pm-11pm
Greene King IPA; Regular Guest Beer
16th century multi-roomed, thatched pub, with bookshop attached. Well deserved reputation for good food.

SOULBURY

Map Reference: E4
Leighton Buzzard 3 miles SE.

BOOT

51 High Road
☎ (01525) 270433
11am-2.30pm; 6pm-11pm
Benskins Best Bitter, Ind Coope Burton Ale; Marston's Pedigree
Comfortably furnished bar and restaurant featuring Victorian antiques and hunting prints. An interesting à la carte menu offers plenty of variety (mussels a speciality in season) and vegetarian dishes are available.

RED LION

Hollingdon (O.S. Ref. 875270)
(Half a mile west of village)
☎ (01525) 270001
Boarded up. Probably for sale as a private house.

SPEEN

Map Reference: D8
High Wycombe 5 miles South. Compact, sheltered ridge village, with a mixture of old brick-and-flint cottages and modern dwellings.

KING WILLIAM IV

Hampden Road
☎ (01494) 488329
Noon-3pm; 6.30pm-11pm
(Closed Sunday evening)
Boddingtons Bitter; Marston's Pedigree
Restaurant with no facilities for large scale drinking, but drinks only are served in the right hand bar, which is effectively the pre-dinner aperitif area. Supper licence till midnight.

OLD PLOW

Flowers Bottom Lane
☎ (01494) 488300
Noon-2pm; 7pm-8.45pm
(Closed Sunday evening and Monday)
Brakspear Bitter

White Lion, St. Leonards   *GG, 1993*

À la carte and bistro restaurant in what is left of a pub dating back to 1650. Drinks not served without a meal.

Chilterns. Excellent garden with separate, safe area with swings, slide and climbing frame, for children. No evening meals on Sunday.

ST LEONARDS

Map Reference: E7
An upland village along winding lanes above Wendover. On the road from Halton to St. Leonards there are some magnificent views, and the Forestry Commission has laid out some good walks.

WHITE LION
Jenkins Lane (O.S. Ref. 919070)
☎ (01494) 758387
11am-2.30pm; 6pm-11pm
Benskins Best Bitter, Ind Coope Burton Ale; Regular Guest Beer

17th century pub with many low beams and horse brasses. Reputedly the highest pub in the

STEEPLE CLAYDON

Map Reference: B4
One of several villages sharing the name of Claydon House, home to the Verney family since the 15th century. The present house is owned by the National Trust and has associations with Florence Nightingale.

CROWN INN
33 West Street
☎ (01296) 730250
Noon-2pm; 7pm-11pm
(Opens 11am-11pm on Saturdays)
Tetley Bitter

From the out of place continental lookalike shutters to the interior which is badly in need of wholesale refurbishment this pub is a serious under achiever. A victim of the current economic climate.

FOUNTAIN
West Street
11am-2.30pm; 5.30pm-11pm

Unable to obtain any details either by personal visit or phone.

PHOENIX
11 Queen Catherine Road
☎ (01296) 738919
Noon-2.30pm; 5.30pm-11pm
(Opens Noon-11pm Friday & Saturday)
Draught Bass; Tetley Bitter

A 16th century thatched and whitewashed grade 2 listed pub with a large garden containing a Wendy house and an orchard. A warm and friendly welcome. Pleasant interior with two bars, one tiled and one carpeted. Darts played in one bar and in also in the separate games room along with pool. Strong ladies darts team, a quiz team and a pool and darts knock out competition every Saturday. Within easy walking of the Swan's Way footpath.

PRINCE OF WALES
Addison Road
☎ (01296) 730512
7pm-11pm
(Opens 11am-11pm on Saturdays)
Boddingtons Bitter; Hook Norton Best Bitter

One-bar village local with games emphasis. 40-seater restaurant under refurbishment - catering should be available from March 1995.

STEWKLEY

Map Reference: D4
Milton Keynes 5 miles N. A straggling village 'street' village, with a few original 16th century and 17th century buildings. It has twice been threatened by airport proposals, which required the removal of St. Michael's the finest Norman church in the county and one of the most unspoilt in England.

CARPENTERS ARMS
High Street South
☎ (01525) 240272
11am-11pm
Tetley Bitter; Wadworth 6X; Regular Guest Beers

Low ceilinged two-bar pub at southern end of village. Small restaurant, off saloon bar. No meals Monday evening. The bar has a good selection of malt whiskies and there is a keen games following including two quiz teams.

SWAN
High Street North
☎ (01525) 240285
Noon-3pm; 6pm-11pm
Courage Best Bitter, Directors; Marston's Pedigree; Morland Old

Speckled Hen

Fine Georgian pub situated in the village centre. Good atmosphere in an old beamed interior which has a separate dining area. Monthly live music on Sunday evening.

STOKE GOLDINGTON

Map Reference: D2
String of houses along the B562 Northampton Road about 5 miles NW of Newport Pagnell

LAMB

16 High Street (O.S. Ref. 837488)
☎ (01908) 551233
11am-2.30pm; 5.30pm-11pm
(Opens 11am-11pm on Saturdays)
Draught Bass; Hook Norton Best Bitter; Morland Old Speckled Hen

Friendly village local with something happening most days. A quiz on Wednesday, live music on Thursday, free pool on Friday and Sunday, regular art exhibitions, theme food nights, a golf society and fishing club as well as skittles, darts, crib and dominoes. Although there is no separate dining area, children are welcome to eat in the lounge.

WHITE HART

High Street (O.S. Ref. 838487)
☎ (01908) 551392
Noon-2pm; 7pm-11pm
(Closes 3pm Saturday lunchtimes)
Adnams Broadside; Charles Wells Eagle

Small two-bar stone built pub of unknown age but the architecture and beams cry very old. The games area, just off the public bar boasts a league winning skittles team as well as a very good darts team, while crib and dominoes are played around a cosy real fire. The pretty, separate restaurant area welcomes the whole family for home cooked meals every lunchtime except Monday and on Thursday, Friday and Saturday evenings.

STOKE GREEN

Map Reference: F10
Stoke Poges 1m N

RED LION

☎ (01753) 521739
11am-11pm
Draught Bass; Fuller's London Pride; Regular Guest Beer

Originally two 17th century cottages for agricultural workers to Stoke Place. The small nook opposite the listed bar frontage used to be the local Post Office window. Note the copy of Grey's 'Elegy' in his own hand above the inglenook fireplace. In the original preserved kitchen is a cast iron range with a brick oven, and the original water pump. Non-smoking room has a collection of litho prints. There is a good quality menu in the á la carte restaurant. A pleasant and historic pub which is well worth finding. No food Sunday evening.

Canalside pub with wooden floor, beamed ceilings and a no smoking area. Mainly a family pub. Very busy in the summer with passing trade from the road and the canal. Excellent childrens room complete with baby changing unit.

STOKE HAMMOND

Map Reference: E4
Almost canalside cluster of houses 3 miles S of Bletchley.

DOLPHIN
Stoke Road
☎ (01525) 270263
11am-2.30pm; 5.30pm-11pm
(Open 12.30pm-2.30pm; 6pm-11.00pm Winter)
Worthington Best Bitter; M & B Brew XI; Greene King IPA; ABC Best Bitter; M&B Highgate Mild; Flowers IPA, Original

Approximately 250 years old this friendly village pub holds regular events. Meals from an extensive menu always available. Games room, large garden with childrens playground.

THREE LOCKS
☎ (01525) 270470
11am-2.30pm; 6pm-11pm
(Opens 11am-11pm in Summer)
ABC Best Bitter; Tetley Bitter

STOKE MANDEVILLE

Map Reference: D6
Suburban village internationally known for its Spinal Injuries hospital and Paraplegic 'Olympics'. Moat Farm was owned by John Hampden, and it was the 'ship money' tax on it he refused to pay in 1635. The church spire is claimed to be the furthest point from the sea in any direction.

BELL
29 Lower Road
☎ (01296) 612434
11am-3pm; 6pm-11pm
Tetley Bitter; Wadworth 6X

Lively and comfortable roadside house. Pool table in the 'Public Bar' end of this one-bar pub.

BULL
Risborough Road
☎ (01296) 613632
11.30am-3pm; 5.30pm-11pm
Draught Bass; Marston's Pedigree; Tetley Bitter

ADNAMS
SOUTHWOLD

Sole Bay Brewery

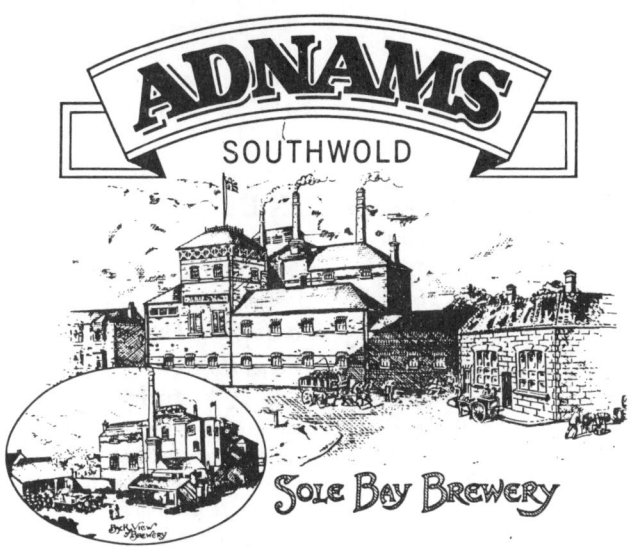

From Suffolk's Oldest Brewery, Britain's Finest Beer.

ADNAMS & CO PLC·SOLE BAY BREWERY·SOUTHWOLD·SUFFOLK IP18 6JW·TELEPHONE SOUTHWOLD (0502) 722424

Village pub, built in 1821, with cosy lounge bar and large garden. Interesting art work featuring various places in Britain. No food Sunday lunchtime.

WOOLPACK
21 Risborough Road
☎ (01296) 613447
Noon-2.30pm; 5.30pm-11pm
(Opens 12pm-11pm Friday & Saturday)

ABC Best Bitter, Ind Coope Burton Ale; Tetley Bitter

An 'olde worlde' half thatched inn with a large garden, originally built in 1752 as a wood house. Excellent friendly atmosphere of a traditional relaxed family pub. Offers a good choice of food from its 'Big Steak' menu and is open all day Sunday for diners.

STOKE POGES

Map Reference: F10
Slough 3m S. The world beats a path to its 'country churchyard' which inspired Thomas Gray to write his Elegy. The grounds of Stoke Place and Stoke Park (now the Golf Club) were laid out by Capability Brown. Stoke is one of the 'Three Hundreds of Chiltern' stewardship of which is involved in formal resignation from Parliament.

DOG & POT
94 Rogers Lane
☎ (01753) 644175
11am-3pm; 5.30pm-11pm
(Opens 11am-11pm on Saturday)

Courage Best Bitter; Regular Guest Beers

Originally called the Dog and Porridge Pot, the present building dates from 1895. The original pub, built in 1759, is now a private house because the lord of the manor objected to a pub on his land. A comfortable single bar with new but traditional styling, seating under the horse chestnut trees at the front of the house as well as a large garden at rear. Live music once a month.

FOX & PHEASANT

Gerrards Cross Road
☎ (01753) 662047
11am-2.30pm; 5.30pm-11pm
Ruddles County; Webster's Yorkshire Bitter

The drinking area is small, with the bar having carved panels and leaned ceilings. The main entrance has sofa seating that leads through to the restaurant carvery. The carved ceiling in the bar gives the interior a Tudor look.

ROSE & CROWN

Hollybush Hill
☎ (01753) 662148
11am-3pm; 5.30pm-11pm
(Opens 7pm Saturday evenings)
Adnams Broadside; Morland Original Bitter, Old Masters, Old Speckled Hen; Regular Guest Beer

Pre-war two-bar pub with single entrance. Plush velour seating in both areas and a cosy and welcoming atmosphere. Landlord is a former aircraft carrier officer, and the pub has connections with the R.N.L.I.

SIX BELLS

Bells Hill
☎ (01753) 643057
11.30am-11pm
Boddingtons Bitter; Wadworth 6X

Modern 60's pub on the edge of a housing estate. Public bar is popular with the young and there is a more sedate lounge furnished with deep red-buttoned seating. The kitchen provides fresh northern-style fish, chips and mushy peas on Fridays and Saturdays as well as good value home cooking. Live music every second Saturday.

STOKENCHURCH

Map Reference: C8
An expanding commuter village originally built around the rural furniture-making industry. Located high up on the edge of the Chilterns with direct access to the M40 motorway, its huge telecommunications mast is visible over a wide area. The Wesleyan chapel in the village was built by Hannah Ball, a local resident who also founded the first English Sunday School here in 1769.

CHARLIE BARTHOLOMEW'S

Wycombe Road

☎ (01494) 485005
11am-2.30pm; 5.30pm-11pm
Draught Bass; Morland Original Bitter; Occasional Guest Beers

Main road village pub, previously called 'The Raven'. Refurbished and enlarged and offering good value food. Sixty seater separate restaurant ideal for larger parties. Families welcome. Smart comfortable bar mainly for over 25's - no loud music or pool tables.

FLEUR DE LYS
The Green
☎ (01494) 482269
11am-3pm; 5.30pm-11pm
Boddingtons Bitter; Brakspear Bitter; Marston's Pedigree; Occasional Guest Beers

Old pub at rear of village green. Very popular with young people. Separate restaurant area. Barbecues in summer. Live music every two weeks.

FOUR HORSESHOES
Oxford Road
☎ (01494) 482265
11am-11pm
Greene King IPA; Tetley Bitter; Flowers Original

Pub in centre of village. Popular with young people, live music and discos regularly. Coaches catered for.

KING'S ARMS
Oxford Road
☎ (01494) 483516
10am-11pm
Brakspear Bitter; Flowers Summer Ale, Original

Large 400 year old hotel with extensions. Collection of prints depicting old Stokenchurch in lounge. Large reception facilities, coaches welcome. No meals Sunday evening.

ROYAL OAK
Church Street
☎ (01494) 483437
11am-2.30pm; 5.30pm-11pm
Boddingtons Bitter; Brakspear Bitter; Wadworth 6X; Flowers Original; Regular Guest Beer

Village local in centre of village. Extended to include food area. Occasional barbecue in summer.

STONE

Map Reference: D6
Almost an extension of Aylesbury towards Thame. Off the main road is an attractive village, including the Norman church of St.John the Baptist, which incorporates a striking font.

COUNTY ARMS
68 Oxford Road
☎ (01296) 748325

11.30am-3pm; 6pm-11pm
ABC Best Bitter; Tetley Bitter; Regular Guest Beer

Comfortable and friendly split-level pub with large public bar.

ROSE AND CROWN
2 Oxford Road
☎ (01296) 748388
11am-3pm; 5.30pm-11pm
(Opens 11am-11pm on Saturday)
Ansells Bitter; Tetley Bitter; Regular Guest Beer

Friendly games oriented village local. Home cooked food available all sessions.

WAGGON AND HORSES
39 Oxford Road
☎ (01296) 748740
11am-11pm
ABC Best Bitter, Ind Coope Burton Ale

Well kept country pub, built in 1900, with strong local trade. Recently renovated with the off-licence being removed and the pub's appearance turned to a more rustic style. The landlord is a Burton Cellarmanship award winner. Live music of various kinds on Saturday nights.

STUDLEY GREEN

Map Reference: D8
High Wycombe 5 miles SE.

STUDLEY ARMS
(O.S. Ref. 788952)
☎ (01494) 483279
11am-3pm; 5pm-11pm
Draught Bass; Charrington IPA; Old Luxter's Barn Ale; Regular Guest Beer

Traditional English pub on main road with top class food in Silks and Studs restaurant and bars. Popular, particularly at weekends.

TAPLOW

Map Reference: E10
Nearby Maidenhead Bridge presents Georgian masonry at its finest, whilst also providing a convenient starting point for a walk along one of the nicest reaches of the Thames. Among the sights is Brunel's red brick railway bridge, incorporating the world's longest brick span; it is also noted for the curious echo produced by the arch on the Bucks side.

DUMB BELL
Bath Road
☎ (01628) 21917
11am-3pm; 5.30pm-11pm
(Opens 11am-Midnight in summer)
Ind Coope Burton Ale; Tetley Bitter

Large 1960's roadside pub with a single long bar popular with the young in the evenings and with families at the weekend. A well kept house with good quality beer which is unusual for this style of pub. Can get very crowded in the evening. Food all homemade. Varied live music on Thursday and discos every Wednesday and weekends.

HORSE & GROOM

Bath Road

Historic 17th century pub on the site of a Post House dating back to the early 16th century. There are 19th century extensions incorporating Georgian windows, stables and bakehouse across the yard. A listed building. Now under the name of 'Sainsbury's' you will see paintings of smiling people in the upper windows. The rest of the pub is obscured by blue hoardings. We hope that one day this historic building will re-open as a pub.

OAK & SAW

Rectory Road
☎ (01628) 604074
Noon-3pm; 5.30pm-11pm
(Opens Noon-11pm Thursday to Saturday)

Courage Best Bitter;
Marston's Pedigree;
Wadworth 6X; Regular Guest Beers

The building dates from the early 1800's. The interior has been opened up to a single bar accessed through the late Victorian porch with bay window frontage. The atmosphere is cosy with subdued lights and decor, being frequented by business clientele at lunchtimes and by locals and younger crowds at evenings and weekends. Food is all home prepared and good value for money.

OLD STATION INN

Bath Road
☎ (01628) 22922
Noon-3pm; 6pm-11pm

Regular Guest Beer

Building dates from 1931 but its origins go back to 1838 when the railway terminated at Maidenhead on the embankment above the pub. Three separate areas in the single bar. Rear garden very suitable for children. Known locally as the 'old tin shack' because the original pub was! It was the works bar for the rail workers.

TAPLOW COMMON

Map Reference: E10
Taplow 2m S. 300 feet above the Thames lies Cliveden, a great mansion set in beautiful surroundings and given to the nation by the Astors in 1942; it was here that Arne's 'Rule Britannia!' was first played. The grounds (NT) are well worth a visit.

FEATHERS INN

Taplow Common Road
☎ (01628) 664646

11am-3pm; 5pm-11pm
Tetley Bitter; Thomas Greenall's Bitter; Regular Guest Beer

Large single-bar pub with several separate seated areas. Listed building over 120 years old, formerly owned by Wellers of Amersham. Family oriented with children welcome, especially in large garden with playground equipment. Very enthusiastic landlord, much in support of CAMRA and the local community.

TATLING END

Map Reference: G9
Just East of Gerrards Cross where the A40 crosses the M25

HARVESTER AT DENHAM
Oxford Road
☎ (01895) 832623
11am-3pm; 5pm-11pm
(Opens 11am-11pm on Saturday)
Courage Best Bitter, Directors; Regular Guest Beer

Previously called the 'Ugly Duckling' - the present name is temporary until a better one is chosen. Comprises a refurbished open-plan bar and 90 seater restaurant.

STAG & GRIFFIN
Oxford Road

☎ (01753) 883100
11.30am-3pm; 5.30pm-11pm
Brakspear Bitter; Fuller's London Pride; Hook Norton Best Mild; Regular Guest Beers

Comfortable pub which was formerly the 'Pennyfarthing' restaurant and then the 'Hogshead'. Five cask ales available including a mild and two guest beers. Petanque played.

THE LEE

Map Reference: E7
Wendover 4 miles W
Pretty estate village in narrow Chilterns lanes, with two churches (the old and the new) sharing the same yard. The manor was the home of the Librty family - note the ship's figurehead representing Admiral Earl Howe glaring at passing motorists; other timbers from the ship were used to rebuild the Liberty shop in Regent Street.

COCK AND RABBIT
(O.S. Ref. 900043)
☎ (01494) 837540
Noon-2.30pm; 6pm-11pm
Fuller's London Pride; Morland Old Masters, Old Speckled Hen; Wethered Bitter, Flowers IPA; Beer with House Name

176

Large country pub with two contrasting bars. A traditional public and a plush, comfortable lounge overlooking the large garden. Regular quiz nights on a Sunday. Cock & Rabbit bitter is 4.2% ABV.

GATE INN
Lee Gate (O.S. Ref. 895054)
☎ (01494) 837368
11am-4pm; 7.30pm-11pm
Adnams Bitter; Marston's Pedigree; Tetley Bitter; Wadworth 6X; Occasional Guest Beers

Large old pub with many wooden beams and a tiled floor. Large garden and car park. Live music Thursday and Saturday.

OLD SWAN
Kingswood, Swan Bottom (O.S. Ref. 902055)
☎ (01494) 837239
11am-11pm
Draught Bass; Butcombe Bitter; Fuller's London Pride; Morland Original Bitter

Isolated old free house with lovely old fireplace and uneven stone floor. Separate dining area to one side. No evening meals Sunday or Monday.

THORN-BOROUGH

Map Reference: C3

Straggling village 3 miles E of Buckingham just off the A421. Claydon brook runs through the village and is crossed by a 14th century bridge.

LONE TREE
Buckingham Road
☎ (01280) 812334
11am-2.30pm; 5.30pm-11pm
Draught Bass; Regular Guest Beers

Set between Bletchley and Buckingham this roadside pub is primarily food oriented with an excellent and original menu. There is a single bar-cum-dining area that is wood panelled, has an inglenook fireplace and exposed rough bricks. An ever changing range of superbly kept real ales, many unusual for this area.

TWO BREWERS
Bridge Street
☎ (01280) 812020
11am-2.30pm; 6pm-11pm
Boddingtons Bitter; Marston's Pedigree; Wadworth 6X; Flowers IPA

Pleasant two-bar village pub fashioned out of local limestone. Dating in part from the 16th century and grade 1 listed. The quieter saloon bar maintains its old world feel with an inglenook fireplace and huge beams. Horse brasses and photos of the village clubs past and present are perfectly at home in here. Whilst in the public bar there is an inglenook fireplace as well, but on a smaller scale, alongside a brace of church pews and other more comfortable seating.

TINGEWICK

Map Reference: B4
About 2 miles W of Buckingham a straggling bottleneck of a village very much in need of a by pass.

CROWN
Main Street
☏ (01280) 848442
Noon-3pm; 7pm-11pm
Hook Norton Best Bitter

L-shaped pub on main road central to village. Large inglenook fireplace and unusual pub furniture (i.e rotating table tops). On reflection this isn't so unusual.

ROYAL OAK
Main Strret
☏ (01280) 848373
11am-3pm; 5.30pm-11pm
(Opens 11am-11pm on Saturdays)

Intends to have real ales sometime.

TURVILLE

Map Reference: C9
Henley 5 miles South. A delightful village nestling in a Chiltern fold, and overlooked by an attractive windmill.

BULL AND BUTCHER
(O.S. Ref. 768911)
☏ (01491) 638283
11am-3pm; 6pm-11pm
Brakspear Mild, Bitter, Special, Old, OBJ

Country pub in most attractive countryside. First licensed in 1617. Open fires in both bars. Extensive menu including vegetarian dishes. Mecca for several motor clubs (MG, etc).

TURWESTON

Map Reference: A3
The far flung reaches of this county. In fact, one more step and you enter the twilight zone of Oxford via the back door of Brackley.

STRATTON ARMS
(O.S. Ref. 601378)
☏ (01280) 704956
Noon-3pm; 6pm-11pm
Courage Best Bitter, Directors; John Smith's Bitter

Former Bellhaven pub chain property as the misleading sign will tell. Somewhat run down exterior in local stone with what might potentially be a characterful interior hidden behind artex and flock wallpaper. A large garden to the rear that could pass for the East Midlands third airport. Possibility of expansion but a little too far from the main road.

The Taste of Oxfordshire, ..in Buckinghamshire!

Sample the Traditional Fine Ales from Oxfords only family owned Brewery, at one of the following Public Houses.

The Diarymaid, Elmhurst Rd, Aylesbury, Bucks

The Papermakers Arms, Kingsmead Rd, High Wycombe, Bucks

The Carpenters Arms, Spittal St, Marlow, Bucks

The Royal Oak, Missenden Rd, Gt. Kingshill, Bucks

The Royal Oak, Ickford, Nr. Aylesbury, Bucks

The Bottle & Glass, Gibraltar, Nr. Stone, Bucks

1782

The Old Fisherman, Shabbington, Nr. Aylesbury, Bucks

MORRELLS BREWERY
Oxford

TWYFORD

Map Reference: B4
Buckingham 5 miles NE.
A dead-end village close to the old Great Central Railway line, it has a Norman church with a magnificent original door. The fondly remembered Red Lion closed in the summer of 1994.

CROWN
The Square
☏ (01296) 730216
Noon-3pm; 7pm-11pm
(Opens 6pm in summer)
Greene King IPA; Hook Norton Best Bitter

Two-bar friendly village local with fireplaces at each end. No food Wednesday evening. Live country music once a month.

SEVEN STARS
Gawcott Road (O.S. Ref. 675268)
☏ (01296) 730520
11.30am-11pm
Eldridge Pope Best BItter; Jennings Bitter; Rebellion Mutiny; Regular Guest Beers

Much altered internally in recent years. Original bar now serves as dining area with main bar up a step. Large central inglenook fireplace. Extensive menu includes vegetarian and childrens dishes. Originally a small coaching inn. Upstairs function room also used as overflow for restaurant. Live bands every Sunday.

TYLERS GREEN

Map Reference: E9
2 miles east of High Wycombe. on the B474 between Hazlemere and Penn.

HORSE AND GROOM

Elm Road (O.S. Ref. 905940)
☎ (01494) 812229
11am-3pm; 6pm-11pm
Morland Independent IPA, Original Bitter, Old Speckled Hen

Two bar pub on main road, with comfortable quiet lounge and large enclosed garden with access from common and children's activity climbing frame. No meals on Sunday.

HORSE AND JOCKEY

Church Road (O.S. Ref. 903938)
☎ (01494) 815963
11am-2.30pm; 5.30pm-11pm
Fuller's London Pride; Ansells Mild, Ind Coope Burton Ale; Tetley Bitter; Regular Guest Beers

Has all the qualities of a good country village pub. Fine collection of horse brasses and livery. Food served at all times.

OLD QUEEN'S HEAD

Hammersley Lane (O.S. Ref. 904937)
☎ (01494) 813371
11am-11pm
Courage Best Bitter, Directors; John Smith's Bitter; Morland Old Speckled Hen; Ruddles Best Bitter; Regular Guest Beers

Traditional pub with a flagstone floor that 'dates back from 1666'. Renovated with tasteful restaurant. Special real ale night on Thursdays.

VERNEY JUNCTION

Map Reference: C4
Named after the Verney family whose railway pioneering efforts brought civilisation to this outpost. Verney Junction remains an outpost to this day.

VERNEY ARMS

☎ (01296) 712784
Hook Norton Best Bitter

Ultra quiet village pub situated in the most northerly outpost of metro-land. Like the railway junction, the pub remains splendidly isolated. A real must for the train spotter.

WADDESDON

Map Reference: C6
Aylesbury 5 miles SE. A largely Victorian village dominated by the ornate Rothschild manor house (NT) based on the Chateau de Blois among others. Note the unusual tall chimneys throughout the village. England's first point-to-point was raced here in 1835. The manor was re-opened in 1994 after 3 years restoration, and wine cellars containing rare vintage claret are now open for the first time.

BAKERS ARMS
27 Baker Street
☏ (01296) 651395
11am-3pm; 6pm-11pm
(Opens 4.30pm Friday and all day Saturday)
Draught Bass; Ansells Mild; John Smith's Bitter

Basic boozer, just off main road. Evening meals only occasionally - ring to check.

BELL
High Street
☏ (01296) 651320
11am-3pm; 6pm-11pm
Draught Bass; Ind Coope Burton Ale; Tetley Bitter

Recently refurbished comfortable local with large public bar. Handy for Waddesdon Manor.

FIVE ARROWS
High Street
☏ (01296) 651727
11.30am-3pm; 6pm-11pm
Chiltern Beechwood; Fuller's London Pride; Regular Guest Beer

Victorian architecture at its most ornate. The name is a reference to the five sons of the Rothschilds. An upmarket small country hotel (6 bedrooms), smartly refurbished with a parquet floored bar. It boasts an impressive wine list and quality cuisine.

LION
High Street
☏ (01296) 651227
Noon-2.30pm; 5.30pm-11pm
Draught Bass; Fuller's London Pride; Regular Guest Beer

Free house, specialising in good value, freshly cooked meals. Large wooden tables allow plenty of elbow room.

WEEDON

Map Reference: D6
Cromwell planned the Battle of Aylesbury here. A country mansion named Lilies houses a colossal collection of secondhand and antiquarian books - prospective buyers must phone for an appointment.

FIVE ELMS
Stockaway

☎ (01296) 641439
Noon-2.30pm; 6.30pm-11pm
(Opens 7pm Saturday evening)
*Greene King IPA, Abbot;
Marston's Pedigree; Regular
Guest Beer*

A tiny, charming, unspoiled country pub on three levels. Its name is now sadly an anachronism. No food Sunday or Tuesday evenings.

WENDOVER

*Map Reference: E7
A delightful small town nestling below the highest edge of the Chilterns. Once represented in Parliament by John Hampden and Edmund Burke, it is now surrounded by residential estates, but the centre retains its old charm. The brick clock tower looks somewhat out of place, but to the west and the south are attractive groups of buildings; in Pound Street (above the High Street) is a long row of timber-framed cottages.*

GEORGE

4-6 Aylesbury Road
☎ (01296) 625089
Noon-11pm
ABC Best Bitter; Tetley Bitter

Wendover's oldest pub situated near the clock tower. The 16th century low beamed interior given over to a large pool/pinball area. Popular with RAF trainees.

KING AND QUEEN

17 South Street
☎ (01296) 623272
Noon-3pm; 6pm-11pm
(Open 12am-11pm on Saturdays)
Hancock's HB; Tetley Bitter

Small 16th century pub at South end of village next to garage with which it shares a car park. Basic public bar with inglenook, comfy lounge. Occasional theme evenings. Ask for scrumpy if you want real cider.

OFFICE

Wendover Dene, London Road
☎ (01296) 624878
11am-3pm; 5.30pm-11pm
*Hook Norton Best Bitter;
Theakston's Best Bitter, XB*

Early 18th century coaching house which depends upon 'passing' trade. Formerly a Charles Wells pub called the 'Halfway House', it reopened as a free house at end of October 1994 following nearly two years closure. Extensive renovations have left the interior layout unchanged. Situated over a mile south of the town.

PACKHORSE

29 Tring Road
☎ (01296) 622075
Noon-4pm; 6pm-11pm
(Open all Friday pm and all day Saturday)
*Morland Independent IPA,
Original Bitter; Charles Wells
Bombardier*

Lively street corner pub with

King & Queen, Wendover *JW, 1993*

inglenook at one end of central bar. Locals pub, keen on sports. Limited snacks lunchtimes only (not Sunday).

RED LION HOTEL
High Street
☎ (01296) 622266
11am-11pm
Draught Bass; Brakspear Bitter; Courage Directors; Young's Special

16th century coaching inn leased from the lord of the manor by Regent Inns. Extensive interior renovation during 1994 resulted in new bar area. Access is via reception entrance from car park or re-instated front door in High Street.

RISING SUN
57 Tring Road
☎ (01296) 622745
Small inn with interesting four seasons motif on frontage. Closed since October 1993 due to non-renewal of licence. Now a private house but currently up for sale.

ROSE AND CROWN
139 Tring Road
☎ (01296) 623235
11am-11pm
Benskins Best Bitter; Tetley Bitter

Nearest pub to RAF Halton. Revamped in early 1995 on 'Mr. Q's' theme (ie. three pool tables, satellite TV and loud music).

SHOULDER OF MUTTON
20 Pound Street
☎ (01296) 623223
11am-11pm
(Closes 3pm-6pm Mon-Wed Jan & Feb)
Boddingtons Bitter; John Smith's Bitter; Morland Old Speckled Hen; Flowers

Original

Early 17th century former hotel, adjoining railway station. Rambling building with large restaurant (open all day Sunday) and extensive garden. Acquired by Devenish from Whitbread in 1993 and now part of Greenalls. Good value bar meals.

SWAN & BREWERS
20 High Street
☎ (01296) 622257
11am-11pm
Greene King IPA, Abbot; Regular Guest Beer

A free house since February 1994, this large pub, which was originally two separate buildings, has been extensively redecorated, including restoration of the wooden floored 'Swan Bar'.

WEST WYCOMBE

Map Reference: D8
A quaint and curious village saved from demolition in 1929 by the Royal Society of Arts, who purchased it from the Dashwoods and later transferred it to the National Trust; thus it has remained largely intact. West Wycombe Park is now open to the public, as are the church and, mausoleum and 'Hellfire' caves on the hill opposite. Sir Francis Dashwood and several eminent 18th century politicians indulged in seances and erotic fantasies with the local maidens, allegedly within the golden ball on top of the church tower.

FRIEND AT HAND
West Wycombe Road
☎ (01494) 525557
Noon-2.30pm; 5.30pm-11pm
Morland Original Bitter; Charles Wells Bombardier

Two-level locals pub with garden and car park upstairs! Originally the building was an inn and railway station combined. Live music Saturday nights.

GEORGE AND DRAGON HOTEL
☎ (01494) 464414
11am-2.30pm; 5.30pm-11pm
(Opens all day Saturday)
Courage Best Bitter, Directors; Regular Guest Beer

18th century coaching inn with an original timbered bar. Two of its bedrooms have four poster beds. Noted for its food; meals every day. Excellent garden. Function room.

OLD PLOUGH
High Street
☎ (01494) 446648
11am-2.30pm; 5.30pm-11pm
(Opens 11am-11pm Friday & Saturday)
Ind Coope Burton Ale; Regular Guest Beers

Unusual pub with upstairs and downstairs bars; the garden is also

Friend at Hand, West Wycombe AG, 1991

upstairs. Free house leased from the National Trust. Folk club Wednesday evening.

SWAN

☎ (01494) 527031
11am-2pm; 5.30pm-11pm
Morland Original Bitter, Old Masters, Old Speckled Hen

Family run traditional unspoiled pub. Beer served by gravity dispense.

Fuller's London Pride; Morland Independent IPA, Original Bitter; Occasional Guest Beers

Rambling roadside pub run by Ian and Kath Price, former licencees of the Grand Junction, Buckingham. If the landlord Ian has to raise his voice to you, you WILL notice because Ian is Buckingham's town cryer.

WESTBURY

Map Reference: A3
The last watering hole on the main road before entering Oxfordshire.

REINDEER

Buckingham Road
☎ (01280) 704934
11am-3pm; 5pm-11pm

WESTCOTT

Map Reference: C6
Waddesdon 2 miles East.

WHITE SWAN

27 High Street
☎ (01296) 651455
11am-3pm; 7pm-11pm
(Open until 4.30pm Saturdays)
Greene King IPA, Rayments Special, Abbot

Typical two-bar village local with public bar mainly used by youngsters.

WESTON TURVILLE

Map Reference: D6
Aylesbury 2½ miles NW. A rambling village with four mediaeval 'ends', once a centre of the duck-breeding trade; a few thatched cottages survive.

CHANDOS ARMS
Main Street
(01296) 613532
11.30am-3pm; 5.30pm-11pm
Greene King IPA; Benskins Best Bitter; Tetley Bitter; Regular Guest Beer

Welcoming country pub at western end of the village, with large L-shaped bar. Disused Aunt Sally at rear of pub, but strong local following for dominoes, darts and cribbage. Large garden at front.

CHEQUERS
35 Church Lane
(01296) 613298
11.30am-3pm; 6pm-11pm
(Closed Monday lunchtime)
Tetley Bitter; Wadworth 6X; Regular Guest Beer

Stone flagged bar adjoining popular restaurant, located at rear of village. Offers high standard of cuisine but no food Sunday or Monday evenings and only bar meals Saturday lunchtimes.

FIVE BELLS HOTEL
40 Main Street
(01296) 613131
11am-11pm
Draught Bass; Worthington Best Bitter; M & B Brew XI; Fuller's London Pride

A narrow frontage hides an extensive building, including two lounge bars, restaurant, accomodation, childrens play area and zoo. Pleasant service in comfortable surroundings.

PLOUGH
5 Brook End
(01296) 612546
11am-2.30pm; 6pm-11pm
(Open until 3pm on Saturday)
Fuller's Chiswick Bitter, London Pride, ESB

Small, plain but spotless pub used by villagers. Keen on games such as Trivial Pursuit and darts etc.

WESTON UNDERWOOD

Map Reference: E1
Pretty village that has won the prestigious best kept village award. Its connections with William Cowper may go further than the name of the pub as he spent some time in this area.

COWPERS OAK

☎ (01234) 711382
11am-3pm; 5.30pm-11pm
Hook Norton Best Bitter; Marston's Pedigree; Webster's Yorkshire Bitter

Typical village local with large garden replete with childrens playground. Northampton skittles for the adults plus two guest beers.

Benskins Best Bitter, Ind Coope Burton Ale; Tetley Bitter; Regular Guest Beer

Originally three cottages dating back to the 1600's, the frontage is listed as is the function room which was a stable. The bar has a beamed low ceiling, original internal doors and flagstones. Good value home cooked food.

WEXHAM STREET

Map Reference: F10
Just to the east of Stoke Poges

PLOUGH

☎ (01753) 662633
11am-11pm
(Opens all day Sunday for diners)

STAG

☎ (01753) 662052
11am-11pm
Courage Best Bitter; Regular Guest Beer

Big two-bar pub with a large enclosed garden. Roomy modernised lounge bar and traditional public bar. No evening meals at weekends. Occasional country & western music.

Chandos Arms, Weston Turville GG, 1994

TRAVELLERS FRIEND

☎ (01753) 662173
11am-11pm
Boddingtons Bitter; Regular Guest Beer
🌿 ✕ ✗ ♟ ♣ ⓼ 🚗 ♪
Comfortable one-bar village pub with games bar to one end. Happy hour 5pm-7pm. Quiz night Sunday evenings (no meals available). Live music every second Saturday.

WHADDON

Map Reference: D3
4 Miles W of Bletchley just off the A421 and taking its name from Whaddon Chase, the forest that used to cover the land hereabouts in the reign of Henry III.

LOWNDES ARMS
4 High Street
☎ (01908) 501706
11.30am-3pm; 6pm-11pm
Courage Best Bitter; ABC Best Bitter; Ruddles County; Tetley Bitter
🏠 🌿 ⇌ ✕ ✗ ♟ 🚗 🛏
An ancient and modern roadside pub on the outskirts of Milton Keynes. Parts of the building date from the latter part of the 18th century and parts from the 1980's, an 11 bedroomed motel in the pub grounds being the most recent example.

WHEELER END COMMON

Map Reference: D9
High Wycombe 3 miles East.

BRICKMAKERS INN
Bolter End Lane (O.S. Ref. 803932)
☎ (01494) 881526
11am-3pm; 5.30pm-11pm
John Smith's Bitter; Old Luxter's Barn Ale; Ruddles County; Webster's Yorkshire Bitter
🏠 🍺 🌿 ✕ ✗ 🅿 ♟ 🚗 🛏
Mainly food trade with standard variety and specials. Carvery upstairs. Good range of vegetarian food. Popular at all times.

CHEQUERS
Bullocks Farm Lane (O.S. Ref. 806926)
☎ (01494) 883070
11am-2.30pm; 7pm-11pm
(Closed on Mondays and Sunday night)
Brakspear Bitter; Hook Norton Best Bitter
🏠 🍺 🌿 ✕ ✗ 🅿 🚗 🛏 ♪
300-year old country pub just over motorway from Lane End. Difficult to find but worth buying a map for. Mainly a restaurant with high class food. Reasonable prices and distinctive service.

WHELPLEY HILL

Map Reference: F7
Chesham 3 miles SW

WHITE HART
(O.S. Ref. 000039)
☎ (01442) 833367
11am-2.30pm; 6pm-11pm
(Closes 4pm Saturday lunchtime)
Draught Bass; Benskins Best Bitter; Regular Guest Beer

Proper country locals pub, always lively. First pub in Europe to stock Southern Comfort. No food on Sundays.

WHITCHURCH

Map Reference: D5
A most attractive village between Aylesbury and Winslow, taking its name from the limestone structure of St. John's church, but chiefly notable for its buildings of mixed stone, timber framing and thatch. Nearby is the decayed hamlet of Creslow, with its surviving 14th century manor house, probably the oldest inhabited building in the county.

CROWN & THISTLE
Oving Road
☎ (01296) 641532
11.30am-3pm; 6.30pm-11pm
(Closed on Mondays)
Courage Directors; Fuller's London Pride; Charles Wells Bombardier; Regular Guest Beer

Small, cosy 16th century pub with stone flagged floor and inglenook fireplace. Occasional beer fesivals (marquee in garden) and special food evenings.

WHITE HORSE
High Street
☎ (01296) 641377
Noon-2.30pm; 5.30pm-11pm
(Opens 5pm Friday and all day Saturday)
Greenalls Cask Bitter; Wadworth 6X

Pleasant local on two levels, with separate games room. A centre for many village sports and societies. Occasional live bands. No food Sunday.

WHITE SWAN
10 High Street
☎ (01296) 641228
11am-2.30pm; 6pm-11pm
Fuller's London Pride, ESB

Attractive part-thatched 16th century pub with large mature garden. Distinctive wood panelling in lounge bar and splendid grandfather clock. Small separate dining/meeting room.

CAMRA

WHITELEAF

Map Reference: D7
Off A4010; Princes Risborough 1 mile SW. A quiet, sheltered hamlet on the Upper Icknield Way. Cut into the chalk in the beechwoods above is an enormous cross with an unusual triangular base. The attractive 9-hole Golf Club also offers real ale.

RED LION
Upper Icknield Way (O.S. Ref. 817040)
(Near A4010)
☎ (01844) 344476
11.30am-3pm; 5.30pm-11pm
(Opens 6pm Saturday evenings)
Brakspear Bitter; Hook Norton Best Bitter; Morland Original Bitter, Old Speckled Hen; Wadworth 6X

Attractive and secluded 17th century pub with low ceilings in pretty village. Noted for its food.

WIDMER END

Map Reference: E8
Off A4128, High Wycombe 3 miles South.

ROYAL STANDARD
Grange Road (O.S. Ref. 882965)
☎ (01494) 712095
11.30am-3pm; 5pm-11pm
(Opens 11am-11pm Friday & Saturday)
Courage Best Bitter; Marston's Pedigree; Ruddles Best Bitter; Wadworth 6X; Young's Special

Lively local off main road. Car park is tucked away down the lane. No food Sunday or Monday.

WINCHMORE HILL

Map Reference: E8
Off A404; Amersham 3 miles NE

PLOUGH INN
☎ (01494) 721333
11am-2.30pm; 6pm-11pm
Theakston's Best Bitter, XB, Old Peculier; Occasional Guest Beers

Large, comfortable pub, owned by Barbara Windsor's husband. The high quality restaurant is named after her. Bar snacks are available in the tasteful lounge bar.

POTTERS ARMS
Fagnall Lane
☎ (01494) 722641
11.30am-2.30pm; 5.30pm-11pm
(Closes 3pm Saturday lunchtime)
Greene King IPA; Regular Guest Beer

Large, L-shaped, pub with satellite TV and separate pool room. Beware the Ruddles Bitter is on 'top pressure'.

THE MARLOW BREWERY
EST. 1993

IPA

REBELLION BEER CO.

MUTINY

Retail Sales : 01628 476594

WING

Map Reference: E5
On A418; Leighton Buzzard 3 miles NE. A large and attractive village, twice proposed as a site for London's Third Airport, with an impressive and well preserved Anglo-Saxon church. Ascott (NT) once the home of the Dormer family, was considerably enlarged by Leopold de Rothschild in Victorian times; the gardens include an elaborate fountain by American sculptor Waldo Story, similar to his work at Cliveden. A group of dormer almshouses is an attractive feature of the village.

COCK INN
High Street
☎ (01296) 688214
11am-3pm; 6pm-11pm
Courage Directors; Webster's Yorkshire Bitter; Regular Guest Beers

An expensively restored free house, one bar, a 60-seater restaurant with an extensive menu, ample parking and good facilities for the disabled. Six real ales always available (including four selections from far and wide). Seasonal beer festivals are held. The building is part 16th century and was once a coaching inn.

DOVE
Aylesbury Road
☎ (01296) 688258
11am-11pm
Boddingtons Bitter; Regular Guest Beers

Re-opened as a free house in January 1995 after being closed for seven months. The bars and kitchen have been redecorated throughout.

QUEEN'S HEAD
9 High Street
☎ (01296) 688268
11am-3.30pm; 6pm-11pm
(Opens 11am-11pm Friday & Saturday)
Tetley Bitter; Wadworth 6X; Regular Guest Beer

Large lively bar with two pool tables; small and much quieter lounge. Separate dining area off lounge, no meals Friday or Sunday evenings. The building dates back to the 16th century, but despite much restoration work it still retains the old look.

SPORTSMAN'S ARMS
45 Littleworth (O.S. Ref. 883230)
☎ (01296) 688254
Noon-11pm
Ind Coope Burton Ale; Tetley Bitter

Small two-bar pub with regular village following and keen on pub games. Occasional live music.

WINGRAVE

Map Reference: E5
Off A418; Aylesbury 5 miles SW.
A hilltop village in the vale, with some fine houses and a duckpond; Moat Lane bears witness to the surrounding wetlands before they were drained. The village school and many of the Victorian cottages were provided by Hannah, wife of Baron Meyer de Rothschild of Mentmore.

ROSE AND CROWN
The Green
☎ (01296) 681257
11.30am-3pm; 6.30pm-11pm
(Saturday hours may vary)
ABC Best Bitter; Regular Guest Beer

Excellent early 17th century traditional three-bar local in an unspoilt style. Stone flagged public bar, small snug and games room. Names of landlords back to 1767 displayed in bar.

WINSLOW

Map Reference: C4
About 3 miles SE of Buckingham on the A413.
Small town with market square, a 17th century Baptist chapel by the cattle market and at one time a railway station. It does have something of a rarity in Winslow Hall which is one of the very few houses by Sir Christopher Wren.

George, Winslow NH, 1994

BELL HOTEL
Market Square
☎ (01296) 714091-712741
10am-11pm

Greene King IPA, Abbot

Dating from the 16th century this hotel has been refurbished and the original building with superb wooden pannelling has gone. Likewise the beers which are an uninspired choice for a free house.

DEVIL IN THE BOOT
Granborough Road
☎ (01280) 812092
Noon-2.30pm; 5.30pm-11pm

(Opens Noon-3pm; 6pm-11pm Saturdays)

Flowers IPA

An old pub with a strange old name which derives from the story of a thirteenth century priest, John Schorne, who claimed to have trapped the devil in a boot. One cosy and relaxing bar. A pub worth finding, but not much in the way of beers for a free house?

GEORGE

Market Square
(01296) 713229
11am-3pm; 6pm-11pm
Banks's Mild, Bitter; Marston's Pedigree

17th century two-bar town pub. Attractive exterior with wrought iron balastrades. Prime position fronting the market square. Popular and often crowded. Pool in back bar. Banks's beers served by electric dispense.

NAGS HEAD

Sheep Street
(01296) 712037
11am-2.30pm; 6pm-11pm
ABC Best Bitter; Tetley Bitter

One almost L-shaped bar replete with a large collection of spoons, a boars head and a dummy or mannequin if you prefer. It has been suggested that the dummy is the corpse of a customer who got on the wrong side of the landlord. As for the boars head, any connections with the landlord have long gone.

SWAN

2 Station Road
(01296) 714924
11am-3pm; 6pm-11pm
Greene King IPA; Wadworth 6X

Corner pub with small bar. Pleasantly bright but affected decor. False vegetation and modern paintings. An attempt at style which doesn't quite come off.

WOOBURN

Map Reference: E9
On A4094; High Wycombe 4 miles NW. A ribbon development along the Wye Bourne between Loudwater and Bourne End. There is still an attractive village green at Wooburn Green, though cricket is not played on it! Further down the valley is Wooburn 'Town' once dominated by a large Victorian paper mill. The flint church incorporates a striking rood screen.

CHEQUERS

Kiln Lane, Wooburn Common (O.S. Ref. 909870)
(01628) 529575
11am-11pm
Eldridge Pope Dorchester, Hardy Country, Royal Oak; Rebellion IPA

Country hotel with small bar area, large restaurant and function rooms.

WOOBURN area

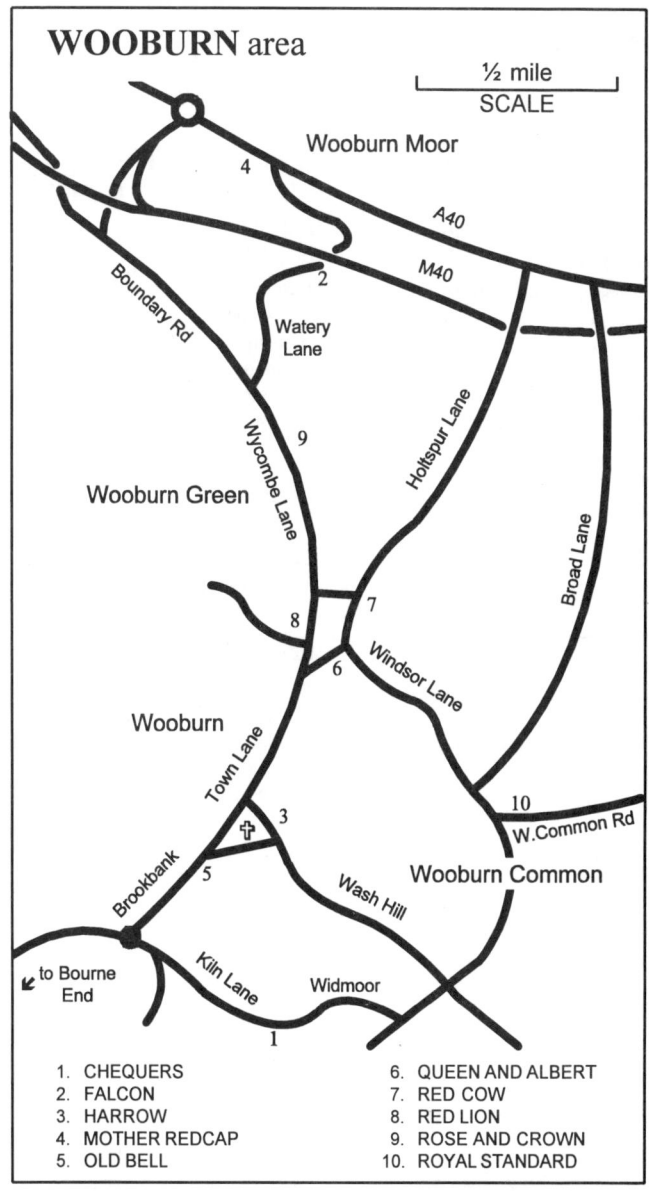

½ mile SCALE

1. CHEQUERS
2. FALCON
3. HARROW
4. MOTHER REDCAP
5. OLD BELL
6. QUEEN AND ALBERT
7. RED COW
8. RED LION
9. ROSE AND CROWN
10. ROYAL STANDARD

FALCON

Watery Lane, Wooburn Moor
☎ (01628) 522752
11am-2.30pm; 5.30pm-11pm
(Opens 11am-3pm, 6pm-11pm Saturday)

Draught Bass; Brakspear Bitter; Wadworth 6X

Single U-shaped bar with ground level cellar. Various memorabilia including traffic lights on bar. Beware low beams. Scenic waterfall opposite door on way in.

HARROW

Town Lane
☎ (01628) 529200
Noon-3pm; 5.30pm-11pm
(Opens 11am-11pm Saturday)
Charrington IPA; Tetley Bitter; Regular Guest Beer

Friendly locals' pub with no frills and gimmick-free. Sharp turn next to Wooburn Church.

MOTHER REDCAP

London Road, Wooburn Moor
☎ (01494) 674215
11am-3pm; 5.30pm-11pm
(Opens 11am-11pm Thursday - Saturday)
Draught Bass; Morland Original Bitter

Games orientated, L-shaped local near the M40. Cockney shows on Sunday lunchtimes with sing-songs. No full meals available Sunday lunchtime.

OLD BELL

Town Lane (O.S. Ref. 909877)
☎ (01628) 520406
11am-3pm; 5pm-11pm
(Opens 11am-11pm Friday & Saturday)
Boddingtons Bitter; Brakspear Bitter; Morland Old Speckled Hen; Wadworth 6X; Flowers Original

Very pleasant, attractively decorated pub with restaurant and good bar food. Now an 'Interpub'.

QUEEN AND ALBERT

24 The Green
☎ (01628) 520610
11am-3pm; 5.30pm-11pm
(Opens 11am-11pm on Saturday)
Benskins Best Bitter, Ind Coope Burton Ale; Regular Guest Beer

Friendly local, popular with all ages. Good value bar food (meals not available on Sundays and not on Monday and Tuesday evenings in winter). Petanque piste available.

RED COW

14 The Green
☎ (01628) 531344
11am-3pm; 6pm-11pm
Morland Original Bitter, Old Masters; Regular Guest Beer

Popular low beamed public bar and lounge and restaurant. Home cooked real food (not available Sunday evening).

RED LION

41 The Green
☎ (01628) 521442
11am-11pm
Boddingtons Bitter; Flowers Original

Boisterous youngster's pub.

ROSE AND CROWN

144 Wycombe Lane, Wooburn Green
☎ (01628) 520681
11am-11pm
Worthington Best Bitter; Boddingtons Bitter; Regular Guest Beer

🐿 ❀ ✕ ♠ ❽ 🚗

Comfortable through room with variety of areas and features. Welcoming domestic atmosphere at front changing to busy games room at rear. Basic menu plus home-made specials. No food Sunday lunchtimes.

ROYAL STANDARD

Wooburn Common Lane (O.S. Ref. 923876)

☎ (01628) 521121
11am-11pm

Boddingtons Bitter; Brakspear Special; Castle Eden Ale; Wethered Bitter; Regular Guest Beers

🐿 🍺 ❀ ✕ ✕ ♠ 🚗

Isolated pub with emphasis on food; large variety (including vegetarian); menu on blackboard. Petanque piste in garden. Now a 'Wayside Inn'. Open all day for food on Sunday.

WORLDS END

*Map Reference: E7
Wendover 1 mile SE*

END OF THE WORLD

Aylesbury Road
☎ (01296) 622299
Noon-2.30pm; 6pm-11pm

Greene King IPA, Abbot

❀ ✕ ✕ 📷 🚗 🛏

Renovated one-bar pub re-opened August 1994, opposite large garden centre, at site of former gibbet. Stone-flagged main bar, small intimate restaurant and spacious tented patio restaurant at rear. Beware fake handpump for cider.

MARQUIS OF GRANBY

225 Aylesbury Road
☎ (01296) 622104
11am-11pm

Tetley Bitter

❀ ❽ 🚗

Large underutilised roadhouse with Grade 3 listed exterior. Closed for eleven weeks in autumn of 1994 and future viability uncertain although Ind Coope have plans for a possible 'Steakhouse'.

WORMINGHALL

*Map Reference: B9
Thame 5 miles SE. A watermeadow village close to the Thame, and notable as the birthplace in the late 16th century of three bishops - all members of the King family. The most striking building is the pub.*

CLIFDEN ARMS

Clifden Road (O.S. Ref. 640083)
☎ (01844) 339273
11.30am-3pm; 6pm-11pm
(Opens Noon-3pm; 7pm-11pm in Winter)

Adnams Extra; Fuller's ESB; Hook Norton Best Bitter; Morrells Varsity; Regular Guest Beer

🐿 ❀ ✕ ✕ 📷 ♠ 🍺 ♿ ♣

Picturesque village local named after Viscount Clifden, Lord of the Manor. Off the beaten track, but well worth finding. It prides itself on not offering 'fast' food, only good food cooked as quickly as they can. Aunt Sally in garden. Occasional live blues and jazz.

WYCOMBE MARSH

Map Reference: E9
On SE outskirts of High Wycombe.

DISRAELI ARMS
Ford Street
☎ (01494) 526760
11am-3pm; 5.30pm-11pm
Boddingtons Bitter; Brakspear Bitter; Rebellion Mutiny; Wadworth 6X; Regular Guest Beers

Comfortable lounge bar with interesting decor including collection of cigarette cards. Restaurant recently extended (to cater for 55 people). Huge menu chalked up over bar including Cajun specialities.

GENERAL HAVELOCK
114 Kingsmead Road (O.S. Ref. 889915)
☎ (01494) 520391
11am-2.30pm; 5.30pm-11pm
(Opens 11am-3pm, 5pm-11pm Friday)
Fuller's Chiswick Bitter, London Pride, ESB; Seasonal Beers

Traditional family pub: smart and friendly. Noted for its lunches. Meals available on Saturday evenings in summer.

HALFWAY HOUSE
London Road
☎ (01494) 451612
11am-11pm
Tetley Bitter

Rambling, ancient pub exactly half way between London and Oxford. No food.

KING GEORGE V
680 London Road
☎ (01494) 520928
11am-11pm
(Times in winter may vary)
Courage Best Bitter, Directors; Wadworth 6X

Roadside pub at an angle to the road (A40). L-shaped lounge and public bar games room. Variety of beams suggests old building extensively renovated. No food Sunday evening.

PAPERMAKERS ARMS
182 Kingsmead Road (O.S. Ref. 895912)
☎ (01494) 523244
Noon-2pm; 5.30pm-11pm
(Opens 11am-11pm Saturday)
Morrells Bitter, Varsity

Comfortable pub between Loudwater and Wycombe Marsh. Handy for sports field.

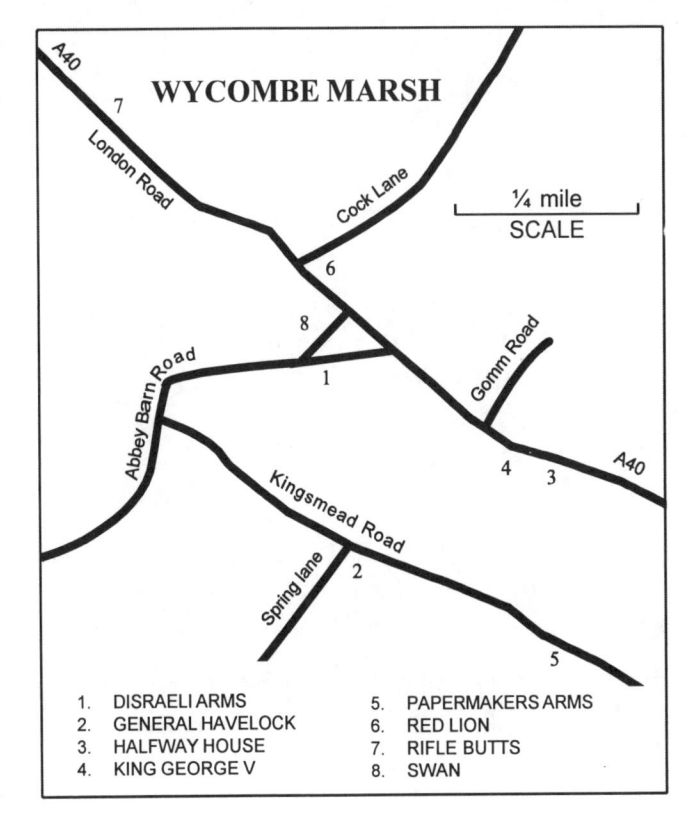

WYCOMBE MARSH

1. DISRAELI ARMS
2. GENERAL HAVELOCK
3. HALFWAY HOUSE
4. KING GEORGE V
5. PAPERMAKERS ARMS
6. RED LION
7. RIFLE BUTTS
8. SWAN

RED LION
551 London Road
(01494) 520727
11am-11pm
Chiltern Ale, Beechwood
Large corner local with modern decor.

RIFLE BUTTS
421 London Road
(01494) 527906
Noon-3pm; 5.30pm-11pm
(Opens 11am-11pm on Saturday)
Ruddles Best Bitter
Sited on former rifle range. Popular with locals in the evening.

SWAN
Abbey Barn Road
(01494) 27937
11am-11pm
Hancock's HB; Courage Best Bitter; John Smith's Bitter
One of the few remaining locals used by young and old. Just off main road. Friendly and distinctive welcome. Landlord claims pub has one of the cheapest pints and most crib teams of any pub in Wycombe area. Check availability of Sunday meals.

General Havelock, Wycombe Marsh   *AG, 1994*

LOST LOCALS

All the pubs listed below are what CAMRA calls "LOST LOCALS" - that is to say pubs which have been closed for redevelopment or conversion to another use. All the pubs on this list have ceased trading since the last CAMRA Guide for the whole county was published in 1984.

It is always sad to see pubs close. They are a vital part of community life and invariably have a loyal band of local customers. Some of them once achieved the ultimate accolade of being listed in CAMRA's Good Beer Guide. Others may have become run down or too isolated to remain financially viable.

Fond memories remain: although the Derby Arms has been closed for about ten years its excellent beer won't be forgotten. Nor if you ever found the Red Lion in Twyford (which closed last year) will you forget the amazing banter that went on in that tiny cosy bar. CAMRA members won't miss the Wellhead near Wendover for its ale but musical headbangers may regret the loss of an important venue.

There are 52 pubs on our "lost list" and several more in the main body of this book which are closed but whose future is uncertain. Some may re-open but that is not generally the case. Many pubs have closed due to the combined effects of the economic recession and the Monopolies Commission's Beer Orders of 1992 (whereby major brewers had to reduce the size of their tied estates).

We should like to think that now that the economic climate is improving pub closures will almost cease. Unfortunately, however, other factors are at work and many pubs are struggling financially. The crack-down on drinking and driving, the tendancy for people to drink supermarket canned drinks or cheap imports from France and changes in social behaviour are all combining to hit the pub trade.

The pubs of this country are a valuable heritage which we should support - and if we don't, the list of "lost locals" will trundle on relentlessly.

LOST LOCALS 1984-95
(and what they are now)

Aston Clinton
Bell	Restaurant
Buckland Wharf (New Inn)	Offices

Aylesbury
Derby Arms	Flats
John Hampden	Pizza restaurant
Prince of Wales	Car park
Seatons (the George)	Building society
Three Pigeons	Demolished
Victoria	Betting shop
Windmill	Non alcoholic pub

Bledlow
Corner House	Antique shop

Bletchley
Bow Bell	Burnt down

Buckland Common
Horse & Hounds	Private house

Chesham
Golden Ball	Offices

Dinton
White Horse	Belgian restaurant

Edgcott
Fox	Private house

Edlesborough
Axe & Compass	Private house

Great Kingshill
White Horse	Demolished (by lorry)

Great Missenden
Red Lion .... Offices
Royal Oak .... Cafe/diner

Haddenham
Waggon & Horses .... Chinese restaurant

High Wycombe
Bull .... Clothes shop
Castle .... Burnt down
Byrds .... Wine bar
Grapes .... Chemists shop
Red Cow .... Shops
Red Cross Knight .... Ring Road
Rose .... Offices
Ye Exchange .... Ring road

Holmer Green
Beech Tree .... Chinese restaurant

Longwick
Duke of Wellington .... Offices

Milton Keynes
School House (Slade) .... Music venue
Station Concourse Bar .... Cafe
Walnut Tree .... Community Centre

Newport Pagnell
George .... Chinese restaurant
Newport Arms .... Italian restaurant

Padbury
Robin Hood .... Private house

Pitstone
Chequers .... Private house

Quainton
Sportsman .... Private house

Ravenstone
Wheatsheaf .... Private house

Saunderton
Three Horseshoes .... Demolished

South Heath
Black Horse .... Gymnasium

<u>Southend Common</u>
Drover .... Private house

<u>Steeple Claydon</u>
Old Sportsman .... Private house

<u>Stony Stratford</u>
Stratford Arms .... Indian restaurant

<u>Swanbourne</u>
Swan.. Private house

<u>Twyford</u>
Red Lion .... Private house

<u>Wendover</u>
Wellhead... Private house

<u>Wingrave</u>
Bell... Demolished

<u>Winslow</u>
Bull.. Private house
Crooked Billet...................................... Private house
Windmill .... Vet's surgery

<u>Wolverton</u>
Royal Engineer .... Shop or fast food

THE BRITISH PUB UNDER THREAT

MILD - Why the poor relation?

A good pub offers its customers a choice of beer styles, i.e. mild and stout as well as bitter and lager.

Some of the tastiest beers in the country are milds - Adnams and Batemans spring readily to mind.

Milds offer value for money as they are usually 10p to 15p per pint cheaper than bitter.

Mild is a traditional British beer generally made with darker crystal malts and less hops than bitter beers. It is normally of lower gravity than bitters and therefore ideal for lunchtime or early evening sessions. It is the original low alcohol drink, although not as weak or tasteless as the 1980's products.

There are about 100 different milds brewed in Britain. Most are in the 1030 - 1035 O.G. range (2.8 - 3.7% ABV) but Sarah Hughes Dark Ruby mild is 1058 (6%). In some areas, the local mild is more popular than the bitter e.g. Brain's in Cardiff and Banks's in the West Midlands.

Some of the milds available in Buckinghamshire - Brakspear's (1030 OG), Morrell's (1036 OG), Ansell's (1035 OG) and Greene King (1032 OG).

So why do the brewers shy away from offering mild. Do they still associate mild with cloth caps and whippets.

Some people find it difficult to understand that a beer which is LIGHT in alcoholic content does not have to be light in taste or colour.

The brewers are not keen to promote mild because they make greater profit margins on lager which is about the same strength on average (and therefore has the same tax liability).

Mild requires care and effort in brewing, storing and serving.

Mild has a limited life in the cellar whereas lager cannot deteriorate further however badly it's treated or however long it remains unserved.

Even some of the main regional brewers, notably Morland, have made the mistake of dropping mild in the last few years. Fullers revived their famous Hock mild in 1993 only to downgrade it to a seasonal ale - look out for it from late April to early June. It is possible for brewers to revive cask mild, if customers ask for it and then support it when it is available.

Unfortunately only a handful of pubs in the county can offer customers the choice of both cask conditioned mild and cask conditioned bitter. It is probably more than a coincidence that those pubs in general have the most character and hospitality.

There is no reason why far more pubs should not offer the choice.

SUPPORT TASTE AND GOOD VALUE

VISIT THE PUBS WHICH SELL MILD.

ASK FOR MILD IN THE OTHERS.

REVIVE CUSTOMER CHOICE!

Cider Asides

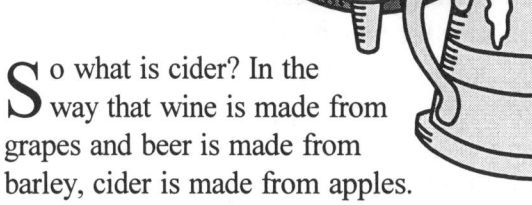

So what is cider? In the way that wine is made from grapes and beer is made from barley, cider is made from apples. There is also a drink called perry which is made from pears. To make cider, all you need to do is get a big load of apples, crush the juice out of them and then ferment it: and the result can be very nice indeed. You can buy cider in lots of places but be aware that most of this is not natural cider. It has been adulterated and altered to make it more 'appealing' and because of this it doesn't taste as good. But will the new cider drinker know the difference?

By now pretty much everyone should know the difference between real ale and the fake beer. The real stuff tastes interesting and the fake stuff is fizzy and bland with a big head on it. Well that's alright, but what about cider then? There are also two types of cider: the real and the fake fizzy stuff. You probably won't realise that because in Buckinghamshire there is very little of the real thing sold and only in a small number of pubs. Look for the little apple symbol in this very guide (it does not mean that the landlord has a personal computer!).

So how can you tell the real from the imitation? It used to be so simple. The real cider was served by gravity from a small dark red plastic barrel or (very rarely) from a beer-type handpump. The fizzy cider was driven by high pressure carbon dioxide out of a fount that looks like one used for lager. This has now changed! There are now ciders that are stored in kegs and then given a blanket pressure. The cider itself may (or may not) be cask conditioned. If the cider is in fact cask conditioned and if the blanket pressure is kept very low then the cider will be very nearly real and hence just about acceptable. But if either of these conditions is not met then the result is a fake cider. Addlestones is often served in this borderline way.

On the other hand Scrumpy Jack is almost certain to be fizzy and served from a totally fake handpump.

Real cider should be almost flat and slightly cloudy. Is there any other way of telling which is which? Well, no there isn't. A common myth is that there is a difference between cider, cyder and scrumpy. All three words are used by different cider makers to mean different things. We can in no way rely on this distinction.

Nor can we rely on determining the quality of the drink by finding out who made it. Although nearly all the fizzy fake cider is made by the bigger and better known producers, some of the best of the real ciders are made by them as well.

The best way to find out about the range of ciders (or any other drink) is to sample a wide range and decide for yourself. For preference on a hot summer's day with nothing very much to do except watch the world go by. Down by the Thames or somesuch. Lovely.

JOIN CAMRA TODAY!

CAMRA Membership gives:

- Monthly copies of *What's Brewing*, CAMRA's entertaining and highly regarded newspaper.

- Generous discounts on CAMRA products and publications (including the best-selling *Good Beer Guide*).

- Advance warning of beer festivals throughout the U.K. and Europe - and discounts when you get there.

- An invitation to join CAMRA's activities such as brewery trips, meetings and socials.

- **ABOVE ALL**, you will belong to a flourishing and successful consumer movement which is acting as a champion for beer drinkers and pub users.

APPLICATION TO JOIN CAMRA

I/We wish to become members of the Campaign for Real Ale Limited and agree to abide by the Memorandum and Articles of Association of the Campaign.

Name(s) ....
Address ....
....
Postcode ....

Signature ....

Date ....

I/We enclose the following remittance for individual/joint membership:

	Individual Annual	Joint Annual	Individual Life	Joint Life
UK and EEC	£12 [ ]	£14 [ ]	£120 [ ]	£140 [ ]
Rest of the World	£16 [ ]	£18 [ ]	£160 [ ]	£180 [ ]
Student/Unwaged	£6 [ ]	£7 [ ]		
Disabled	£6 [ ]	£7 [ ]	£60 [ ]	£70 [ ]
Retired	£6 [ ]	£7 [ ]	£60 [ ]	£70 [ ]

Send your remittance (payable to CAMRA Ltd) with this application form (or a photocopy) to:

The Membership Secretary,
CAMRA Ltd., 230 Hatfield Road, St.Albans, Herts., AL1 4LW

CAMRA LOCALLY

This guide has been compiled by the combined efforts of four local branches. For information about CAMRA in your area, the contacts are as follows :

Aylesbury Vale & Wycombe Branch (Aylesbury, High Wycombe, Marlow and Beaconsfield areas):

>Bryan Spink   Tel : (01296) 25764
>15 Bedwyn Walk
>Aylesbury
>Bucks HP21 8EQ

Mid Chilterns Branch (Amersham and Chesham areas):

>Chris Pontin   Tel : (01442) 834899
>48 Hyde Meadows
>Bovingdon, Hemel Hempstead
>Herts HP3 0ES

Milton Keynes & North Bucks Branch (Buckingham, Milton Keynes and Newport Pagnell areas):

>Barry Mayles   Tel : (01908) 370036
>106 Hunter Drive
>Bletchley, Milton Keynes
>Bucks MK2 3LU

Slough Windsor & Maidenhead Branch (Taplow, Burnham and Iver areas):

>Bob Keegan   Tel : (01753) 550948
>43 Hillside
>Slough
>Berks SL1 2RW

Further copies of this guide, priced £ 4.95 each incl. postage and packing, may be obtained from :

>John Wood   Tel : (01296) 625215
>10 Warneford Avenue
>Halton, Aylesbury
>Bucks HP23 5QD

Cheques should be made payable to:-
CAMRA BUCKS GUIDE.

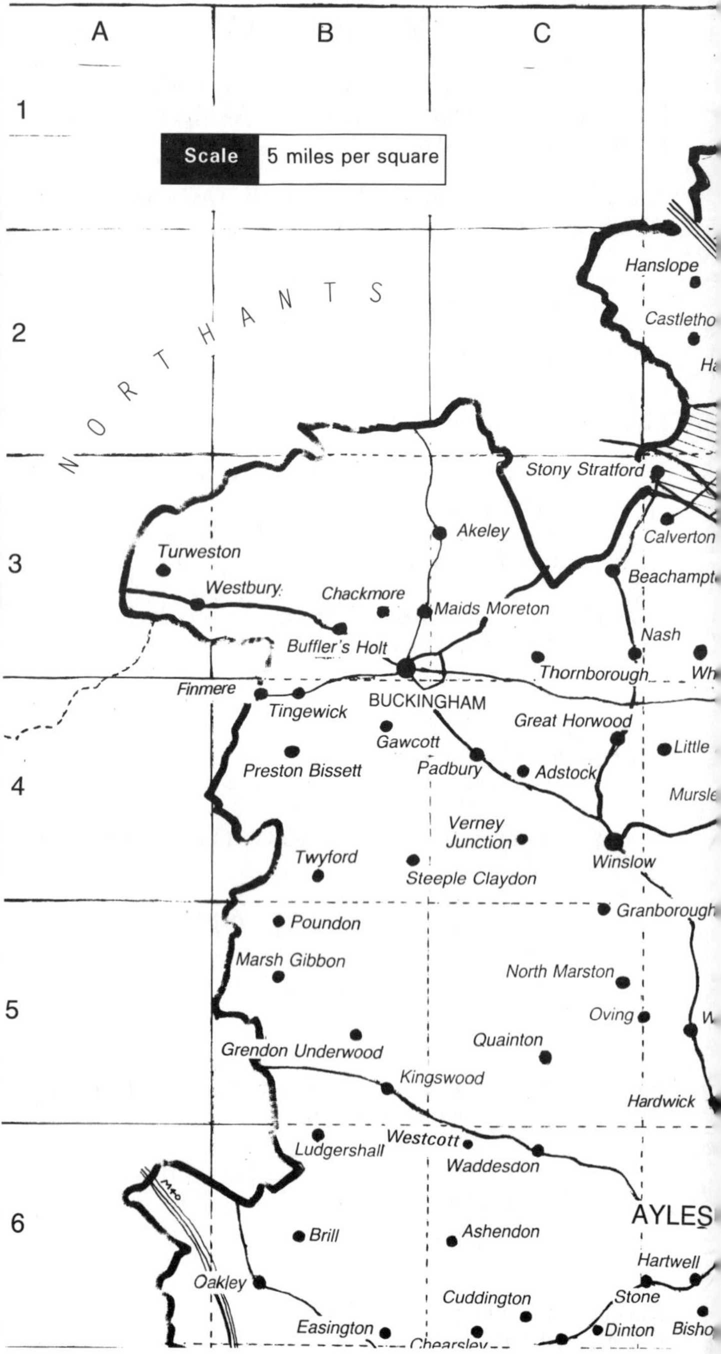
A
B
C
1
2
3
4
5
6
Scale
5 miles per square
N O R T H A N T S
Hanslope
Stony Stratford
Calverton
Beachampt
Akeley
Turweston
Westbury
Chackmore
Maids Moreton
Buffler's Holt
Nash
Thornborough
Finmere
Tingewick
BUCKINGHAM
Great Horwood
Gawcott
Preston Bissett
Padbury
Adstock
Verney Junction
Twyford
Steeple Claydon
Winslow
Poundon
Granborough
Marsh Gibbon
North Marston
Oving
Grendon Underwood
Quainton
Kingswood
Hardwick
Westcott
Ludgershall
Waddesdon
M40
AYLES
Brill
Ashendon
Hartwell
Oakley
Cuddington
Stone
Easington
Dinton
Chearsley

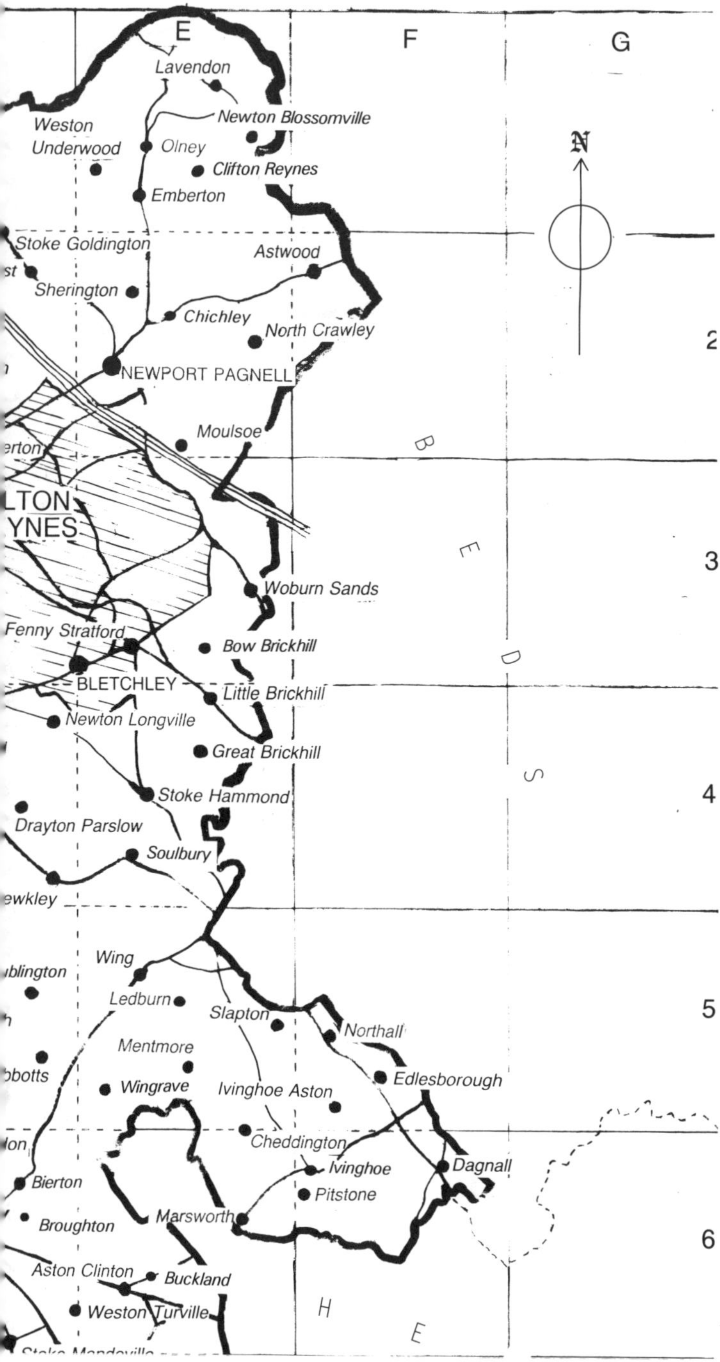
E
F
G
2
3
4
5
6
Lavendon
Newton Blossomville
Weston Underwood
Olney
Clifton Reynes
Emberton
Stoke Goldington
Astwood
Sherington
Chichley
North Crawley
NEWPORT PAGNELL
Moulsoe
B
E
D
S
H
E
LTON
YNES
Woburn Sands
Fenny Stratford
Bow Brickhill
BLETCHLEY
Little Brickhill
Newton Longville
Great Brickhill
Stoke Hammond
Drayton Parslow
Soulbury
Wing
Ledburn
Slapton
Northall
Mentmore
Wingrave
Ivinghoe Aston
Edlesborough
Cheddington
Ivinghoe
Dagnall
Pitstone
Bierton
Marsworth
Broughton
Aston Clinton
Buckland
Weston Turville

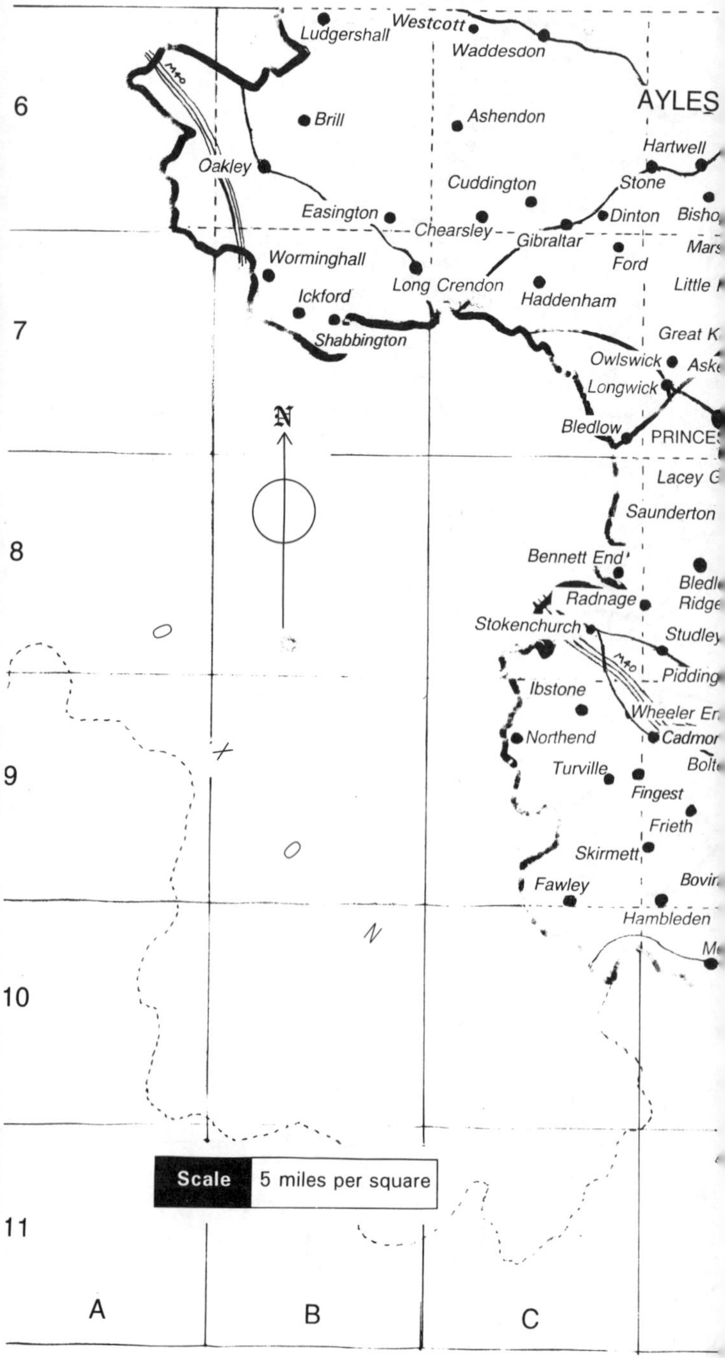

Westcott
Ludgershall
Waddesdon
AYLES
Brill
Ashendon
Hartwell
Oakley
Stone
Cuddington
Easington
Dinton
Bisho
Chearsley
Gibraltar
Mars
Worminghall
Ford
Long Crendon
Little
Ickford
Haddenham
Shabbington
Great K
Owlswick
Aske
Longwick
Bledlow
PRINCE
Lacey G
Saunderton
Bennett End
Bledl
Radnage
Ridge
Stokenchurch
Studley
Pidding
Ibstone
Wheeler Er
Northend
Cadmor
Turville
Bolt
Fingest
Frieth
Skirmett
Fawley
Bovir
Hambleden
M40
Scale
5 miles per square
6
7
8
9
10
11
A
B
C

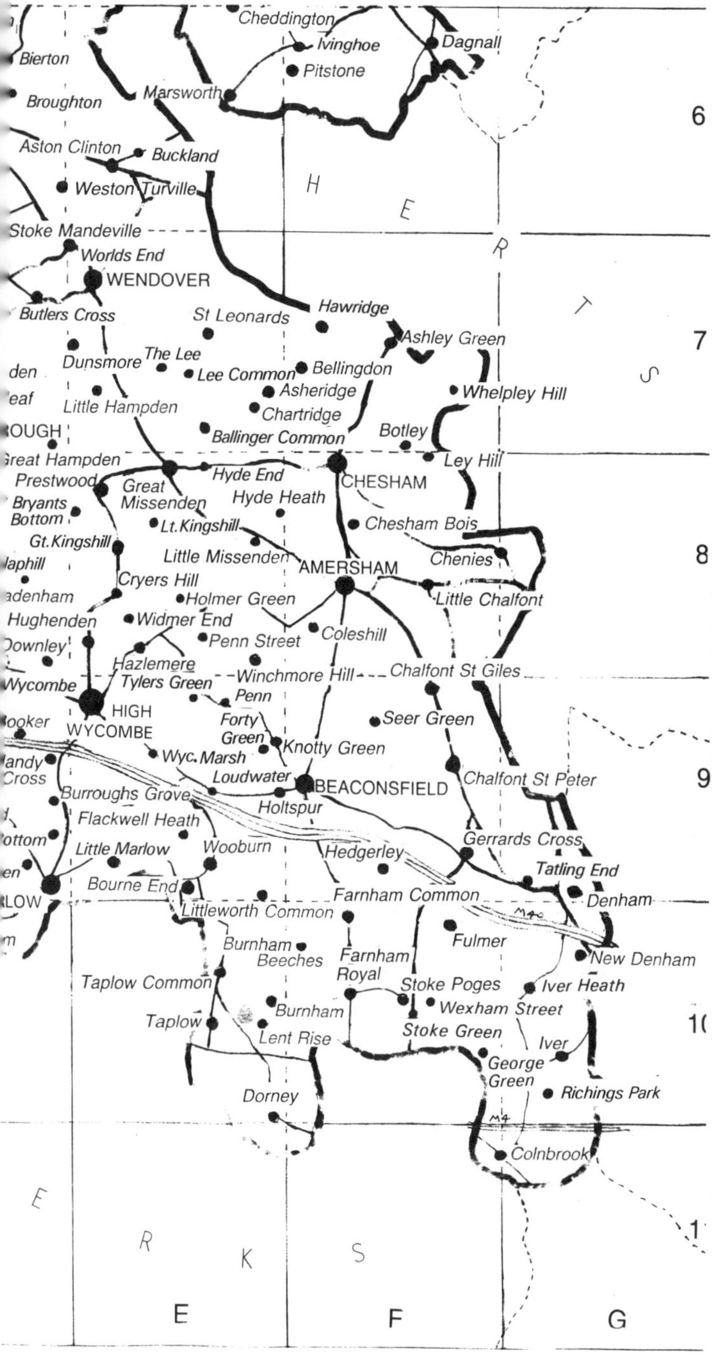
Cheddington
Ivinghoe
Dagnall
Pitstone
Bierton
Broughton
Marsworth
6
Aston Clinton
Buckland
Weston Turville
H
E
Stoke Mandeville
R
Worlds End
WENDOVER
T
Hawridge
Butlers Cross
St Leonards
Ashley Green
7
The Lee
Dunsmore
Lee Common
Bellingdon
S
Asheridge
Whelpley Hill
Little Hampden
Chartridge
Botley
Ballinger Common
Ley Hill
Great Hampden
Hyde End
CHESHAM
Prestwood
Great Missenden
Hyde Heath
Bryants Bottom
Lt. Kingshill
Chesham Bois
Gt. Kingshill
Little Missenden
AMERSHAM
Chenies
8
Cryers Hill
Holmer Green
Little Chalfont
Hughenden
Widmer End
Penn Street
Coleshill
Hazlemere
Winchmore Hill
Chalfont St Giles
Tylers Green
Penn
HIGH WYCOMBE
Seer Green
Forty Green
Knotty Green
Wyc. Marsh
Chalfont St Peter
9
Loudwater
BEACONSFIELD
Burroughs Grove
Holtspur
Flackwell Heath
Gerrards Cross
Little Marlow
Wooburn
Hedgerley
Tatling End
Bourne End
Farnham Common
Denham
Littleworth Common
M40
Burnham Beeches
Farnham Royal
Fulmer
New Denham
Taplow Common
Stoke Poges
Iver Heath
Burnham
Wexham Street
Taplow
Lent Rise
Stoke Green
Iver
George Green
Dorney
Richings Park
M4
Colnbrook
E
R
K
S
E
F
G

NOTES